Women and Health

CULTURAL AND SOCIAL PERSPECTIVES

MOTHERHOOD
IN
BONDAGE

By

MARGARET SANGER

Foreword by

MARGARET MARSH

Ohio State University Press

Columbus

The reprinting of this book was made possible with the help of The Ohio State University Libraries.

Copyright © 2000 by The Ohio State University.
All rights reserved.

Originally published in 1928 by Brentano's, Inc.

Library of Congress Cataloging-in-Publication Data

Sanger, Margaret, 1879–1966.
  Motherhood in bondage / Margaret Sanger ; foreword by Margaret
  Marsh.
      p.   cm. — (Women and health)
  Selections from letters sent to Mrs. Sanger by mothers in the United
  States and Canada.
  Originally published: New York: Brentano's, 1928.
  Includes bibliographical references.
  ISBN 0-8142-0837-1 — ISBN 0-8142-5036-X (pbk.: alk. paper)
      1. Birth control.   2. Pregnancy.   3. Women—United States—
  Social conditions.   I. Title.   II. Women & health (Columbus,
  Ohio)

  HQ766.S325 2000
  363.9'6—dc21   00-032366

Cover design by Paula Newcomb.
Printed in the United States.

*The paper used in this publication meets the minimum requirements
of the American National Standard for Information Sciences—Perma-
nence of Paper for Printed Library Materials. ANSI Z39.48–1992.*

9 8 7 6 5 4 3 2 1

TO

Havelock Ellis

Note

For invaluable assistance in preparing the material contained in this volume for public presentation, I am deeply indebted to various members of the staff of the American Birth Control League. I am especially grateful to Mrs. Mary Sumner Boyd, for her skillful analysis of the letters, and her sympathetic discrimination in the selection of letters of particularly vital significance, her splendid fulfillment of a labor requiring infinite patience and deep human sympathy; to Mrs. Bertha Potter Smith, who for several years has brought order out of the chaos of an avalanche of incoming appeals, and has helped in the consequent correspondence; and to Miss Anna Lifschitz, who has for so many years taken charge of the endless details involved in the work of mobilizing and coördinating the ever-accumulating masses of human documents. To these collaborators and to all who have encouraged me toward the publication of this volume, I wish to extend my deepfelt thanks.

MARGARET SANGER

Willowlake,
Fishkill, N. Y.
September, 1928

CONTENTS

CONTENTS

Foreword

Reproductive Rights, Reproductive Freedom,
and Margaret Sanger's Motherhood in Bondage

"I was married when I was fourteen years old," a typical
letter in this book begins, "now I am a mother of sixteen
children . . . and am on my way with the seventeenth." Another woman writes, "I have been married twelve years
and I am twenty-six years old," providing details of a life
of too-frequent pregnancies, births, stillbirths, and miscarriages. *Motherhood in Bondage*, first published in 1928,
is a compilation of 470 of the letters sent to Margaret
Sanger during her first fourteen years as the most famous—
some would have said infamous—voice for women's right
to birth control. These letters, chosen to buttress her conviction that women's inability to gain access to inexpen-
sive, reliable, *female-controlled* contraception was the root
cause of most social ills, demonstrate that poor women
were both desperate for useful contraceptive advice and
determined to gain some control over their reproductive
lives.

At the time this book appeared, Sanger claimed, she
had received more than a quarter of a million letters like
these from married women exhausted from measuring
their days in pregnancies, miscarriages, abortions, and
births; from single women contemplating marriage but

unwilling to accept the idea of yearly pregnancies; and from men whose marriages disintegrated, they believed, because their wives constantly feared another pregnancy.[1] Although the letters are undated, most of them seem to come from the years after the publication in 1920 of Sanger's first book, *Woman and the New Race*, which made her name nearly a household word in the United States.

Margaret Sanger, a Woman Rebel

Margaret Sanger (1879–1966) coined the term *birth control* and made it her single-minded cause during a career that spanned much of the twentieth century. Historians have disagreed about the exact nature of her legacy—some view her as a failed radical who abandoned her principled beliefs in order to win the medical profession's approval, while others paint a more sympathetic portrait of a leader willing to make some compromises in the interests of a large and laudable goal.[2] Nearly all agree, however, that the birth control movement was one of the most important forces in the transformation of heterosexual behavior and attitudes in the twentieth century. Today, women expect to be able to control their fertility, to choose to bear or not to bear children, and even—albeit unrealistically—to conceive at will. This is a dramatic change from the past, when heterosexual intercourse and reproduction were invariably linked. Although contraception had been practiced for millennia, it was only in the twentieth century that it became possible virtually to ensure that a woman could engage in intercourse without fear of pregnancy.[3] Not all of this was Margaret Sanger's doing, of course, but she played a pivotal role.

Born in 1879 in Corning, New York, Margaret Louisa was Anne and Michael Higgins's sixth of eleven children and the third of four girls. Anne Higgins was a devout Irish Catholic who was devoted to her children and apparently adored her handsome, roistering, freethinking, church-hating husband, a stonecutter who spent more time debating with his neighbors the merits of his favorite iconoclastic agitators than he did carving the funerary monuments that provided the family's precarious living. Margaret also admired her father's beliefs, and in later years she often credited him as the inspiration for her own refusal to conform to conventional thought. Perhaps. Equally likely, as her biographer Ellen Chesler suggests, her mother's relentless childbearing—unchecked by equally relentless ill health—profoundly shaped both Sanger's drive for women's reproductive freedom and her intense antipathy for the Catholic Church.

Anne Higgins, having spent her life cleaning, sewing, cooking, caring for her large family, and indulging her freewheeling spouse, died in 1899 of the tuberculosis that had plagued her for decades. She was fifty years old, "worn-out and emaciated," as Chesler notes, "her only solace, perhaps, that it was Good Friday, one of the holiest days of the year."[4] Margaret was then just nineteen. Her two older sisters Nan and Mary had gone into domestic service, where Mary would remain for the rest of her life. (Nan later became a private secretary.) These sisters, wanting Margaret to have greater opportunities than were available to them, had provided the tuition for her to attend a private boarding school to complete her high school education. Although she was able to stay for only two years, leaving before she could earn her diploma because funds were lacking to finance her final year, her education was complete enough for her to land a teaching job in New Jersey. In the middle of her first year at the new job, however, her father called her home to nurse her mother during her final illness. And she stayed at home, reluctantly, for another year, when she finally escaped for good, moving first to White Plains, near New York City, to study nursing, then taking additional training in New York itself.

In New York she met William Sanger, an idealistic young architect with radical political sympathies. They married in 1902, and Margaret had three children in eight years. The family at first lived in the suburbs, moving to the city in 1910. In New York she worked part-time as a nurse and midwife among the city's immigrant poor, helping to support her husband and children. The couple soon became a part of an exciting "bohemian" subculture in which radicals and intellectuals, as well as their miscellaneous hangers-on, mingled in Greenwich Village cafés and each other's apartments. Her new friends and acquaintances included John Reed, the young journalist who later would witness and praise the new Soviet Russia, write about it in the classic *Ten Days That Shook the World*, and then die tragically young; "Big Bill" Haywood, leader of the Industrial Workers of the World, an organization known familiarly as the "Wobblies"; and Mabel Dodge, one of the more conspicuous of those young men and women who, living on their families' affluence, were smitten by the radical working class and its leaders.

Perhaps the most influential of the radicals Sanger met in the years before World War I was Emma Goldman—anarchist, free-lover, and a cultural icon of rebellious youth fleeing from their middle- and upper-class backgrounds into the bohemian life of New York's Greenwich Village.[5] At the time they met, Goldman had been speaking out on women's reproductive rights—daringly including the right of single women to free sexual expression—for several years. Although it remains unclear whether she provided explicit instruction in contraceptive practice in any public way, we do know that she did so privately.[6] For Goldman, women's right to control their reproductive lives was one aspect of her larger vision of absolute social, political, and personal freedom based on the philosophy of anarchism.[7]

Whatever Goldman's influence on Margaret Sanger, in the latter's hands birth control was transformed from one element of a larger philosophy into *the* essential precondition for women's freedom and independence. Sanger plunged into the cause, precipitating her first arrest in 1914, for violating the "Comstock Law"[8] with an article in her journal *The Woman Rebel*. When she fled the country to avoid trial, her husband and Emma Goldman took up the cause. William Sanger was arrested in 1915 (while his wife was still in Europe) for distributing Margaret's contraceptive manual, *Family Limitation*, and Goldman went to jail in 1916, also for providing contraceptive instructions. When Margaret returned, the charges against her were dropped, although she would soon be arrested again, as was her sister Ethel Byrne, for operating a birth control clinic. This time, she was convicted. Becoming estranged from Sanger during these years, Goldman later claimed that although she actively battled for Sanger's freedom, Sanger never returned the support when Goldman was arrested. For her part, Sanger had decided that in order to achieve her goals she needed to distance herself from the anarchists and socialists who had earlier inspired her.

From 1915 until her death, Sanger made birth control her only cause. She soon expunged its roots among the anarchists and claimed that an abortion tragedy inspired her lifelong quest. In justifying her passion for women's right to birth control, she regularly told the story of Sadie Sachs, a woman Sanger said she nursed who died from a botched abortion because neither her health nor her family finances could support another birth. No doctor, Sanger claimed, had been willing to provide the contraceptive information that could have saved her from the abortionist who killed her.

Sadie Sachs herself may never have existed and may instead have been a composite of the hundreds of poor women Margaret attended in childbirth or after their abortions. This story nevertheless provided a vivid and simple explanation for Sanger's single-minded focus. The reality was somewhat more complicated. As this brief history shows, Sanger no doubt was inspired in part by the tragedy of women who died as Mrs. Sachs did. But she had also been influenced by women like her mother, whose health was destroyed and life probably shortened by her unconstrained childbearing, as well as by the example of her radical friends.

Margaret Sanger's name would become synonymous with the birth control movement for half a century. When she began her crusade, she had intended that clinics, staffed by nurses, would provide women with the information they needed. But the court case that came out of her arrest for opening the first birth control clinic (in Brownsville, N.Y.) directed her along a different path. Even though she had served her sentence, she decided to appeal her conviction. Although she lost her appeal in 1918, in upholding the conviction the New York Court of Appeals surprisingly provided an opening for legalized birth control by interpreting existing law to allow for physician-prescribed contraception on broadly defined medical grounds. The ruling meant she could not rely on nurses, but Sanger plunged ahead with a different agenda. Reluctantly concluding that if her vision of available contraception were ever to become a reality she would have to gain the support of physicians, she aggressively pursued medical legitimacy.[9] This did not mean, however, that she abandoned her position that access to birth control, on an unfettered, democratic basis, was both a fundamental right of all women and the bedrock foundation of social progress. For the next half century, as she traveled from political radicalism to conservatism, she never swerved from that belief.

Consumed by her life's work, Sanger relegated her personal relationships to a secondary place. She did not follow in the footsteps of her older sisters, who never married, but she was surely no better suited to conventional domesticity. Whether the Sanger marriage would have lasted longer had Margaret not found her husband's financial irresponsibility all too reminiscent of her father's behavior is not clear. What is clear is that she grew thoroughly tired of him long before their divorce, which she finally obtained—against his wishes—in 1921, after a long separation. She married again in 1922. Her new husband, Noah Slee, was a wealthy businessman. During their courtship she referred to him in letters to friends simply as "the millionaire." This marriage brought Sanger substantial financial assets for the cause of birth control as well as a husband who, according to Chesler, tutored her "in the habits of businesslike punctuality, reliability, and caution that made possible her transition from the birth control movement's wild-eyed and controversial pioneer to its preeminent, if still controversial, professional leader."[10]

During the 1920s her *public* persona became more conservative, and if her politics could not yet be described as such she did begin more overtly to seek allies among the wealthy, many of whom were committed to birth control on the basis of their belief that *they* already knew how to control the size of their families, but the poor were entirely too prolific. She also courted the eugenicists, an influential group of academics and social observers who worried about the decline in the birth rate of the middle classes at a time when the poor were having large families. The eugenicists were adamant in their conviction that social class, ethnicity, and race were directly related to a couple's "fitness" to reproduce. Sanger's personal beliefs were only partly in accord with theirs. Although she generally defined the so-called unfit in individual rather than social terms (unlike the eugenicists), she did nevertheless insist that men and women with physical or mental disabilities, or whose families had a history of such disabilities, should not have children. And she did seek the support of these extreme eugenicists, sometimes coming perilously close to espousing their racist and ethnocentric views.[11]

By the time Sanger completed *Motherhood in Bondage*, she had left her radical past behind. Her principal institutional base had become the Margaret Sanger Research Bureau, which was also a birth control clinic now headed by a physician, Hannah Stone. *Motherhood in Bondage* was designed to gain public and professional support for birth control by making it clear that contraception could stabilize families, enable the poor to enjoy social mobility, and help to prevent violence against wives and children.

Contraceptive Knowledge and Practice

Skeptical readers of *Motherhood in Bondage* today may question whether the women and men who wrote to Sanger could really be as ignorant of contraceptive methods as these letters suggest. Even many doctors, Sanger implies, were unfamiliar with birth control techniques. How could that be? Did Sanger exaggerate the ignorance of both the public and the medical profession in order to make a political point? Were Americans as uninformed of birth control methods as this book suggests? And if contraceptive information was really unavailable, how had family size declined so dramatically in the nineteenth century—from an average number of births in 1800 of 7.04 to 3.56 by 1900?[12]

Historians respond to these questions in several ways. It is highly likely that periodic abstinence and abortion accounted for at least part of the decline in the birth rate in the nineteenth century. However, we also know that from about the 1830s until the 1870s, contraceptive information was widely available to Americans of all social classes. Perhaps the most widely used contraceptive "method" was coitus interruptus (popularly known as withdrawal). Of course, it was not consistently reliable, but even a 50 percent effectiveness rate would reduce a woman's number of pregnancies. In addition, popular medical authors suggested (and often sold through the mail) such items as condoms (new techniques in the vulcanization of rubber had made available moderately priced synthetic condoms by the middle of the nineteenth century), douches, sponges to be soaked in solutions designed to kill the sperm and inserted into the vagina before intercourse, and "womb veils," an earlier version of the diaphragm. Popular literature also advised that women had a so-called safe period in which they would be unable to conceive; however, physicians actually knew almost nothing about the timing of women's fertility. As a result, most of them believed that women were most likely to conceive just before or just after their menstrual period, so they advised women that it was "safe" to have intercourse during the middle days between menstrual periods. This is actually the time in which women generally are at their most fertile.[13]

Today, when Americans expect contraception to be nearly foolproof, douching, withdrawal, and periodic abstinence would never be sufficient. In the nineteenth century, however, married couples generally sought merely to limit the number of children to the three, four, or five considered manageable. In such a context, these methods did have an impact. For those determined not to bear a child, the option of abortion was widely available as well.[14]

The historical record reveals what methods were *available*, and one can assume from the wide array of products that there was a substantial market; but historians know less than they would like about the actual couples who used them. Aside from the scattered letters between couples, sisters, and friends, there is only one "survey" to which we can turn. Beginning at the end of the nineteenth century, California physician Clelia Mosher asked forty-five married upper-middle-class women about their contraceptive habits. Most acknowledged using some form of contraception. Besides withdrawal and periodic abstinence, the women mentioned condoms and douching as other preferred contraceptive means.[15]

By the time Dr. Mosher started her survey, public contraceptive information had become more difficult to obtain than it had been earlier in the century. In 1873 the distribution of such material became illegal, as the nation, or at least the opinion leaders in the Protestant middle class, declared war upon "obscenity," which included contraceptive information and devices. The federal law that enshrined this principle was popularly called the "Comstock Law," after its chief proponent, Anthony Comstock, a self-styled purity reformer and head of the New York Society for the Suppression of Vice. States soon passed their own "little Comstock" laws, and although drug stores and itinerant sellers still dispensed contraceptives, doing so had become an illegal activity. The manufacture of contraceptives had been driven underground as well, and there was no way to ensure the quality or efficacy of the products.[16]

Adding to the barriers set up by of a dearth of formal information, young women may have been embarrassed to turn to mothers or older sisters. Throughout much of the nineteenth century, particularly in the middle class, a cultural proscription existed against "excessive" sexuality within marriage. In an era in which romantic "friendships" between women (and between men as well) were not only tolerated but encouraged, and in which some psychosocial diseases in both women and men were "treated" medically by what most of us nowadays would view as stimulation to orgasm, it was nevertheless considered immoral for married couples to engage in "excessive" intercourse without reproductive intent. Physicians stood ready to pronounce on the appropriate amount of intercourse allowable—generally once or twice a week—beyond which a man's strength and a woman's health, not to mention the morality of both, would be endangered.[17]

By the time Margaret Sanger began her birth control crusade these attitudes had come under widespread attack. One popular magazine declared in 1913 that "Sex O'Clock" had struck in America. Although historians have argued persuasively that the Victorians were never quite so prudish or "Victorian" as our contemporary public image would have them, men and women of the mid to late nineteenth century maintained a public reticence about intimate matters. By the second decade of the twentieth century such restraint had come to seem increasingly old-fashioned. Partly because of an urban working-class youth subculture that flaunted sexuality, partly because of the glamour of bohemian lifestyles adopted by youthful and not-so-youthful middle-class rebels, partly because of the new direction toward personal freedom that feminism had taken, and partly because of the aggressive frankness of the anti-vice crusaders of the first decade of the new century, sexuality emerged as a public topic of discussion. Marriage itself came under increased pressure to satisfy an ever-expanding number of emotional needs, including that of sexual satisfaction for both husband and wife. [18]

Margaret Sanger insisted that such satisfaction was possible only in the presence of reliable contraception. During the years in which she was receiving the letters that fill *Motherhood in Bondage,* the women (and men) of her social and economic class did in fact know how to prevent pregnancy with some considerable success. The two most popular methods required the cooperation, indeed the active engagement, of the male partner. A man had to choose to employ a condom, often viewed as an impediment to full male satisfaction; coitus interruptus required him to control his responses. Sanger did not believe that most men could be counted on to take contraceptive responsibilities as seriously as women. But the individually fitted diaphragm, Sanger's method of choice, required a visit to a physician. (In Europe, nurses fitted diaphragms, but both legal constraints and attitudes of physicians in this country meant that the only way she would be able to get medical support for birth control was to agree that prescription would be left to doctors.) Diaphragms, as a result, were more readily available to middle- and upper-class women than to the less affluent.

Poor and working-class women, Catholics, black and

white rural women, and first-generation immigrants tended to bear more children than did middle- and upper-middle-class native-born, urban and suburban white Protestants. Although at least one historian of birth control has claimed that larger families among the poor resulted from their inability to think "systematically" about the future, or "to plan on the basis of long term consequences of present acts,"[19] most historical evidence suggests that poor women, even as late as the 1920s, in reality possessed little knowledge of the techniques of contraception. The sociologists Robert and Helen Lynd, whose 1920s study of Muncy, Indiana, found almost universal contraceptive use among the "business classes," discovered that fewer than half of the working-class wives attempted any form of family planning; of that half, fully a third said that their efforts were limited to being "careful" in the timing of intercourse. Many of the women had no idea that fertility could be controlled and asked the interviewers for information. Other studies confirmed the observations of the Lynds. In the rural South, where fertility rates were the highest in the nation, women seemed the least knowledgeable. As late as the 1930s and 1940s, Southern rural whites and blacks rarely employed contraceptive devices.[20]

Mothers "in Bondage"

Most, although not all, of the letters in *Motherhood in Bondage* are from women. Few had access to information about contraception from any "official" medical source. Whatever knowledge they might be able to acquire would have come from mothers, sisters, neighbors, or husbands. Although it is impossible from the letters to know who the letter writers were in terms of their race or ethnicity, since few letters include that information, it is not difficult to envision the circumstances under which these women married, conceived, and reared their children. Many of these letters appear to have come from mining settlements, mill towns, and poor rural communities. Families lived in tight quarters in small houses that often lacked plumbing or even a pump to bring water indoors. A number of the women who wrote were —or at least perceived themselves to be—isolated from family and neighbors, either literally or because of their social circumstances. Some of them seem to have been ostracized by their neighbors, although it is not clear why.

Their husbands were miners, poor farmers (at least some of them sharecroppers or tenant farmers), field workers, railroad brakemen and switchmen, and laborers. Wives frequently contributed to their family's support. Notes one, "I do all my housework, live in a cellar on a homestead. For wood and water I go outside. . . . I take care of milk and chickens, also have a garden, besides I have to do most of the work of running a small grocery store and post office which takes hours of my time every day." Some worked in cotton and silk mills, returning to their long hours of work soon after giving birth, leaving their infants in the care of older siblings. Still others took in laundry or, like the woman quoted above, kept small stores. Given the fact that this was the so-called Roaring Twenties, a time of affluence before the deprivations of the Great Depression, the extent of material deprivation among these families may seem staggering. However, the prosperity of the twenties was neither as deep nor as broad as some observers believed. Middle-class urban and sub-urban dwellers, riding the crest of a new consumer econ-omy, did indeed enjoy considerable prosperity until the depression set in at the end of the decade, but agrar-ian America fared less well. Good economic times never touched some parts of the nation, and in others its appear-ance had been so fleeting as to leave little trace. The women who tell their stories in these letters had little or no acquaintance with the antics of the young Jazz Age flapper or the comforts of the middle-class suburban family.

The women who tell their stories in *Motherhood in Bond-age* all too often grew up in households marked by poverty and violence, only to find themselves repeating the cycle in their own marriages. Marrying at what we would con-sider today a startlingly young age, they serve as a reminder that teen-aged motherhood is not a new phe-nomenon. Unlike many of our own age's young mothers, these adolescents were married, but they were no better prepared for the hardships of rearing children with few re-sources. "I got married at twelve years of age and now I'm twenty-three years old with six children," states one. Mar-riages at fourteen and fifteen were not uncommon. Appar-ently, as Sanger's appendix indicates, 80 percent of those who wrote to her pleading for contraceptive information had been married before the age of twenty, most of them between sixteen and nineteen. Some had married to escape emotional and physical abuse at home, but their husbands and children were unable to provide them with the com-fort they sought.

A number of the women write of happy marriages, with

considerate and caring husbands who joined their wives in seeking a way to prevent unwanted pregnancy. But others present grim portraits of married life. One very unhappy wife endured treatment that we would identify as rape, although she would never have used the term: "It is one thing certain, my husband won't give up his right as a husband, for I've pleaded for it as my very life seemed to hang on it, each intercourse is very painful, at times almost deathlike." Another notes in her request for a specific contraceptive measure that "it would have to be something that I can do without my husband knowing for he thinks breeding machines are what all women are." Too many of the women had husbands who drank to excess, beat their wives and children, and—should their wives attempt to limit their "marital rights" out of a fear of pregnancy—took up with other women.

Other women complained of "happy-go-lucky" husbands (a term used both by the letter writers and Sanger herself) who regularly impregnated their wives but then spent all of their leisure with male cronies, leaving the women to care for and to worry about the children. Such neglect could be heartbreaking. The night her third child was born, says one, her husband "run off to the show till midnight." After the fourth arrived, the next day he "run seventy miles to go fishing with other men and how I was wishing I were dead." Sanger is unsparing in her criticism: "The careful reader will note that it is the carefree happy-go-lucky father who is as a rule most violently opposed to contraceptive measures." She could have had her own father in mind: although Michael Higgins was charming and does not seem to have ever been intentionally cruel, he certainly put his pleasures above the needs of his family. Perhaps she heard echoes of her mother's experience when she considered these letters.

Unable to keep from becoming pregnant, these women wrote, they used whatever means came to hand to terminate unwanted pregnancies. To the reader of today, the number of abortions some of these women underwent may seem shocking, given that most abortions—with the exception of therapeutic abortions performed for what were deemed serious health reasons—were illegal until 1973. In spite of its illegality, however, an abortion was not inordinately difficult to obtain in the 1920s.[21] Still, to find that it was so much easier to get an abortion than to gain information on reliable birth control is sobering. By the 1920s Sanger had reversed her earlier approval of abortion, now opposing it on the grounds of its danger to a woman's health. (She was not opposed to those performed in hospitals for medical reasons.) Not only does she devote a section of the book to what she calls "Desperate Remedies," but she also liberally includes references to abortion throughout the book. No doubt should remain in the minds of her readers that unwanted pregnancy led women to compromise their health—indeed, to put their lives at risk. "I am just up out of bed from an abortion, the twelfth one," writes one thirty-six-year-old mother of four, "and my health is gone." Another, married just six years with two children, mentions her "twelve miscarriages . . . all brought on through abortions and I nearly died from blood poisoning three times."

Not all of the references to abortion in this book may be evident to today's reader. Medical terminology of the day termed a miscarriage a "spontaneous abortion," and the women themselves sometimes elided the distinction between a miscarriage and an abortion. But for the most part, when a woman in this book had a miscarriage, she used that term or, quite often, the word "mishap." If she had an abortion, she used that term or the common euphemism, "operation." When a woman says bluntly, "I got rid of it," she might be referring to an abortion procured from a physician, midwife, or abortionist, or to a self-induced one. "Causing a miscarriage" generally meant taking drugs to induce abortion.

A woman who wanted to terminate a pregnancy in the 1920s had several alternatives. She could induce a miscarriage herself. Orange sticks, slippery elm, and rubber catheters were available at most drug stores. Women also used, according to historian Leslie Reagan, "knitting needles, crochet hooks, hairpins, scissors, and button hooks." Needless to say, the use of these items could easily result in the perforation of the uterus and trigger infection. These infections could even lead to death. Many doctors and midwives, who shared the popular belief that an abortion was not immoral if it occurred before a woman could actually feel the movement of the fetus—the folk term was "quickening"—would perform illegal abortions. Therapeutic abortions, legally performed by doctors, generally in hospitals, were considered legitimate medical procedures. The most common indicator for a therapeutic abortion was uncontrolled nausea and vomiting. Tuberculosis and other serious medical conditions also served as indicators. In the 1920s and 1930s, it was less difficult to obtain a therapeutic abortion than it would become in the

1940s and 1950s, but poor women often did not have access to such medical care.[22]

Some drugs, including time-honored herbal recipes derived from common plants, were considered effective in provoking miscarriage. In 1914, in the first edition of her pamphlet *Family Limitation*, Sanger herself offered a medicinal recipe to "bring on the menses"—actually, the text suggests, it would prevent an embryo from implanting in the uterus. Rural women also may have had knowledge of botanical abortifacients handed down through the generations. While a number of historians have discounted the efficacy of such recipes, John Riddle persuasively argues that scientific studies have confirmed the abortifacient properties of some of the more popular herbal remedies used for that purpose.[23]

The women who had undergone numerous abortions were clearly worried about the effect on their health and appealed to Sanger for very precise instruction in contraceptive methods, since very few of them would have had access to the relatively small number of birth control clinics operating in New York (under Sanger's own aegis), Chicago, and Los Angeles. Sanger and the other women who answered this correspondence generally responded first by sending a copy of her pamphlet on contraceptive technique, *Family Limitation*, which provided simple instructions for methods that would not require a physician. These instructions should have been of particular use to rural women, since some of the spermicides could be made at home using ingredients available through most druggists. Because Sanger had become convinced that the diaphragm was the best contraceptive, by this time she and her staff had also compiled a list of sympathetic physicians to whom they could refer her correspondents. Much of the medical establishment, however, continued to be hostile to Sanger in the 1920s. Few physicians believed that contraceptive information was a right of every woman, and in 1925 Morris Fishbein, the influential editor of the *Journal of the American Medical Association*, wrote that no birth control method existed that was "physiologically, psychologically, and biologically sound in both principle and practice." Many doctors continued to believe that the practice of contraception led to permanent sterility. Even as late as 1936, most of the nation's medical schools still provided little or no training in the prescription of contraceptives.[24]

Sanger hoped that by publishing these letters she would rally support for birth control and at the same time counter critics who perceived her work as contributing to a decline in morality. Sanger's first argument, both in her own introduction to each section and in the more powerful weapon of the words of the women themselves here in this book, was that poor women did not choose to spend their lives pregnant or nursing and that, given access to birth control, they would use it. The repetition of similar stories lends emphasis to the argument. Poor as many of these writers are, they seem determined to find a way to exert control over their fate by choosing how many children they would bear. They were exercising responsibility, seeking information that would enable them to attain a better life for themselves and their children. "I don't know any of the pleasures of life," writes one, "but that don't keep me from hoping for them someday."

A second argument was designed to counter the criticism of her erstwhile comrades on the left that she had turned away from social reform and was in league with those racists and eugenicists who argued that the poor should be discouraged from having too many children because their prolific unions were "degrading" the nation. Although Sanger's prejudices against the handicapped led her to conclude that they should not have children, she did not believe—or at least did not display in this book—any notion that entire groups of people, such as immigrants, African Americans, or the poor, could be described as unfit. The letter writers make that point in several ways, especially in the chapter called "The Struggle of the Unfit." They detail their own suffering from tuberculosis, heart "trouble," strokes, describe their syphilitic or alcoholic husbands, mention children who are blind or deaf, and ask for help in preventing conception. While there is no doubt that Sanger attempted to win eugenicists to her cause, in this book at least she takes a more moderate stance by choosing letters that enable her to make the point that the so-called unfit know who they are and would not have children if they could help it. This was a different position from the one taken by eugenicists, who included among the "unfit" poor whites in the South, Catholic and Jewish immigrants and their children, and the descendants of enslaved African Americans.

Especially noteworthy are the letters included in this volume that address surgical sterilization, given the publication of *Motherhood in Bondage* just a year after the shocking decision of the Supreme Court upholding involuntary sterilization. By the 1920s thirty states had passed compulsory sterilization laws. Promoted by eugenicists, these laws were designed to prevent those deemed unfit for motherhood from bearing children. Some young women were sterilized without their knowledge, and nearly all who were sterilized had little or no choice in the matter. Women who had become pregnant outside of marriage, who were incarcerated in reformatories for unconventional sexual behavior, or who were believed simply to have a family tendency toward a mental or physical handicap fell victim to this practice. In 1927, the Supreme Court in *Buck v. Bell* upheld the constitutionality of compulsory sterilization laws. More than 12,000 women endured compulsory sterilization before the practice came under attack after World War II; still, an uncounted number of additional women remained subject to what one historian has called "quiet coercion."[25]

The dividing line between compulsory and voluntary sterilization could sometimes seem so fine as to be almost imperceptible. Did the young pregnant wife who writes that her doctor "sentenced me to be sterilized" because she wanted to terminate a pregnancy face compulsion? Did the fact that she refused to agree to sterilization in exchange for an abortion make the physician any less coercive? "Being a poor girl and as I don't quite understand all this sterilizing business, I went to another doctor who helped me out of the pregnancy [that is, performed an abortion]. I also asked her what she thought of it [sterilization] and she had different ideas altogether." Having found a second and more sympathetic physician from whom she obtained an abortion made it possible for this woman to avoid sterilization, but what if there had been no other doctor?

The sterilization issue could cut two ways, however. Another woman with two children who sought sterilization was unable to persuade her doctor. While not categorically refusing to accede to her wishes, he told her not only that she was "too young" at twenty-two to make such a decision, but also "that after the operation I will have no sexual desire and that I will be lazy also that I will become stupid and wouldn't care for anything." She did not trust his assessment: "I think that if I was sterilized I would be very happy and would have no cause for worry. My husband is also willing, but I want to know the truth about it first."

These two letters dramatically illustrate that poverty and lack of education did not keep women from seeking to control their reproductive lives. Indeed, this is the third and perhaps most powerful refrain of this book. Although in *Family Limitation* Sanger had endorsed the use of condoms, her preferred method—the diaphragm—did not require male cooperation. Sanger was not anti-male, but her own experience suggested that men were not always dependable. However much men loved their wives, she believed, there was a "vast contrast between the psychology of fatherhood and motherhood." A man's experience of parenthood, she argues here, "is an experience fundamentally vicarious in character, never at closest grip with the great biological drama of reproduction." There are distant echoes of the nineteenth-century voluntary motherhood movement in Sanger's words. Women who had espoused voluntary motherhood had insisted that because women bear the children, they alone should have the right to say when and how.[26]

The Impact of Motherhood in Bondage

Sanger was very disappointed by the immediate reception of *Motherhood in Bondage*. She had hoped that it would have a major influence on the public and policy makers alike. But its sad stories were not comfortable reading for the prosperous middle-class, book-buying public at the time. Many of them, satisfied in their own immediate prosperity, had come to believe that the poor suffered because they lacked the will to succeed. The book's sales were dismal, and Sanger's husband apparently bought up all the unsold copies and gave many away. Nevertheless, she believed in the book, keeping a reserve to send, as David Kennedy reports, "to thousands of persons who she felt needed convincing about birth control— including all the bishops attending the 1934 Protestant Episcopal Convention."[27]

The book's failure to become a best-seller when it was published does not diminish its historical importance. *Motherhood in Bondage* has brought alive for subsequent generations the determination and hope, as well as the fears, of hundreds of women about whom we would otherwise know very little. The letters, of course, do not allow for unmediated access to the ideas or feelings of the writers, having been specifically selected for this book to illustrate a particular viewpoint. Moreover, some of the letters—the reader has no idea which—are excerpted, and

not a single letter is dated. Internal evidence rarely en-
ables the reader to know when it was written. Finally,
there is no way to tell how representative these women
were of other women in their social and economic groups.
The very fact that they initiated correspondence with a
major public figure out of a desire to transform their lives
suggests that they might not be entirely typical.

These limitations notwithstanding, the letters are a precious historical resource. They not only shed light on the
marriages, families, and material circumstances of women
who would not otherwise have left written records but also
demonstrate the participation of these women in one of the
most important movements of the twentieth century—for
reproductive rights and reproductive freedom. Given that
the foot soldiers of the birth control crusade in the United
States were largely middle- and upper-class women with
the time to join and staff voluntary organizations, and (in
later years) men for whom work in the birth control field
provided professional opportunities, it can be too easy to
view the movement as irrelevant to the poor and working-
class women who continued to have a higher birthrate
than those in better economic circumstances. These letters
challenge such an interpretation, as one student of the papers of the American Birth Control League in the 1920s
perceptively noted. "Women of the working-class have
participated actively in the birth control movement," said
Francis Vreeland, "but their efforts have been of a different kind from those of the upper-middle class women. . . .
[T]he main response of women of the poorer class . . .
was by letter to the main agitators, usually looking for
help."[28]

While it would be true to say that Sanger believed wholeheartedly that birth control would give women more control over their reproductive lives, she seems naive in her view that social problems such as poverty and unemployment can be resolved merely by changing individual reproductive behavior. She did not see these problems as structural ones requiring societal as well as individual solutions. To acknowledge that failing, however, does not diminish her actual accomplishments. Margaret Sanger, of course, was not the only birth control activist of the twentieth century. Throughout the country, other women and men engaged in contraceptive advocacy, from the physician Robert Latou Dickinson early in the century and Mary Ware Dennet, Sanger's rival in the 1920s, and a host of others. Still, Sanger remains for many the symbol of the birth control movement.

In the 1920s and afterward, Sanger did become more conservative in her politics and made questionable alliances with those whose agendas were racist and ethnocentric, but she never abandoned the core of her feminist belief that before women can be free they must have control over their own sexuality and reproduction. Late in her life, she encouraged her friend Katherine Dexter McCormick to finance the research that led to the creation of the birth control pill and even came to admire John Rock, the Catholic physician who was the co-developer (with scientist Gregory Pincus) of the first oral contraceptive.[29]

Sanger viewed the birth control pill—which received approval from the Food and Drug Administration in 1960—as the fulfillment of her mission, a birth control method completely in the hands of women and undetectable by men. The separation of sexuality from reproduction, a goal since the beginning of her career, seemed to have been achieved. It was her unswerving commitment to that goal that marked Sanger as a true revolutionary, because birth control so fundamentally challenged deeply held societal beliefs about the nature of family life, the relationship of sexuality to morality, and conventional gender roles. It is not necessary to venerate Sanger uncritically to understand that she was indeed one of the major figures of the twentieth century, whose vision was one of the principal forces behind the dramatic social and cultural changes in demography, family organization, and sexual behavior that marked the twentieth-century quest for control of fertility.

MARGARET MARSH

Notes

1. Margaret Sanger was never a slave to the literal truth, as her autobiographies demonstrate. However, we do know that thousands of women wrote her throughout her career, and by the 1920s the volume of correspondence was heavy enough that she employed a staff to read and answer the letters.

2. David Kennedy, *Birth Control in America: The Career of Margaret Sanger* (New Haven: Yale University Press, 1970); and Linda Gordon, *Woman's Body, Woman's Right: A Social History of Birth Control in America* (New York: Penguin Books, 1977), are critical of Sanger, each for different reasons. Ellen Chesler's recent biography is both thorough and compelling. *Woman of Valor: Margaret Sanger and the Birth Control Movement in America* (New York: Simon and Schuster, 1992). While not uncritical of her subject, she argues convincingly that Sanger remained a feminist committed to women's reproductive rights. James Reed, *From*

Private Vice to Public Virtue: The Birth Control Movement and American Society since 1930 (New York: Basic Books, 1978), remains one of the best studies of the principal leaders in the field of contraceptive rights. Reed, like Chesler, is sympathetic to Sanger's conflicting allegiances. The account of Sanger's life herein is derived from these sources. Thanks to the dedication and years of hard work on the part of the scholar Esther Katz and her colleagues at the Margaret Sanger Papers Project, interested students and scholars can have access to a microfilmed edition of her papers, comprising 101 reels in two collections. In addition, the project has completed the first of its subject-focused electronic editions of the Sanger papers, *The Papers of Margaret Sanger*, ed. Esther Katz, et al. (Columbia, S.C.: Model Editions Partnership, 1999), ⟨http://adh.sc.edu/ms/msabout.html⟩. Among the fascinating documents now available is the first edition of Sanger's pamphlet *Family Limitation*, which describes and recommends contraceptive measures, and the distribution of which sent her husband Bill Sanger to prison in 1915.

3. This is not to say that contemporary contraception never fails, because it does, and the failure rate varies not only by method used and by the user's care but also by the user herself. Still, this century is marked by the ability to separate heterosexual intercourse and reproduction in a way heretofore unthinkable. An excellent study of nineteenth-century contraception is Janet Farrell Brodie, *Contraception and Abortion in Nineteenth-Century America* (Ithaca: Cornell University Press, 1994).

4. Chesler, *Woman of Valor*, 41.

5. Two good feminist biographies of Emma Goldman are Alice Wexler, *Emma Goldman: An Intimate Life* (New York: Pantheon Books, 1984); and Candace Falk, *Love, Anarchy, and Emma Goldman* (New York: Holt, Rinehart, and Winston, 1984).

6. Falk, *Love, Anarchy, and Emma Goldman*, 141, suggests that Goldman had discussed methods of contraception, while Wexler, *Emma Goldman*, 209, says that before Sanger was arrested in 1914, Goldman had avoided publicly discussing birth control technique. Goldman was often arrested, Wexler notes,

and believed that birth control was an issue not worth the trouble of arrest. After Sanger's arrest, however, birth control became a free speech issue for Goldman, and she *was* willing to risk arrest for free speech.

7. I have described this vision, held not only by Goldman but by other women anarchists as well, in Margaret Marsh, *Anarchist Women, 1870—1920* (Philadelphia: Temple University Press, 1981).

8. The Comstock Laws are described below.

9. See Chesler, *Woman of Valor*, 158—60.

10. Ibid., 244—45. Chesler's outstanding biography shows that Sanger did not embrace monogamy, except publicly, even after marrying Slee. She continued to have numerous love affairs, but her work always took precedence over any of her romantic entanglements.

11. See, for example, Kennedy, *Birth Control in America*, 115; Chesler, *Woman of Valor*, 215—17.

12. Margaret Marsh and Wanda Ronner, *The Empty Cradle: Infertility in America from Colonial Times to the Present* (Baltimore: Johns Hopkins University Press, 1996), 31, 77.

13. Reed, *From Private Vice to Public Virtue*, chap. 3, and Brodie, *Contraception and Abortion*, esp. chap. 7, provide very good summaries of the contraceptives available in the nineteenth century.

14. James Mohr, *Abortion in America: The Origins and Evolutions of National Policy, 1800—1900* (New York: Oxford University Press, 1978); Leslie Reagan, *When Abortion Was a Crime: Women, Medicine, and Law in the United States, 1867—1973* (Berkeley: University of California Press, 1997); and Brodie, *Contraception and Abortion*, provide the three best sources on abortion law and practice in the United States in the nineteenth century. Reagan's book is also one of the best sources for the twentieth century.

15. Clelia Mosher's survey has been edited and published, with a title supplied by the editors which she herself would never have chosen. Clelia Mosher, *The Mosher Survey: Sexual Attitudes*

of Forty-Five Victorian Women, ed. James MaHood and Kristine Wenburg (New York: Arno Press, 1980.).

16. There are a host of books and articles about Anthony Comstock. Brodie, *Contraception and Abortion,* chap. 8, has a very good summary of the Comstock Law and its impact.

17. For orgasm as medical "therapy," see Rachel P. Maines, *The Technology of Orgasm: "Hysteria," the Vibrator, and Women's Sexual Satisfaction* (Baltimore: Johns Hopkins University Press, 1999).

18. See, for example, John D'Emilio and Estelle B. Freedman, *Intimate Matters: A History of Sexuality in America* (New York: Harper and Row, 1988), esp. chaps. 10–12; Kathy Peiss, *Cheap Amusements: Working Women and Leisure in Turn of the Century New York* (Philadelphia: Temple University Press, 1986); Carl Degler, "What Ought to Be and What Was: Women's Sexuality in the Nineteenth Century," *American Historical Review* 79 (1974): 1479–90; Nancy Cott, *The Grounding of Modern Feminism* (New Haven: Yale University Press, 1987), esp. 156–59; Marsh and Ronner, *The Empty Cradle,* 110–22.

19. Kennedy, *Birth Control in America,* 123–25.

20. Chesler, *Woman of Valor,* 72; D'Emilio and Freedman, *Intimate Matters,* 246–47.

21. Leslie Reagan has done a great service both to the history of women and the history of medicine by documenting the fact that for most of the twentieth century many women and general practitioners continued to believe—the Catholic Church and the gynecological establishment notwithstanding—that abortion during the first three to four months of pregnancy was morally legitimate. Attitudes shifted dramatically in the 1940s and 1950s, and abortions, both illegal and therapeutic, became much more difficult to obtain. Reagan, *When Abortion Was a Crime,* esp. 162–75. See also Rickie Solinger, *The Abortionist: A Woman Against the Law* (New York: Free Press, 1994).

22. Reagan, *When Abortion Was a Crime,* 43–44, 63–63, 75–76.

23. John Riddle, *Contraception and Abortion from the Ancient*

World to the Renaissance (Cambridge, Mass.: Harvard University Press, 1992). See esp. chap. 15, in which Riddle discusses the decline but not eradication of such herbal knowledge from the seventeenth to the nineteenth centuries. Brodie, *Contraception and Abortion*, 226, also argues that "these medicines were often effective" but goes on to emphasize the risks they posed, including, "at times, acute danger to a woman's life."

24. Fishbein is quoted in D'Emilio and Freedman, *Intimate Matters*, 244. See Marsh and Ronner, *The Empty Cradle*, 114—15, for the idea that contraception led to sterility.

25. Elaine Tyler May, *Barren in the Promised Land: Childless Americans and the Pursuit of Happiness* (New York: Basic Books, 1995), 96—97; Chesler, *Woman of Valor*, 216—17; D'Emilio and Freedman, *Intimate Matters*, 215.

26. Voluntary motherhood was the nineteenth-century term for the belief that women alone had the right to decide when and whether they would conceive and bear a child. The best discussion of voluntary motherhood is in Gordon, *Woman's Body, Woman's Right*, 95—115.

27. Chesler, *Woman of Valor*, 267; Kennedy, *Birth Control in America*, 168.

28. Frances Vreeland is quoted in Reed, *From Private Vice to Public Virtue*, 123.

29. With Wanda Ronner, I am currently writing a biography of John Rock. For more information on him, see *The Empty Cradle*, chapter 5. Also see Loretta McLaughlin, *The Pill, John Rock and the Church* (Boston: Little, Brown, 1982).

CHRONOLOGY

Important Events in Margaret Sanger's Life
before the Publication of Motherhood in Bondage

1879 *Born Margaret Louisa Higgins in Corning, New York.*

1902 *Marries William Sanger.*

1910 *The Sangers move to New York City.*

1914 *Begins publication of* The Woman Rebel; *is arrested under the* Comstock Law; *writes* Family Limitation; *flees to Europe to avoid prosecution.*

1915 *Returns from Europe to face trial.*

1916 *Charges against Sanger in 1914 case dropped; opens first birth control clinic in the United States in the Brownsville section of Brooklyn, New York, with her sister, Ethel Byrne; both arrested.*

1917 *Founds* Birth Control Review. *Ethel Byrne is tried and convicted in the clinic case; engages in hunger strike in prison. Sanger also convicted; serves 30 days.*

1918 *Judge Frederick Crane of the New York Court of Appeals upholds Sanger's conviction but also rules that the law allowed physicians to prescribe contraceptive measures on broadly defined medical grounds.*

1920 *Publication of Sanger's first book,* Woman and the New Race, *a popular success.*

1921 *Organizes the nation's first Birth Control Conference; opens birth control clinic headed by Dorothy Bocker, M.D.; divorces William Sanger.*

1922 *Founds the American Birth Control League; marries Noah Slee. Publication of* The Pivot of Civilization.

1926 *Publication of* Happiness in Marriage; *Hannah Stone, M.D., becomes director of Sanger's New York Clinic.*

1927 *Supreme Court upholds the legality of compulsory sterilization in* Buck v. Bell.

1928 *Publication of* Motherhood in Bondage.

Introduction

Thousands of letters are sent to me every year by mothers in all parts of the United States and Canada.

All of them voice desperate appeals for deliverance from the bondage of enforced maternity.

The present volume is made up of the confessions of these enslaved mothers. Selection has of course been necessary, since time after time the same tragedy of motherhood is repeated.

A word of explanation may seem necessary concerning my motives in publishing this painful and often heartbreaking testimony.

For several years popular editions of my book, "Woman and the New Race" have circulated widely—even into the most remote and inaccessible outposts of this continent. That book carried in simple and elementary terms the message of Birth Control as the surest instrument of the emancipation of enslaved womankind. Responses to this message continue to come to me in an unending stream. They have made me realize with increasing intensity that whoever kindles a spark of hope in a human breast cannot shirk the responsibility of keeping it alive. To these women, my name has become a symbol of deliverance—and I say this without vanity or egotism. Their tragedy lies not alone in the apparent hopelessness of their bondage, but in the fact that they have unburdened their souls to me, a stranger, because in their intuitive faith, they are confident that I might extend help denied them by husbands, priests, physicians, or their neighbors. The careful reader will discern in not a few of these appeals a fervent quality that suggests an inarticulate prayer.

That peculiar intensity of the appeal indicates, I am convinced, their despair—and the forlorn hope that has been kindled.

It is my hope that the intelligent reader will be sensitive to the message these records voice. For this reason I have decided to present them with the least possible editing or revision. I have abridged certain letters, and give excerpts from others, only from the effort to save space, to avoid monotonous repetition, or insignificant detail.

Repetition the readers will find, but significant repetition. It builds up the unity of this tragic communal experience. Despite all the differences, the story of motherhood in bondage is, by and large, the same story,— the same pattern of pain, except here producing the same cry for deliverance.

Having kindled the hope which is expressed in the letters which daily cover my desk, I cannot shirk the further responsibility of extending every aid it is within my power to proffer. It is my conviction that the publication of these profoundly human documents will do more toward the alleviation of the poignant miseries attested to than any other immediate step. Indifference is inevitably the result of ignorance. If the great, prosperous and generous American public is brought to a realization of the tragedies concealed in the very heart of our social system, I am confident that it will recognize the importance of measures advanced which aim to prevent their recurrence in the future.

At times I have been discouraged and disheartened by the deliberate misrepresentation of the Birth Control movement by the opponents, and by the crude tactics used to combat it. But at such moments invariably comes back into my mind the vision of the enslaved and suppliant mothers of America. I hear the low moan of their cry for deliverance—a vision ever renewed in my imagination by the perusal of these letters. Painful as they are, they release fresh resources of energy and determination. They give me the courage to continue the battle.

Similarly, when I am confronted with arguments against Birth Control, arguments which are as a rule presented by learned theologians or indefatigable statisticians, this dim far-off chorus of suffering and pain begins to resound anew in my ears. How academic, how anæmically intellectual and how remote from throbbing, bleeding humanity all of these prejudiced arguments sound, when one has been brought face to face with the reality of suffering!

An easy and even a pleasant task is it to reduce human problems to numerical figures in black and white on charts and graphs, an infinitely difficult one is it to suggest concrete solutions, or to extend true charity in individual lives. Yet life can only be lived in the individual; almost invariably the individual refuses to conform to the theories and the classifications of the statistician.

In selecting a comparatively small but representative number of the thousands of letters from enslaved mothers who have appealed to me, I have resisted a temptation to classify, or to attempt to reduce complicated human problems to a rigid system of percentages or decimals. It would likewise be a fallacy to seek to draw general conclusions from the insufficient and usually fragmentary testimony presented. Although the squeamish may denounce this book of human documents as an unnecessary exposure of human horrors and clinical cases, its essential value consists precisely in the uncanny power of these naïve confessions—unguarded, laconic and illiterate as many of them are—to make us see life as it is actually lived close to the earth, without respect for the polite assumptions and conventions of sophisticated society.

This power to bring the reader close to the heart of motherhood in bondage makes these records dramatic— they possess all the naked power of old folk-ballads or tales. Some are stark and almost Biblical in their brief narration. They are as poignant in what they leave unsaid— but which we can read between the lines—as in their amazing revelation of fact. What writer of fiction has more briefly or more heart-breakingly revealed the tragedy of a whole life? One young woman has written in a few lines: "My mother died when I was only seven and father worked me in the fields just the same as the house until I was eleven then he put me out of a home just simply told me he didn't want to see me there when he got back from town. So it meant for me to go which I did and no one told me anything. I was just kicked from one place to another. . . ."

But out of all the varieties of experience and humiliation recorded, a definite unity emerges. Each letter contains the record of a woman caught in the toils of unwilling maternity, enslaved not only by the great imperative instincts of human nature—hunger and sex—but hopelessly enmeshed in this trap by poverty, heredity, ignorance, the domination or the indifference of the husband, the timid passivity of the family physician, and the ever-increasing complications of successive pregnancies.

Even when it is carried out in the best conditions provided by modern hygiene and prenatal care, childbearing is an extremely hazardous undertaking. It is a comfortable assumption of the majority of unthinking people that all children in America are brought into the world surrounded by the care and attention which is given to the birth of babies of the upper middle classes. Such people do not realize that it is still possible in these United States for women to milk six cows at six o'clock in the morning and to bring a baby into the world at nine. The terrific hardships of the farm mother are not to the least degree lightened by the problem of maternity. Unmitigated hardships go on as usual, and if she and her newborn infant survive, it is only to face them anew, and with additional complications.

Whatever the disadvantages suffered by the poor city mother, these records indicate that they are as nothing as compared with those of the lonely farm slaves condemned to unwilling pregnancies, brutally bestial lords and masters, and an almost total deprivation of the ordinary comforts of life. "I have to carry my babies to the field," writes a Southern farm woman, "and I have seen their little faces blistered by the hot sun. . . . Husband said he intended making our girls plow, and I don't want more children to be slaves. I work in the field, wash, cook, sew, iron, and in fact everything. All the poor Southern

INTRODUCTION

farm women do." The social and charitable agencies which
operate in the great cities and even the smaller towns of
America cannot, or do not, reach the victims of such conditions in the country. The only possible solution for the
country woman would be her own control of her reproductive powers. Again and again, in these letters to me, these
women have prayed for deliverance, and have expressed
pathetic willingness to make any sacrifice to gain their
emancipation from the bondage into which they have been
cast.

The records I have chosen for publication are by no
means exceptional. I have not picked them out to harrow
the finer feelings of the readers, but rather because they
are typical of certain definite phases of enslaved motherhood in America. They illustrate concretely how every
social and economic problem of our civilization is complicated and rendered more difficult of solution by being so
closely interwoven with that of slave maternity. The letters fall naturally into a number of distinct groups, which
are indicated in each successive chapter. We shall see, if
we have the patience to read attentively, how impossible
it is for the family burdened by an ever increasing brood
of unwelcome babies to extricate itself from the mire of
poverty. We shall see how girl-wives, burdened with premature pregnancies and childbirths, are dragged down into
this mire, and are made prematurely old by the clash of
instincts and environments over which they have no control. Another group of letters reveals the pathetic tragedies of that type of woman who cannot escape from the
cruel trap of maternity, whose life is spent in a veritable
succession of incessant pregnancies and childbearing. In all

1

of them we may read of the terrible cost of bearing children—the inestimable waste of human energy and human effort.

One great student of the problem of reproduction has declared that mankind goes on bearing its young as it did in the Stone Age. Primitive man, alas, may have gone about this important racial business with crudity and brutality. But he was not confronted in addition with the problems of congenital defect, of weak bodies unfit to carry on the race. In a certain number of the records here presented, we discover women not only enslaved by poverty and instinct, but cruelly smitten by hereditary diseases and physiological defects—which they wish to avoid transmitting to their children.

Despite their limitations, their lack of education, these mothers reveal themselves strangely conscious of their duty to the race, of the sacredness of their maternal function, of their realization that the life-stream must be kept clean and fresh. Because of this, their appeals ring with an irresistible pathos, a stabbing intensity that cannot fail to bring tears to the eyes of any but the most calloused cynic.

Others reveal the tragedy of childhood—the mother's desire to save her own children from the disastrous trap of life into which she herself has unwittingly fallen; the tragedy of the unwelcome child, of the neurasthenic mother who breaks down under the excessive burden under which she labors; the discouragement of the father; the lowering of the standard of living which the family had once so courageously set for itself.

Still another group confesses that no matter how great nor how protracted the punishment, there is no cessation of that ruthless, relentless force which might be made so tractable a slave, but which uncontrolled becomes so inhuman a master. Some tell of husbands who look upon their wives as mere breeding-machines; others of husbands loving and considerate, who do everything in their power to cooperate, yet who are always defeated by the timid passivity of the family physician who feels that his duty is accomplished when he has given a perfunctory warning of impending dangers.

There is pathos in those recitals of the young wife's effort to retain the romantic love of her husband, even though her youthful beauty has been immolated on the altar of enforced maternity and made a living sacrifice to the cruel gods of reproduction.

Those confessions of self-imposed continence throw new light upon an ignored aspect of marriage in America. These narratives indicate to what lengths husbands and wives are willing to go when they have become awakened to the penalties of excessive child-bearing. Deprived of more humane methods, they are driven to deny Love itself in order to sustain life.

The American public has shuddered with horror at recent exposures of the tragedies of womankind in India and the cynical bestiality of the white slave traffic in South America. But because women are enslaved in distant lands, we should not jump to the facile conclusion that they have attained freedom in our own country. It is an easy gesture to point to the millions of dollars expended annually upon charities and philanthropies, to repeat the current platitudes concerning our national prosperity and the well-being of the working classes. The fact remains, as the testimony I herewith present proves, that here in our own country we are countenancing a type of slavery that is a disgrace to American ideals and that constitution which guarantees to every citizen the right to life, liberty and the pursuit of happiness.

In presenting this testimony to the jury of the intelligent American public, I am violating no misplaced confidence. Nothing essential to the truth has been suppressed; but details by which the writers might be identified have been withheld. The letters are published with the earnest hope that this book will help toward the eradication of the conditions so poignantly depicted in them.

Motherhood
IN BONDAGE

I

Girl Mothers

TO American minds there is something shocking in the child-marriages which take place in India and China. To force girls who have not yet attained their full physical development into marital relations is rightly condemned as barbaric. It is as destructive to the normal growth of the individual as any system of child-labor. The whole trend of Western civilization is toward the lengthening of the period of childhood and adolescence. Well-rounded development demands adequate preparation for the duties of wifehood and motherhood.

I have chosen as the first group of records a series of letters which show that right here in America, despite all our high ideals, all our efforts at the suppression of child-labor, all our legislation raising the "age of consent," child-marriages and child-motherhood continue to exist. Relatively speaking, these cases are as bad as those recorded of India. One of the writers was married at the age of twelve and became a mother before she had attained her thirteenth birthday. In my records are several cases of girls married at the age of thirteen, and no less than two hundred and fifty between the ages of fourteen and fifteen.

The whole experience of mankind, crystallized into customs and traditions which retard marriage until the potential mother has attained full mature strength, tends

3

to safeguard the next generation, to insure to the children-to-be a rich heritage of health and strength. Here we may read the confessions of young, immature girls seeking in an early marriage an escape from the hardships of life which even as young children they are forced to suffer; who hope to find in marriage romance, joy, happiness, the fulfillment of all their secret dreams. Almost as soon as they have attained the period of adolescence, they are thrust into the bitter realities of maternity.

The following records show how relentlessly the processes of nature assert themselves. Conception takes place almost immediately. The natural building-up of the frail body which should take place during the adolescence is prevented by the early pregnancy. The function of maternity overburdens the capacity of the girl mother. The youthful victim can never regain the strength lost in this initial depletion; for, as the records show, the first pregnancy and childbirth are followed in rapid succession by repeated ordeals. Six children at the age of seventeen years is one shocking example given. Another is struggling at the age of fifteen with two babies. Another young mother of twenty-one years testifies that she has already given birth to eight infants. If this were the end of the inhuman tragedy, it would indeed be bad enough. But the present records are supplemented by those of older women who have sacrificed their whole lives, up to the menopause, with an endless succession of pregnancies and childbirths and miscarriages.

Early marriage may be said to promote normal development; but early marriage does not necessarily imply premature and wasteful maternity. A girl who marries at a relatively youthful period may well continue natural and normal growth within the marital relation as out of it. With a loving husband who is her close companion she may be able to enjoy all the delights of youth and fulfill her duties as a wife, happily in the security of the husband's protection. A few years of comradeship and mutual adjustment and education in the realities of life are a necessary prerequisite to the serious function of parenthood. A happy family can be founded only upon the permanent basis of mutual affection.

As a general rule, motherhood should not be thrust upon a young woman before she has attained the age of twenty-two. And certainly few young men are sufficiently developed to face the responsibilities of fatherhood before their twenty-fourth year.

The problem of the child mother can be solved satisfactorily only when we help her to help herself—to give her the means of avoiding overcrowding; the crowding of one function upon another, the curtailing of the period of normal growth, and substituting for this period the function of chance and premature pregnancy. The farmer would refuse to jeopardize the lives of his livestock in this fashion. But here are records which indicate that there are American husbands who do not show their wives the same consideration.

Here are twenty-eight typical cases of child-motherhood as it exists in our own United States:

One

I was married at the age of twelve years. One month before my thirteenth birthday I became the mother of my first child, and now at the age of thirty I am the mother of eleven children, ten of them living, the youngest now seven months old. My health has been poor the past two years now and I don't believe I could ever stand it to have any more. Please won't you send me information so I won't have to have more children, for we have more now than we can really take care of.

Two

The reason I send for information is because I think if any woman needs help I am the one. I am seventeen years old. I married when I was thirteen years old and I am the mother of six children. My first baby was thirteen months old when another one was born, then ten months after that I had twins and ten months later another set of twins. Now I am to have some more. My husband gets awful cross with me when I get this way, because, like you say in your book, he thinks we have got plenty. It is also wearing me down. I never feel well.

Three

I am a girl fifteen years old, married, and have two children. My father left my mother with ten children, three sets of twins; and I the oldest one had to find some way to make a living. I married a poor man and he is a poor provider and I don't want to bring no more children here in poverty.

Four

I am coming to you for help, so please help me, a poor young woman. I am a young woman of seventeen years

and I have three small children, the first is two and a
half, the second is one and a half and the third is three
months old. I married at only fourteen years old and
dont know what to do. I work so hard that I am almost
dead. Thinking "Woman and the New Race" was a book
that tells how to don't have children, I sent for it. I read
it but I dont see anything about how to don't have children, so I am coming to you for help.

Five

I feel that I must write you and see if you can help me.
I married when only sixteen and after ten months was
the mother of a little girl. I did not want more children
so soon but sister told me it was terrible sin to prevent
it. And I had no mother to take the matter to as mother
died when we was quite small. So there was no other one
for me to ask and I felt there was nothing that I could
do, so after eleven months I had another little girl that
was very little and sickly. It is now three months old and
has been sick every day of its life. I am now only eighteen
and the mother of two puny little girls and I feel that I
can bear no more soon, as I have all my life been little
and sickly, and since my children came I have seen never
a well day. Since the birth of my last baby I have blind
and nervous spells. I would rather die than to have another one soon. I know I would never get over it and I
can not give the two babies that I have got half the care
they should have on account of my health, so I pray if
there is any way you can help me that you will. I am trying to keep away from my husband all I can but it causes

quarrels and trouble between us all the time. I pray that you will free me from this trouble.

Six

Is there really a living creature who could read your book "Woman and the New Race" and not see the truth of every word in it? I feel that any woman who could set forth a work like that would not deny me the information I ask, law or no law. I am nineteen years old, have been married two and a half years and my second baby is just two months old. I love my babies, my husband and my home. Life and the work it brings would be nothing to me if I could only feel sure I would have no more children right away. I do not want another for a few years. But my babies are girls, and my husband wanted a son and I want to give him one, but I would like to wait until my little girls are better on their way in life and I am more mature and stronger. I can feel myself becoming weaker and if I had another baby within the next couple of years it would only be detrimental to the child and the rest of the family as well as myself. I left high school at the age of seventeen to marry a poor man and never have regretted it. I have done all my own work and borne my own children happily and with never a complaint, but I live in constant dread of another baby soon, and so does my husband. He has kept away from me for long periods but I cannot ask that of him forever. In the hospital where my babies were born every woman there was trying to find out the same thing. They asked doctors, nurses and each other. They were all in constant dread of more children. Such a condition is deplorable in this age of freedom in everything else.

Seven

I am a mother of one little girl only twenty-two months old and am looking for another every day. I am only seventeen years old. My husband is forty. He has his leg broken in the ankle joint and hasn't walked a step since last October. I am his second wife. He has one girl twelve years old who stays with us and three grown sons and another daughter who is fourteen. I am the only dependence at home to work. I am the fifth child among eleven and have always had a hard time. I feel that it was a Godsend to me when I found you out. I feel as my suffering from bearing children will be ended after this one, for I am sure that you are going to help me through this struggle. When my little girl was born I was only fifteen years old and my time was very hard. I am asking you for the remedy to save me from this awful pain and sin of bringing children to the world without any way to care for them. Oh, it is terrible to think of! I had rather die than have this to do. We are very poor people. It has taken almost everything we had to save my husband's leg. There is but very little left, only enough for us to barely live on, and no one to work but me, and how am I to work for so many little children myself, with a crippled husband?

Eight

I was only fifteen years old, and a year ago the third of December I was married to a man thirty-six years old.

I never gave childbirth a thought; my only thought was of a home and a dear husband. I had a child in nine months and one week's time and me being so young it was hard on me. The doctor said that I must surely find some means to avoid having more but he said I would be a fast breeder.

Nine

I married when I was fifteen, have been married only four years and have three children already. I was married in July, 1920, and in April 1921, my first child was born, just eight days before my birthday when I would be only sixteen. Then in December, 1922, my second one came and March, 1924, my third. Now I don't want any more. God knows I don't. I think I could raise these to be good Christian women if I didn't have any more. I get weaker every time. Before I was married I was always called so healthy, but now I am just a nervous wreck. We do not own a roof over our heads and to my notion we never will if we keep having children this close always. We are able only to have help three weeks after one is born, and one time we couldn't get any at all. My husband did what little cooking there was to be done. He is only getting $2.50 a day and that is all we have. I am not able to take in washings or anything to make a little more.

Ten

I am seventeen years old and two months ago gave birth to a poor little thin baby girl and a month later went to the hospital and had a tubercular growth cut out of my face. When I became pregnant I weighed eighty-seven pounds. Was deathly sick the whole nine months and when I was confined suffered hell. I had pains every six minutes for fifteen hours and hard labor pains every two or three minutes for another fifteen hours and not one drop of chloroform. My baby's head was mashed almost to a pulp. For days she was never laid down on her head. My bones are set so close together that they almost had to be pried apart before she came. You don't know how grateful I would be if you would send me information. My husband is thirty-eight years old. We have a farm of forty acres and work from morning till night to make ends meet. We cannot afford to have help and I am just dragging around wondering how long it will be before I will have to give up.

Eleven

I married when I was but fifteen years old. My health is bad. I am sick all the time and have children fast. I have got to where I lose them. I am not strong enough to carry them. The doctor has told me I have tuberculosis, and I can't hardly live half of the time and I would be more than glad if you will write me a letter in plain language so I can understand. I don't believe it will be any sin when anyone can't keep them when they get that way. The doctor says I will never carry another till time any more. You know my health is a wreck and I am just twenty-two years now. I have not seen any pleasure in my young days. I don't mind what I paid for your book so much good reading in it, if I could just understand the main part.

Twelve

I am young, very young, and soon will be the mother of two babies, for the first child is not fourteen months old. I am sure you will be surprised to know that I am only seventeen years old. I married at fifteen years, and gave birth to my first child when I was sixteen, and when she was nine months old I had to wean her for this other baby.

I never associated with bad girls, and although many young girls in this town have doctors to give them medicine or perform operations to rid them of babies, I know that is wrong. That is why I will soon have two babies. But it is so hard, so wearisome and dangerous to go through with what I've been through and I would just simply hate to have to undergo this again soon but I do not know how to prevent it and have no one to tell me, in fact I don't ask, but I am humbly asking you, Is there any way you can help me? My husband is good to me, but $12.00 a week is just barely enough to keep us alone from poverty, and he is only two weeks older than I am, so you see we are both only children.

Thirteen

I would like for you to help me not to have more babies. I would rather do anything than have another. I don't think anything is sweeter than being a mother. I'm twenty-six years of age, the mother of eight children, the oldest being eight. Had one set of twins, boys. I have three that can't walk. Now have never known anything but to have two very little ones at a time. I can't nurse them so therefore they are not stout. My husband also isn't a stout man. My two youngest are in a baby hospital now, I mean besides a baby eight weeks old.

My children have been anywhere from seventeen months, twenty, and twenty-four months between them. One baby was fifteen months when the twins came. There were twenty-one months between them and the next. She was not quite thirteen months when the next one came. The doctors say that she will never be well any more. They don't think she will live long. She is two years and four months. Well there is the one next to her she was fourteen months between her and the last. I love being a mother, but they are not well and I see more than ever that my health is breaking so that's the reason I want help.

Fourteen

I am twenty years old, am the wife of a brakeman. We have one boy, he will be three, one baby boy dead, was born at seven months, lived eighteen days. Have had two miscarriages. I was married at sixteen. My husband only works steady about three months. He has a fine education but even work that takes educated people is full, so the rest of the year he does anything he can get to do, which isn't much and it's all he can do to provide for me and the boy we have. I would like to have another child some day but not until I can have a home and can afford another. But I live in fear all the time. My husband is kind and very good, but like myself, he doesn't know what to do. It is terrible that the human race should be so ignorant. If only the women would wake up and demand that knowledge. I just won't have another until I can take care of it like I should.

Fifteen

I would like advice from you how can I control from not getting pregnant so soon. It's three years I'm married and I got three children and I menstruate right along. My smallest baby is three months old and I'm afraid I'll get pregnant any time from now on. So please give me some kind of advice because I cannot support what I got and when they are four I don't know what to do. I'm only twenty years of age. I'd like to have a rest for at least a good while for I have a very hard time when I get a child. I get badly tore and from getting a year apart it's worse.

Sixteen

I have three children and they are all babies yet and they are a little more than I can manage as my baby is eight months old and the oldest one is a little over three years old, so you can see for yourself I have my hands full. My husband is just a laborer in the mills and we are in so much debt as the mills are just working half-time and I do not know the day I have had a dress or any clothing at all. I just wear whatever I get given to me from my sister and I do not want to have any more children for a while so I can go out and help my man to get our debts paid. I am young yet and I can wait for a while to have more children. I am not twenty years old yet. I think I have had my share for a while, don't you? I would not care if we could afford it, but I have not got the doctor paid for the last one yet.

Seventeen

I was a high school girl of seventeen when I married a farmer, fourteen years ago. I am the mother of eight living children, one baby dead and a three months miscarriage. I am thirty-one years of age and have spent almost all of my married life nursing and carrying babies. I would like you to advise me what to do to prevent from having any more children. My oldest child is thirteen and my youngest five months. I love my children and would give my life for them. But what good would that do, who will teach and care and sacrifice for them as a mother will? I know it was my ignorance on this important subject that has put me where I am, but I must learn all I can for I have three little girls who will need to know about these things and it is them I must learn to care for and save from my fate. My oldest child, a boy, was born February, 1910, when I was eighteen years, a sickly child weighing four pounds at one month. Second child a girl, born November 1910, lived ten hours. Third, a boy, born May, 1913, weighing six pounds. Fourth, a boy born May 1914, weighing ten pounds. Fifth, a girl, born November, 1915, weighing eight pounds. Sixth, a boy, born 1917, weighing twelve pounds. Seventh, a girl, born July, 1918, weighing eight pounds. Eighth, a boy, born 1920, weighing ten pounds. Ninth, a three months' miscarriage and the tenth child a girl born March 1923, weighing eight pounds. As you can see, I have only nursed and weaned one child until I was pregnant again. I have always suffered and worked and never enjoyed myself without this fear of being pregnant again. I love my husband as much as ever and we never quarrel or have hard feelings. We both work hard to make an honest living for our children. I have hired help when I need them most, but I want my home, my husband and children to myself, to raise as we wish without being spoiled with hired help. I want to teach my girls and to get advice for myself. My mother is old-fashioned and thinks children should not know too much and never told us girls what to expect at our sick times or when we were married. I have asked my doctor many times but never get any satisfaction from him. I think I have been down to the valley of death enough times. So please answer and give me some hope.

Eighteen

I have been married seven years and have had all kinds of trouble. I was married when I was fifteen years old, for my mother was left a widow at thirty-two years and could no longer make a living for us children and we all had to get married very young. My first baby I only carried seven months and had a miscarriage and do not know whatever caused it, and suffered a good bit with it. She was a girl, and three months after that I was pregnant again and while carrying her I had to be in bed every two weeks with appendicitis. Two months after the girl was born I had to go through an operation. I am having children one right after the other. I feel worn out and sick all the time. I have six children now and my youngest is seven months old. I want to get help before I am troubled with pregnancy again for I don't think I can go through this again. My husband is a poor miner and complains about his back all the time but has to work hard for if he don't we would all starve.

Nineteen

I am a girl twenty-one years old, yet the mother of four children. The oldest not yet five, the youngest a babe of three months—two boys and two girls. I was married when I was only fifteen, my first born when I was sixteen. Although I married young I was fortunate enough to get one of the best men on earth, but he, like myself, is ignorant of prevention. We are farmers with limited means and have all the children we can do for now. My husband went to our family physician but he told him nothing could be used that would not be harmful to me. May God help you to help me as you have helped other mothers, is my earnest prayer.

Twenty

I am a riting you to help me if you can. I am only twenty-four and the mother of five mighty healthy children but I have all the children I care for, as many as I feel like I can ever care for. As you know the more any one has the weaker they get. I am well and stout to what lots of people are that has as many children as I have but still I am not as stout as I was four or five years ago. I know as young as I am if I keep bringing children in the world I soon wont have any strength at all. My mother died when I was eight years old and in a year my father married again and my step-mother wasn't as kind to us children as she ought to of been, so I married when I was thirteen and in August before I was fifteen I had a little boy born to me. I have ben trying ever since to find some way to keep from having any more but it all ben in vain but I hope you have a way to help me. My husband dont think there is any way to keep a woman from having children without doing something that will injure her health but I dont think having children like I am is doing me any good or him either. I feel sure we woulden of had the children we got if I could of done any thing with him. I talked and pleaded with him and tried to show him where it was wrong to bring so many children in the world, but not one thing could I do with him. It looks if he dont care just so he can get his wants filled. I tell him lots of times he has got me to the place where I wish I had never seen a man.

Twenty-one

I have been married twelve years and I am twenty-six years old so you see I was just three days of being fourteen when I was married. That seems awful young now, doesn't it, altho it didn't then. We were married only one year and ten days when a baby girl came to our home and we were very happy and I got along very well, could take care of baby and do my housework. In less than two years a baby boy came and I didn't do so well then. I thought maybe it would be some few years before another would come but only eighteen months another boy, and I was very bad and the doctor said I couldn't keep on, I was too young, but gave no advice. It lacked only a few days being two years till a baby girl was born dead and I was so bad for three weeks before she came till I didn't want to get well myself. It seems that I just couldn't go on and about the time I began to get some strength back we had another baby girl and I was in bed three months after she came. I never had any milk at all for her and we had to raise her on a bottle and the last time I just worried until I became almost insane. I just suffered till I did not care whether I lived or died, although I loved my husband and babies dearly. My husband looked like he did all for me he could, worried as I did. We tried lots of things but nothing was any good. We didn't have anything only what my husband could work and make. It was very hard on us and babies too as the doctor said I couldn't get that way for three years, so last summer I miscarried at two and a half months and I haven't been able most of the time to do my housework as I am in fear of that all the time I can hardly rest at all.

Twenty-two

I hardly know how to commence but I am coming to you for advice and help as many other poor helpless women have. I would be perfectly happy if not for the same old thing—too many babies too close together. My third baby was born a week after the first one's third birthday. Just three babies in three years and I am only twenty-two years old and I made the mistake of nursing the first one six months after I got pregnant. I pitied him so I hated to wean him and was too ignorant to know I was doing him harm and now he isn't stout and the second one is very nervous and I am also so nervous sometimes I don't know what to do. Actually I get so nervous at times I get sick and now I am afraid I am pregnant again and my baby only eight months old. And I don't know how I'll ever get along for I'm always in misery for six months before my children are born and then to do all the work for them and carry another baby around too, up until the last day as I always have done and the last time I was confined I thought I'd go crazy for the other two babies didn't get half decent care and cried pretty near all the time I was in bed. I have a good husband who would do anything to help me if we only knew how.

Twenty-three

I wonder if you will kindly give me some advice on Birth Control? I have been married not quite four years and have four children, the eldest of which is not three years of age and I feel that I must conserve my strength for a few years for the sake of my children. My home is ninety miles from the nearest hospital and too far from a physician to ever have attendance at child-birth. We have to be grateful for a neighbouring woman to give me her companionship—not assistance—in my time of need. I will be so glad if you could give me some advice or literature on the subject.

Twenty-four

I am twenty-two years old the mother of six children and give birth to a baby every year and it has begun to weaken me. I have been married four years and have six children, one or twins every year or so. I really have more than I can take care of and it puzzles me sorely to ask for help.

Twenty-five

I am the mother of four small children ranging in ages: two, three, four, five, only one year apart and have had two miscarriages since the last child which is two years old. I have kidney trouble and am ruptured. The rupture doesn't bother me only when pregnant, then it is almost past endurance. My husband is also in poor health. I have consulted doctors upon this subject, but of no avail. They only say there is ways but they don't know. I have tried many ways but they do no good. I am almost discouraged. We are trying to pay for a home but it is a very hard matter to save anything as we have so many doctor bills and I am not able to work.

Twenty-six

I was married three days over nine months when my first baby was born and less than a year and five months I had another baby. Another one and a half year I had the third baby, the oldest three years and had three children. I done a lot of worrying when my third baby was to be born, but that baby lived only two months. About two months after that baby was dead I had to have an operation and about ten months after that I had another baby, but she was stillborn as I was so weak and worried when I was carrying her. The doctor even took my tonsils when I was four months carrying this, as I was so weak and nervous and two months after all this I has my womb cleaned and sewed up. And inside of ten months I had another baby. She is now three years old and I think I have had an awful rest, but I am scared stiff I'll be caught again. We have all we can to care for our three children we have now. My husband don't want any more. If we can get out of it. He has worked hard to keep me out of it. I suppose this letter it just trouble for you to read but it feels good to have some one to tell this to for me. My mother had twelve children, ten living, and I was the oldest and always took care of children at home and then didn't get any rest when married.

Twenty-seven

I am the mother of seven living children and been

married eleven years and have had two miscarriages. I have a tumor now growing in my right side. I nearly die with it. My baby is now six months old. My aim is to try to keep from getting pregnant until I have an operation.

II

The Pinch of Poverty

"WE are poor." How can we live—eight children, I and him on one dollar per day?"

"Our children are not going to school now for we cannot buy the shoes for them. . . ." "So poor that we have suffered for the want of eats and clothes. . . ." "The four of us are huddled in one little room about eight feet square." "We are always in debt. . . ." "We both have lots of gray hair already, we are old at twenty-six. . . ."

Such are the bitter cries of these slave mothers who, in addition to being caught in the trap of enforced maternity, are forever harassed by the sharp pinch of poverty.

Here, in the group of documents which follows, we are confronted with no new problem. It is merely another aspect of the same problem viewed from another angle. We see women of the same class and character as the girl mothers—women who have felt the pinch of poverty from their own childhood, who have looked toward marriage as an escape from the hardships and struggles of their own families. But the effort to establish and maintain a decent standard of living has invariably been cancelled by the swift arrival of babies.

The drama of life for these women has become a desperate, ever losing struggle against pregnancy on the one side and poverty on the other. Each new baby is less welcome than the last. Its chances of surviving the perils of infancy are correspondingly lessened. As the children grow older, the expenses of the family increase and the burden of debt becomes heavier and heavier. Even in villages and in the country, the growing family is forced to huddle together in one or two rooms. The younger children are clothed in the worn out garments of the older. One mother records the impossibility of sending the children to school because shoes are too expensive, and the roads muddy. Another revolts against the thought of bringing more children into the world to suffer the hardships she herself has been through. Another confesses herself an old woman at the age of twenty-six, worn out by her terrible struggle for a bare livelihood.

In this environment of poverty, of destitution, of hunger, of debts, of anxiety, often of physical and mental defect, and always of fear, the advent of each new baby is looked upon as a calamity. Who can express surprise that children born under such conditions come into the world with a handicap of physical and psychical defect, and are practically doomed before their birth? Poverty pure and simple—if it ever is pure and simple—without the complications of ignorance and ill health, may be—as our opponents assert—an advantage, a "spur to ambition," instead of an evil. But poverty multiplied by ignorance, hunger, disease, congenital defect, cannot be a proper breeding-ground for the future generations of America.

What arguments can the opponents of Birth Control summon to refute the human documents I submit below?

One is tempted to ask what benign Providence is pleased by this unwilling, suffering submission to one of the blindest of the forces of Nature—a force tyrannical and almost diabolical in its destruction of human hopes and in its inexplicable power to interweave into a hopeless tangle all the bonds that keep mankind in slavery.

One

I have been married twelve years and am the mother of seven girls. The oldest is ten years old and you know what I suffered. We are poor. We can't care for what we got half the time for them to be healthy. I got one dead. My oldest one living has got heart trouble. My youngest one is seven months old. I'm just twenty-eight years old. We are working on the shares this year. My husband is a hard worker and tries to make an honest living. And, let me tell you I have to work to make ends meet. I saw, chop wood, plow and have my little kids to tend to for they are not large enough to help me but a little. Oh, I have a hard time. We are never out of debt. I never get to go anywhere for I never got a dress nice enough to wear or I'm always in a family way. Oh, it is hard on poor women to be in my shape. It is just one baby after another. I can't stand it much longer and work like I do, trying to keep a little to eat and wear. I pray you to help me. If I could stop having babies long enough for these to get where they could walk, Lord, how glad I would be. I know little babies are sweet but when you can't clothe them like they are to be and then they are sick. Lord what trouble mothers do have. Please, pray help me if you can. If you don't, I don't know who will.

Two

I have two little children, and I am like a lot of other poor mothers, I have two too many, so that is why I am writing to you. I have been nothing but a nervous wreck since my first baby was born. We live in a two-room box car and you can imagine our circumstances. I have a good husband and he is proud of his family, but my life is not worth living, nervous, poor and sick all the time. The doctor says not to worry but that is easy to say. When a person has a constant worry for fear they will have more babies and not able to take of them. I am a Christian and I do not want to bring on an abortion, ruin my health or go to hell for murder. But I don't think God wants me to have babies when I can't take care of them.

Three

I am a woman and I have eight children. I am twenty-nine years old. I feel as I am fifty-nine. My baby is eleven months and fourteen days. I never go over a year before I'm pregnant again, so please write me a letter at once. I can't attend these eight children that I have and they are not able to do anything for themselves. Lord, what am I to do with any more. I am a poor woman. I can't work far out for I have always got a young baby. My husband only makes $1.00 per day, some days nothing. How can we live—eight children I and him on $1.00 per day? Please tell me what to do to prevent having any more children. What can I do with those poor miserable children?

I have not the means to do for them, neither the physical strength to do for them. I have got a goiter growing on my neck. The doctor says it came from the strain from childbirth, but yet they won't stop me from having children, as they would rather see me suffer and die. Every time I have a child it gets larger.

Four

I have already six children and one miscarriage and my oldest is only nine years old and my baby is one year and eight months. Now I am in constant fear that I will get that way again for if I do, it is going to be terrible for I have to have an operation, for having my children so close together had put me in such a condition that I can hardly do my own work, and an operation is almost impossible. In the condition we are in now we cannot afford it. We are living on a farm which is all new land; we have only ten acres clear on it. We have no income nowhere, and seven miles from the nearest town. Our children are not going to school now for we cannot buy the shoes for them and its too wet to go with their poor ones.

Five

We have always been poor, so poor that we have suffered for the want of eats and clothes. This spring I lost my oldest son four years old which took me down very badly as I have not been in the best of health since he was born, and now to think I had to lose him. I have two more younger. It is not because I do not want any more. I would be so glad if I could be in the condition to have another so I could have one named after the one I loved so dearly. Right now I want to tell you the conditions we are in, so you will see why I am driven to ask you for advice if I can get it. This spring we were in $2,000 debt before we had our bad luck with the boy, when the expenses we got for him came to $300.00 more. My husband got $4.00 a day during the summer months, but now there has not been any work for about a month. There is a big grocery bill that should have been paid, as I expect every time I go to the store after a little sugar or soap that they will refuse me. My husband has paid out all the money he earned this summer which was not much. Now it is getting cold and we should have warm clothing such as winter underwear and stockings, but where will we get it, I've asked myself a thousand times. Seems like we will just have to freeze and huddle up to the stove all winter. Our house is so cold in the winter time. We feel the wind blow right through it. My husband could go out to work about twenty-five miles away but that would leave me with the chores to do and my baby is too small for me to leave in the house alone and she is a cross nervous baby and has to be on my arms all the time.

Six

I hope and pray that you will get this letter and open your wonderful heart and help a poor devil like me. I can't tell you all my troubles because it would take more paper than I have got. I am twenty-six years old. I have had five children, four living. (My husband is deaf and

I know he is the biggest drunkard in this world.) He don't care for himself nor his family, rambles around and spends all his money. He gives us a little something to eat and that is all. My kids are small and I have to take in sewing to get some clothes for me and my kids to wear. The charitable people give us some old clothes sometimes, so I manage to hide our skin. Somehow my last two kids are almost twins. I be so nervous all the time, my heart is bad. I have to have them by myself. He won't pay the doctor and I know if I get that way again I surely will die. My oldest boy nine looks awful pale and sickly. My next is six and can't talk. The next, a girl, is ruptured in the stomach. The next is one year old. There is nothing wrong with him as I know yet. I want you to help me. If I was able I wouldn't ask this of you. You couldn't help anybody that needs it any worse than I do. For God's sake, answer this letter and tell me what to do. I would rather die than have any more children for a man like my husband.

Seven

I have six children now and have had to live in two rooms for a long time for we did not have enough money to have better. My husband works but he is not well and is sick nearly half the time and when I am in the family way I am sick for the first three months and in bed the last two. I am only thirty and have a daughter thirteen years old. I lost one at about three months along and have been sick with my heart ever since. That was three months ago. My oldest boy is not very bright and I dread to have any more. So if you would only be kind enough to tell me what to do to help myself from having any more children I would be awful grateful. I was only sixteen when I was married and have never been allowed to know anything and now I don't know much but I feel I am my own boss now and will try to get all the books that I can afford to get and teach my children to know what they ought to know.

Eight

This is a call for help. I have been married three years and have two sweet babies, one two years and the other just a few months old. The four of us are huddled in one little room about eight feet square. At night there is no way of ventilating the place and I think it's a crime; I think children deserve something better than that. My husband don't care for children, and says if another one comes he will clear out. I have another sister deserted by her husband for the same thing. Please advise me what to do.

Nine

I have three children, my oldest is only three, the next is only one and will be two shortly, and my baby is six months old, and he is helpless. Doesn't have any use of himself, and I am thinking that I may get in family way again. God knows I cannot bear it. My husband is not well. He was gassed while in France and losing weight all the time, going downhill. We are poor. We haven't one thing on earth. My husband worked for wages until he found that he could not stand it any more. We are trying to farm this year though we had to have help. Everything we have, house, fixtures and all belong to the landlord and I wanted to stay where I could help. Can't you help me and give me peace? I am afraid, afraid to bring any more in the world. My baby is awful sweet though it hurts to think of his condition. I am twenty-two years old and awful weak. I weigh about one hundred pounds.

Ten

We are poor family and cannot afford to have any more children. We have three now, just regular steps and stairs, and we are always in debt. My husband is a fisherman, and he hasn't caught hardly any fish all winter, and we are so far in debt that we certainly will be lucky if we ever get out again, and we never will if I must keep on having more babies that we cannot support. I'm only twenty-seven years old and my husband is thirty. Work is terrible scarce around here.

Eleven

I am a mother of seven children, my baby four months old. I am only thirty-five years myself and perhaps can have just that many more if I don't find someone to help me out. As I am a farmer woman, I have to work all year round. We just bought the farm seven years ago and have $4000 debt yet, so we feel we can't hire a man, besides raising a large family, so I have to take a man's place. I am not very strong. Since my last baby is born I have so much headaches and the baby isn't well either. My only wish is that I won't have to have any more children.

Twelve

I am the mother of four little ones, the oldest only six years old. They are all puny little things, and need so much care and I am not strong enough to care for them, although I try, as we are not able to hire help. The baby is five weeks old. I am so nervous and weak I can hardly stand, yet I have all the care of the children, cooking, washing to do. My husband is a hired man on a farm. His pay is $50.00 per month. What can we do for our children? We can't even dress them comfortably and feed them as they should be fed, although we try so hard. My man goes to work at six in the morning and comes back at seven in the evening so he can't help me any. He isn't strong, only weighs one hundred twenty-five pounds, while I weigh one hundred pounds. It is an awful thing for us to bring more children, little weak things like ourselves, with no way to make a living only their two hands, into the world to be knocked and brow-beat all their lives. I cry and pray and be careful and it all does no good. I have one of your books and don't see why there isn't more people like you in this world. I am only twenty-six years old, my husband the same, so we have a long time yet ahead, although we both have lots of gray hair already, we are old at twenty-six. What a burning shame when I think of how rearing children has brought us down from what we were. I can't see why I should be denied the information I ask for.

Thirteen

I was married at the age of eighteen. Now I am married for seven years and I have four children, they are a year and a few months apart. My last baby girl came this year just one year and four days from my little boy. It's only a week and three days ago since she was born and I am up already doing work because a lady helped me just for five days and I can't afford any other help.

Won't you please in God's name help me? I want to raise the babies I have to be good men and women but if I have any more babies before these are any older I don't think I can because my health is failing. If I only knew what kind of life I was to lead I would have never married. I am a little over twenty-four and already skinny, yellow and so funny looking and I want to hold my husband's love. He is twenty-nine and oh, I love him and the babies I have. He tried to help me but somehow I got caught anyway and a baby came. We didn't have any money to get rid of it and now when I look on her little innocent, red face I am glad I didn't kill it. If you help me I swear I will do anything you want me to.

When you was in Chicago I wanted to go to see you but I had no nice clothes and I knew I would make you feel ashamed if I went dressed shabbily, but how can I dress on $25.00 a week and four mouths to feed, my husband and myself and rent in a basement, $12.00. Oh, if I could see you I would kneel and kiss your hands and you

34

would help me. I swear by all that's holy I will not bring you trouble if you help me. My mother bore eleven children and nine are living so you see I never had it good always work, work and poor like anything. I only went to seventh grade, maybe I wouldn't have seen seventh grade but I wasn't of age to quit.

Fourteen

I thought I would write you a letter. I am sorry I can't help you in subscribing for the Birth Control because my husband is a miner. He is out of work and has been for sometime. The mine where he works shut down for good. I keep putting off writing, I thought I could get some money for to help you but could not. We have not got our home paid for yet and likely to loose it. You know how it is with a family of eleven to do for I am sure. But maybe I can help some way, I am for you. One thing, I got three girls and I don't want them to go through what I have if I can help it. We are poor people and have a hard time I can stand it better than I can stand to see my children suffer what I have.

Fifteen

After seven years of married life, I have had six children. At the age of twenty-six, I look forty, just through ignorance of Birth Control. Being poor, I have no way of enjoying myself. It's the wash-tub one day; the sewing machine the next. You can picture two young people and the children we have.

Sixteen

I have five children, a girl and four boys, my oldest seven years and baby ten months. Our family is so large and my husband gets such small pay we can hardly live. We could not send our little boy to school because we could not buy shoes for him. I am a cripple, was almost burned to death when a child, which makes caring for the little tots and house work hard for me. I had to get up when baby was eight days old because we could not pay for help and I haven't been well since.

Seventeen

I am so worried, I do not know what to do so have come to you for advice. I am nearly 25 years old and have been married two years and a half and have two children, a boy nineteen months and a baby girl three months old. Now I am worried to death for fear of becoming pregnant again. I dearly love children but could never be able to care for any more right now. I haven't even gained my normal strength from having the first baby. He was barely six months old when I became pregnant again. I do all my housework, washing and cleaning. My husband is in poor health and cannot do any kind of strong work. He is bell-boy in a small hotel at present so we cannot afford to hire help of any kind. I want to give my children a fair chance in this world. I have suffered poverty all my life. My father died when I was two years old leaving my mother with four small children and penniless. I know what it means to go out in the world and earn a living without an education. Why should I raise a lot of children and have them suffer?

Eighteen

I am almost at my wits' end now. I married when nineteen years of age and after fourteen months my first baby was born. We sure were proud too, but since then we have five more little ones each coming twenty-one months after the other, we have been married a little over eleven years and six children. I am almost frantic with the cares and worries. My husband is an honest and steady worker and is doing his utmost to keep his family in the things most needed but no one knows how hard it is. Both he and I have to do with almost nothing to keep the children clothed, my husband's wages average between $125.00 and $135.00 a month and it keeps us going to keep going, we can't afford a large family as we cannot provide for them. My baby is a year old and if no more babies come I could go out to work and help my husband, but as it is it's impossible and I beg you Mrs. Sanger if you can please help me find a way to prevent pregnancy. I have appealed to our family physician and he knows the conditions of our family, but when I beg him to tell me what to do he would only say: "to abstain." I love my husband and I certainly would not refuse him what rightfully belongs to him. Can you blame me? Were my husband of a disagreeable disposition I would have turned coward and ended it all, but as it is he does his best both for the children and me and we certainly love our family. If no more babies come and time goes on there is a bright future in store for us.

Nineteen

I was married in May, 1917, and as I was not very strong my first child, a girl, was born at eight months. In seventeen months I lost a seven months' pair of twin boys. In sixteen months more another little girl came to us and six months ago, a boy. I am very sickly and suffer terribly during the entire time I carry my children.

Sometimes we have no help at all during confinement, my husband caring for me and the baby and doing the housework until I am up. Then afterwards I am so weak I am not able to care for the children as they should be. My husband helps me what he can, but he is not strong either and can hardly make a living for us. He is bothered with rheumatism. Three years ago I thought I would lose him, and he has been unable to work at all much of the time since that. We are very poor and were it not for the kindness of relatives in helping us I do not know how we would get along. I would like your advice as to how to keep from becoming a mother as we do not see how we can care for any more.

Twenty

I am a striking miner's wife. We have been out on coal strike here for three years and live in tents and we don't get any clothing at all from our union. What few things we get other people give them to us. During my three years in tents I have lost two children and have two left. One is two years old a little boy, and the other one is two months old. It is a girl. Sometimes friends send us shoes and clothes. I am only twenty-one years old. I cannot take care of any more and I am waiting patiently for a reply.

Twenty-one

I am twenty-two and a mother of four children, one dead and three living. I often cry to see that I am in that miserable way. That's why I come to you for advice. I had my last baby three months ago and it died. My husband is in bad health. He hasn't been able to work for five months. We were forced to move in with mother and father for the high rents that we had to pay. Some times I didn't even have enough for my babies to eat. Oh, how I cry to see my babies in this way. I don't know what I'd do if I had another baby that I know I can't take care of any more.

III

The Trap of Maternity

THERE is a certain type of mother who can best be described as a "breeder."

She is endowed by Nature for the function of motherhood. Often gifted with a splendid physical constitution, she seems to inherit a predisposition to pregnancy. These women often tell you that their mothers and their grandmothers gave birth to ten, twelve, fifteen or more children.

These women are caught early, and never released from the trap of involuntary maternity.

The case-histories I have chosen to present for the consideration of the reader in the present chapter are representative of the hardships and sufferings endured by these martyrs.

These mothers may be fairly said to exemplify the typical American mother—the mother worshipped in our popular songs, stories and motion-pictures. They reveal themselves heroically willing to make any sacrifice to their children. They work like slaves to provide food, clothing, shelter and education for the ever-growing brood. The majority of them are uncomplaining, long-suffering, thinking first of the well-being and the future happiness of the boys and girls they have brought into the world.

Yet for the greater part of their married life they are compelled to fulfill a double duty. For all the time they are "slinging pots and pans," milking cows, or engaging in the heavy manual and physical labor of farm-life, they are bringing an apparently endless stream of children into the world.

Pregnancy succeeds pregnancy in endless succession. Hardly is one child weaned than another is on its way. The double drain on the health of the mother is easy to imagine: she has neither the time nor the energy to devote to the living children in the most critical and delicate stage of their development. Nor can she, on the other hand, conserve her strength, health and vital force to assure a rightful heritage of well-being to the unborn child she is carrying. From this slave mother is exacted a triple tax: her own health is broken down; the well-being of her older children is jeopardized; and the last-born infants are brought into the world with progressively decreasing chances of survival.

In the appended documents we find the confessions of women, the majority of whom have passed their thirtieth year, and many of whom are approaching or past forty, who have enjoyed no surcease from the endless drudgery of childbearing, who have given birth to eight, ten, or twelve children, and who are pathetically begging for release from the long slavery they have suffered and are still enduring.

Many of them, as we see, could at one time have been described as "child mothers." Most of them have married early, and although the mothers of exceptionally large families, are still young in years.

All their sacrifices, all their drudgery, all of their mute, inarticulate heroism, and even their soldier-like descent into the valley of the shadow of death bring no reward.

Poverty closes in about them. Instead of being an occasion for inward rejoicing, the advent of each new baby sharpens their realization that happiness is only a receding mirage. Is it any wonder that so many of these mothers trapped by maternity confess that life hardly seems worth living?

These documents give us something that we cannot obtain from any number of "maternity surveys" or "biometric" computations of vital statistics—the secret, never-told factor of maternal anguish and sacrifice.

Reading them, one cannot refrain from asking if this philanthropic and humanitarian nation of ours can long consent to recruit its citizens of 1938 or 1948, or for the rest of this century, at such an inestimable cost of human well-being and health.

Leading authorities on maternal hygiene teach us that even under the most favorable conditions, and even for those women best suited physically and psychically for the function of maternity, at least two years should elapse between one birth and the inauguration of a new period of pregnancy. Some claim three years. This spacing, experience has taught us, is necessary for the health of the child already born, for the mother, and the child-to-be. The violation of this fundamental rule of maternal hygiene and its dire consequences may be noted in the documents I submit herewith:

THE TRAP OF MATERNITY

One

I am thirty-five. In seventeen years of married life have brought eight children into the world and went down in the grave after three I failed to get. We bought us a little home to start with and oh, the struggle! Have both worked like slaves, I with my own efforts have kept the family in what we had to buy, have sold $300.00 worth of butter, eggs and chickens. He raises what he can for us to eat and saves a little and in this way we have managed to pay for our little home, but have no conveniences whatever. Sometimes I've had only my husband to wait on me when the children came and in every instance have been on the job, slinging pots and pans when my baby was two weeks old and strange to say am still well. I have six children in school and two under my feet, am milking five cows, sell from seventy-five to one hundred pounds of butter a month, fit a package for parcel post every day.

I have milked six cows at six o'clock and brought a baby into the world at nine.

My baby is nine months old and the thoughts of another almost kills me.

Oh! tell me how to keep from having another. Don't open the door of heaven to me and then shut it in my face.

Oh! please tell me, I feel like it's more important to raise what I have than to bring more.

Two

I was married when seventeen, and am thirty-two now, and have eight boys and will be confined again in two months.

I have tried everything everyone told me that was no injury to my health but just the same I get pregnant anyway. Am not able as I used to be for to work for my family but work all the time.

My husband's father is with us. He is about as helpless as a child, with the shaking palsy. Has been that way for twelve years and every year is getting worse. My children are all living but one—he died when fourteen months old. They all are healthy and bright and have all their features all right but it's about enough for to work and make a living for we live on my husband's father's farm. My husband works away whenever he can get work for there is not enough money on the farm to keep the children. My oldest boy, fifteen, is still at school.

Three

I am a young woman in years but an old woman in feelings. I have ten children and two doctors told me with the last one, now five months old, that I was good for five or six more babies if I could live through it. And besides the babies I've had pneumonia five times and gallstones real bad. I have six sisters in the same condition and Birth Control would be such a blessing to them. My husband always told me it was a sin to do anything to keep from having children, but I know better. My little baby has been sick all it's life I am so tied down I can't do anything and not able to do anything, and my husband is not strong.

We are poor people. You know that by the size of my family we do not have what we need, just what we can get. I get desperate sometimes and feel like killing myself to get out of my troubles, then I am ashamed of my weakness and I am determined to stay and care for the little helpless things I've brought into the world, but many the times I've got desperate and almost crazy. I never see a well day or a restful hour.

I don't want my husband to know I use Birth Control. The reason I am not pregnant again now is I just refuse to be, but it makes my husband very mad at me.

All of my friends, or nearly all, have eight or ten children. My children are all close together, some of them have thirteen months between them. I am always sick and tied down. Have three babies on hand to attend to all the time and fast as one can begin to get down and out of my arms another little one comes.

One of my sisters, forty years old, has had twelve and is still having babies. Our mother had fifteen. Grandmother fifteen. And I've tried remedies, but they are no good.

Four

I am one of the many who bear children too often.

I love them dearly but I am only twenty-eight years of age and to give birth to my ninth child in about three weeks. Only have four living children, but they are winners.

I was married in December, 1912, to one of the best men. He is a model husband, very good to me, and not a bad habit. I gave birth to my first baby February, 1914. It was a seven months baby and only weighed three and one-half pounds, with most of clothes on. He is now a big boy and perfect as one could wish. In July 1915 I gave birth to an eight months baby girl, five and one-half pounds. She was taken from us in January 1916, after only five hours' illness. July 1916 I had another six and one-quarter pound baby girl. She was a beautiful child and was very fat and strong, but died of pneumonia on May 1917. December 1917 my third girl was born. She weighed eight pounds. Is now bright and very well. December 1918 I lost one at six weeks, January 1920 I gave birth to another boy. He had the "flu" at six weeks and died. My next boy was born April 1921. He weighed nine pounds, and is now lively and strong. My next child was a boy born November 1922. He is small, but fat and well. You see that is very close, and I am so nervous this time. I do not sleep over two or three hours any night and as soon as I lie down I am so short of breath. I am not usually sick very long, but have chills for quite a time after. I dread this birth worse than any yet. My husband feels awful bad about it, although he loves his family. We were careful before the last two or three came but I get pregnant so very easily.

He says this must be our last and I pray it may be for I sure cannot stand it. He is very good to me and feels so bad for me and helps me in every way he can and I also have many labor-saving helps about the house. I appeal to you to tell me how I can prevent having any more children. I am not of the money class but have a comfortable home. I do not wish my baby to die but want a nice baby as long as I must go through with it but we pray to God to not send any more. I do not think it cruel to prevent it but it is cruel to cause abortion for if there isn't life then there would be in time.

Five

I am the mother of nineteen children, the baby only twenty months old. I am forty-three years old and I had rather die than give birth to another child. The doctor does not give me any information at all, only to be careful. This letter may sound unreasonable, but the records will show that it is true. I have five boys and seven girls living. Two daughters married. One has four children and the other one has five daughters. Have bad health. I need the information for them as well as myself, so for my sake and the sake of humanity please give me the proper information.

Six

I am writing to see if you can help me. I was married when I was fourteen years old and now I am a mother of sixteen children, fourteen living and two dead and I am on my way for another child, three months, and I was sick with this one two months in bed and I am not able to stand on my feet yet. The doctor said I ever have another child I should die, but I am on my way with the seventeenth. One child is married and I have thirteen to take care of and I am not able to do anything. I am only thirty-nine years and all wore out.

Seven

Please help me how to avoid having children and what is the safest thing to do as I think the sun will never shine for me. Am married seventeen years and had nine children and five miscarriages. Had two twins they died. They were seven months' babies and one girl dead, four years old. My baby is eighteen months old and I have girls four years old, ten years, and fifteen years, and a boy thirteen years and a boy seventeen years. All go to school but two. My seven months' babies died and I was that way in ten months again. In sixteen months I had three babies. I suffered untold agony, had fainting spells. My husband is out of work seven months and there are eight of us to keep. The mine is shut down. We are in poor circumstances.

Eight

I am the mother of ten living children and had three miscarriages in two years. And am going to be thirty-nine years old in December. Sure say I have more than my share of children, and with them comes no end of work. My husband goes away from home to work, as it keeps him a-hustling and yet we have nothing, and I do sewing and washing for others to help get along. It sure is a task to bring up a large family, as you ain't able to send them to school, or learn a trade, which costs something. They have to start in life by working when they are' twelve years old, to help buy their clothes. But what's a poor woman going to do? *We ain't living, just merely existing, that's all.* I started out in this world to work at eleven years of age and married at fifteen, and have worked hard ever since, not seeing any good times ahead.

Nine

I have tried so hard not to become pregnant but now I am pregnant again after having given birth to fourteen children. It seems to me it was more than one woman should be asked to. It sure makes my heart and hands full. Husband has cancer of the stomach and I have wanted to be all the comfort to him possible but now my heart is broken and makes me feel like giving up. The oldest child is twenty-four and my last baby was three and now I am along three months again. What should a woman do? It sure seems like a woman should have a limited number of children. I love babies but how can one do justice to a little bunch like this. I some times do not see how I ever have stood it all. I don't see why the law should not be in favor of contraceptives, unless it is that it is in man's hands and he does not have to suffer the consequences.

Ten

I am thirty-four years old and the mother of twelve children. In two months expect another baby. Is there anything I can do if I live through this sickness? One of my babies is just learning to walk, the other, a dear little boy of fifteen months old, is helpless. He is going to be a cripple. We love children but my husband can't earn enough to keep them as we would like to.

Eleven

I am certainly interested in Birth Control if there is such a thing. I have been married thirteen years and have seen myself pregnant every summer but one. I have four living children and expect to be sick again within the next two weeks. Am getting so rundown physically and mentally that I am at the point where something must be done. I have tried so many remedies and used double preventive when others have used the one and were OK. One other thing I wish to mention is that I do not nurse my babies. I am wandering the world for a preventive without an operation and wondered if there was anything you could do for me.

Twelve

I am forty years old, had eleven children. The oldest twenty-three is feeble-minded, seven died when small, but the oldest takes more care than the three others together. Two years ago I had dropsy when my last baby was born and the doctor told me I had to look out so I would not have any more as it would kill me, but the doctor was not allowed to tell me how to keep out of it, so you see I live in constant fear, so please have pity on me and tell me what to do as I have to live for the children's sake.

Thirteen

I am nearly forty years old, and the mother of eleven children, besides four miscarriages. My oldest one is sixteen and one half years and the youngest one just four months. I have eight living, all boys but one. She is eight years old and there were five younger than her. She weighed twelve pounds at birth as did three of those younger ones. The other two were twins and weighed seven and nine pounds. My others weighed ten, ten and one-half and eleven pounds. Now I feel as though I had done my share of baby-raising. This baby is very restless at night and I lose many hours of sleep. I could not nurse my last six children, or rather five for my next to the last one the doctor let die at birth, it's head being born a whole hour before it's body. My milk is so poor in quality that they lose weight on it, but I guess it is nothing to be wondered at when you think of six children and three miscarriages in eight years. Do you think so? Now can you tell me how to avoid having any more. I am in constant fear of getting that way, yet I won't give my husband any excuse to go elsewhere.

Fourteen

I have given birth to twelve children and had terrible confinements, one child was born dead, caused from being born double, which almost caused my death. I just raised six, the others dying in infancy. Married at fourteen, a widow at thirty-eight. If I had the right kind of knowledge I might have married again, but was afraid of having more children. My daughter is tubercular and has had nine children, five living, My son has been married eight years, and has five children, his oldest seven and six. Pick cotton as we live in the cotton belt. I would have given worlds, if they had been mine to give, some way to have governed the size of my family when I was young and could have made something of myself, besides a child-bearing machine and drudge. My husband said it was cheaper to raise children than it was to go into society. It might have been cheaper in dollars, but not in suffering and anguish.

Fifteen

At the time I purchased your book I was mother of eleven children and I thought then that would be the end of my child bearing life, but since then another child has been born and another is on its way, so now I turn to you as I must have your advice. I will appreciate any information that you may give me. I think that it is also my duty to give my daughters any advice that I may receive from you. I work in down town office during the afternoon of each day that I am able in order to earn money to help to keep the little tots fed and clothed. I have been unable to convince my husband of the utmost necessity for us to stop our reproductive acts.

Sixteen

A mother of to-day is truly in need of a friend like you. Especially women like me, that have slaved continually from morning to night, having hardly any pleasure at all. While in my younger years my parents died leaving my brothers and I alone in this wide world, with poverty right in our midst, working hard daily. When I became eighteen years of age I married and found happiness, about a year afterwards I gave birth to my first child, a difference of two years my second child, and we were so happy until finally I became so discouraged that I wanted to die. I am now thirty-eight years ten months, and the mother of ten living children, two of my children dying in infancy. I am very nervous at times, and to think that all my children were born in poverty, and sorely neglected for I was unable to give them the proper care. My husband is good to me, laboring very hard daily to make a decent living. But oh! the struggles are almost unendurable, under the present conditions. Ignorance on this important subject has put me where I am. None of my friends ever told me anything, and I'm sure they knew for they married as long as I am, and have only one and two children, and seem so happy, have ideal homes and everything to their hearts' content.

Seventeen

I have given birth to ten living children, have had three miscarriages and am now pregnant four months. I do all my own work so we will save that much more to try and educate these children as best we can, so they can be independent and make a good living for themselves. My strength is giving out and if I could stop having children after this one comes I think we could manage nicely as I feel I have one of God's best men. He does not drink, smoke nor chew, and spends all his time with me and children when not at work. He helps me in every way he can, but at that it is too much for us both. My oldest son is fifteen years and my baby ten months. If you can teach me how to prevent any more children I will be evermore indebted to you.

Eighteen

I am thirty-eight years old and have brought nine children into the world, one of which died in infancy. The babies were all close together. Also have had two miscarriages. I have tried sleeping apart from my husband but he insists upon his sexual satisfaction so does not help a great deal. We are poor and my husband takes most of the money for his comforts and needs and I and the family have to go without. My mother helps me a great deal in getting clothes for the children.

Nineteen

I am thirty-three years of age, have been married a little less than fourteen years and have given birth to seven children, six of whom are living, one dying at the age of two years and four months from influenza, almost five years ago. Have also had three miscarriages during this time and am now pregnant again expecting to be confined in about one month.

I do not feel that I have shirked the responsibility of

motherhood but do feel that I have all we can provide for and feeling that you can instruct me in what to use as a contraceptive I am writing to you begging for this information. My health is still good and I have a great desire to retain it for the balance of my lifetime in order that I may be able to raise my family and also enjoy life as I should like to.

Twenty

I have had ten children in fifteen years of married life. Have eight living. They are all very healthy children. The doctors told me I was just the one to have them, but I just won't no more. We have not the money to do it. Two hundred dollars a month will not do it right. I want them to have a good education more than I ever had. Now the doctors tell me if I have any more children my health will be gone.

I also made myself have a miscarriage, very near lost my life. That was three months ago.

Since then I have refused to have a thing to do with my husband. He says he does not blame, but I don't know how long it can last. I know he can leave and for myself I do not care, but I could not work out to earn enough to take care of the children. The oldest is fourteen, the baby is sixteen months. I am only thirty-three years old but I look ten years older I cannot do my work any more like I used to. If it wasn't for my oldest girl, she is fourteen, I don't know what I would do, but I can't ask too much of her.

Twenty-one

I am the mother of ten children, the oldest is eighteen years old and my health is ruined. If I feel well one day I feel bad the next. I want to go to the hospital in the fall for repair work and I am constantly dreading pregnancy.

Twenty-two

Please have pity on me and send me some advice as I cannot get any from the doctors here.

I have seven children and I feel that is enough for one woman to raise. That is almost more than we can feed and clothe properly. Husband and I, and the children too, work hard but we would rather give the children we have a good schooling than to be bringing more babies every year or so.

That was my dream when I was a girl, but with ten brothers and sisters I did not get much.

The outlook was dark and I married at sixteen. I was lucky to get a good man who has ever been good to me. Have been married twenty years and gave birth to nine children. Two died in infancy, the rest are all stout and healthy and would make useful men and women some day. We are starting the oldest boy in school and college. He is seventeen years old. The baby is eighteen months old and as I am only thirty-six years old myself, you know that means two or three more babies. My health has been bad for the last six months and I dread another pregnancy.

I live twenty miles from town and cannot get a doctor; most always use a midwife, can't afford to go to a hospital. I suffered death a dozen times with my last child.

Birth Control is the salvation of the poor and as the working man and his family is in the majority, that makes for a better country to live in.

Twenty-three

There isn't anyone that could appreciate help or advice in any way more than I. I have five children, the oldest seven years old and if I could just manage to not have anymore I might live to see them or help send them through school. I almost faint away at the thought of bringing another child in this world when I am not able to care for the ones I already have and cannot hardly feed and clothe them. I manage to send my oldest one to school but it is just do without for the rest of us. I would give anything if I knew how I could prevent having any more children, not that I do not care for the children, but I am just broken down and we haven't anything, always had so much sickness, until we have never got a start. I married when only seventeen and haven't known anything but having children ever since.

Twenty-four

I am asking for some advice concerning my future welfare. I am the mother of ten children. I gave birth to the tenth on June 11. The baby was born dead. I suffered untold misery and came near flooding to death, and feel awfully bad yet not able to be up and doing this writing. I have eight stout robust children. The ninth one is twenty months old and weighs only nineteen pounds, has four teeth, and not walking. I gave nourishment for him only three months. I would rather not bring the dear little things into the world if they are not healthy and stout. My health is so run down and I am so weak I can not expect the children healthy.

Twenty-five

I am writing you for advice as I know you will help me in our condition. We need help now. Neither one of us able to work. My husband has been down, not able to work since last August. I am afraid he will lose his mind. He is thirty-eight years old.

We have been married twelve years and are the father and mother of seven children and will be another one in five months if nothing happens. The last ones were twins. They are ten months old and can't sit up yet and have not got any teeth either. I have so many I can't take care of them like I ought to. I am down with my back nearly all the time. I just can't hardly go. I have not got any strength hardly, my nerves feel all strained to death. If you can tell me how to stop having any more I will be one thousand times glad. I have tried hard to learn something to stop having so many but everything I tried failed. If I could have learned something long ago I never would have had this many. It is breaking me down fast. I was sixteen when I married. I am now twenty-six years old. I guess I take after my mother. She had thirteen, my grandmother had eleven. She is sixty-nine years old. My oldest sister had eleven children. My next sister has eight.

IV

The Struggle of the Unfit

SENTIMENTALISTS never tire of expatiating on the glories of motherhood. Maternity, they tell us, is the birthright of every woman. Salvation arrives with the birth of the first child, and life becomes ever more radiant with the arrival of each new "pledge of affection."

But here is an almost endless series of cases which demonstrate that certain women ought to be totally exempt from the ordeal of maternity. If indeed there is a certain class of women predestined by Nature to the high calling of motherhood, it is no less evident that there are others completely unfit for it.

The forty or so cases presented in this chapter are among the most painful which have ever been sent to me. They record the frightful toll exacted from women unfitted either by physical defect, by psychic abnormality or defective heredity to undertake the serious task of bearing children.

There is something so pitiable in the grim recital of accumulated sufferings they have been through that one is forced at times almost to avert one's gaze, surfeited with the terror and the agony of these tortures. What account of the horrors of any battlefield can equal in intensity these inarticulate cries from the inferno of maternity?

No one individual in any war is called upon to suffer time after time the wounds and lacerations described by these unwilling mothers. Bleeding and wounded, and often only half-alive, they are dragged from death, only to be forced to repeat, a few months later, the same intense pattern of suffering. It is no surprise to find so many of them declaring that they would prefer death to a repetition of the protracted anguish they have experienced.

They do not, it is true, tell the whole story. It is evident that many of them do not realize the complete nature of their congenital defects. This ignorance renders them the more pathetic. Certain of these cases show how their frail and defective constitutions have revolted from the start against the ordeal of pregnancies. Puerperal insanity is not unusual, as well as other psychoses of pregnancy. In some cases, definite physical malformation is evident, so that the infant must almost literally be torn from the mother's womb. Again and again we read of lacerations and other dire complications of parturition. Partial paralysis, "milk leg," varicose veins, and neurasthenia in its protean forms, are all recorded. Physical and mental recuperation from the ordeal is slow, and in certain cases, incomplete. The woman submits to the following—and seemingly inevitable—pregnancy in a depleted physical and mental state.

The infant reflects the debility of the mother. Sometimes she is unable to nurse it, and it weakens and dies. In other cases, it begins its feeble struggle for life in an environment which must doom it from the start to a miserable existence.

If it is objected that the cases here presented are of too clinical a nature, too abnormal, too exceptional, for general reading, we must point out that the majority of them have been due to the community's refusal to help these victims of enforced maternity to help themselves. The careful reader will note that most of them express a desire to do everything in their power to forestall the recurrence of their ruinous ordeals; that many of them have made appeal after appeal to their doctors. The latter, as a rule, have been indifferent, contenting their conscience with the simple advice "don't get pregnant again."

My unshaken conviction is that most women of the type represented in the following records, women who have been disciplined by suffering and educated by sorrow, and who possess the native intelligence to express themselves as clearly and as accurately as these letters indicate, are fully competent—and more than willing—to be instructed in hygienic methods of contraception.

They are not responsible for the inhuman tortures they have suffered. They are the victims of the bland indifference of American society. No civilization worthy of the name can permit the perpetuation of a system of disastrous breeding upon human beings which would be condemned immediately by the federal government if it were practiced by breeders of livestock.

One

My baby is fourteen months old and I expect another again shortly. I am fond of children but I dread having them so close together, and I do not care to have so many, for I am dreadfully nervous and get hysterical at times. My health is dreadful all during the nine months. I am not able to do my work, everything is neglected. I get so bad at times I cannot control my nerves. I have prayed and tried and tried but it seems like all in vain. I get so at times that I cannot stand just a little baby's cries. It works me in such a state that I pull my hair and scold and whip him merely for nothing. If someone would not take him away God only knows that I may injure him. Then after all is over, I sit and cry and worry for hours to think of what I have done. The baby is getting so he is afraid and does not care for me and is also getting so nervous he cannot sleep. He jumps and cries in his sleep. So kindly give me some advice to keep from having so many, for I dread bringing these innocent babes into this world for me to abuse, for I am almost insane and dreadfully nervous at times, especially while I am in this condition. If I do not get some advice or consolation, I do not know what will become of me. I do not want to be a burden and worry to my husband for he is in constant fear for baby. I cannot have anyone stay with me for it seems like the more around me the more nervous I am. I have often wished I had never been born and feel as though the only relief I would have is to take poison and put myself out of the misery I am in. Kindly give me some advice or consolation.

Two

I am only twenty-seven years old, have been married ten years, have seven children and expect to give birth to another in about three months. Also have been in hospital seven times for bladder trouble, blood poisoning, operations and a lot of other troubles all caused by having children. My health is dreadfully poor and I never know from one day to another what will happen. The last three times of pregnancy I have had threatened miscarriages and been in bed for from three weeks to three months. We are only poor people, are not able to hire any help, only one man to earn our support money; am now under the doctor's care, have been from time last baby was born. She is now only eight months old. I do wish you could give me some information how to keep from getting pregnant.

I have got so discouraged I want to die. It would also be lifting a great care from my husband's shoulders. It is killing him as well as myself, because he works day and night trying to make enough to feed us to keep us going. I hope to hear from you in the near future as you are my last deliverer but death.

Three

I have been thinking of leaving my husband; the housework and childbearing is too much for me. I am twenty-four years old. I was married six years ago. Ten months after my marriage, a healthy baby boy was born to us and we were glad, but I was very sick. One year after I had a false conception, and in July 1921, another baby boy. He is not sickly, but delicate; and within thirteen months a baby girl was born, and the doctors had a hard time to save my life; and now another baby is to be born in a few months. I am small; I weigh about eighty-five pounds; and have never been as strong as the average girl or woman. I have to do my own housework, as we cannot afford to have it done. I am nervous and in a run-down condition.

I have consulted several different doctors and they have told me not to have children, that I was too small. They have told me of no preventive. One doctor discouraged me by telling me that I would die if I had any more children. But if I know of some preventive so that I would not get pregnant for at least a few years, it would give me courage to go through my confinement soon, no matter what the doctors have told me. I think it would give me a new lease of life.

Four

I am the mother of six children, the oldest ten years, and the youngest two months, and I myself only twenty-seven years old. I am an old broken-down woman as far as health goes. I am not able to take care of my children, let alone doing my own work. I have been to three of the best doctors in our city and they all tell me I have tuberculosis, and they have had me in bed several times for the rest cure, and yet none of them will tell me anything to use as a preventive—though it is childbearing that has made me this way. Now I am writing to you to see if you can help me, for I feel that I shall die if I get in the family way again.

My husband is very good to me and can provide for all we need. It is not that we do not want children, but I am not able to take care of them. I have to have a hired girl all the time. It seems too that I have no safe periods as some women seem to have, but get pregnant no matter how careful I am. So if you can help me, I will thank you with my last breath.

Five

I am now the mother of three living boys and am only twenty-three years old and have been married five years last January first. At the time I was married I was eighteen and very, very ignorant of sex relation between married couples. With my first baby I became pregnant as soon as married. I had several doctors for pregnant sickness, as I could eat or drink nothing without vomiting until at last I vomited nothing but blood. Then I was ordered to the hospital where they kept me alive by nourishment through the rectum.

Six

When I was married I was very healthy, never had a sick day and at the time I was ordered to the hospital besides pregnant sickness I was on the point of a nervous breakdown. My baby came in September; he was not full time, only weighed six and a half pounds and was always sickly until he was about two years old. In November after he was born I was weak and miserable and fainted at the least excitement and went to a doctor. He said I was pregnant again and in February I miscarried and had hemorrhages after miscarriage. In April after the miscarriage I found to my horror I was pregnant again; I could eat or drink nothing, as with my first baby, only I was in a more rundown condition to start with. We live on a farm of over two hundred acres. I have two children both very young. When the second baby was eleven months old, I was pregnant again, besides I was milking from seven to ten cows night and morning, nursing one baby and cooking for three men most of the time and sometimes four. Had my hands so full and heart also. I was so irritable and nervous and my husband and I could agree on nothing.

Seven

My husband is of a passionate nature and I am not strong and lost all vitality after my baby was born and I became anemic. I was a living ghost, no one knew me, for before I was married, which was at not quite seventeen years of age, I weighed 138 pounds; had a good form as I was solid and did not look it. But as soon as I got married I became pregnant the first day. I didn't know anything, as mother never discussed anything with me, even the first time I menstruated I didn't ask; a girl friend told me. Then I want to tell you how I suffered while pregnant. From morning till night it's nothing but vomiting. I got so I couldn't look at anything to eat. If I would be putting it to my mouth, I would vomit. Light headed, dizzy, weak, I had to give up housekeeping. They fed me on egg nog, forced it into me. Husband and his family mad with fury that he has such hard luck with me, didn't feel sorry for me but for him as he had to pay doctor bills, which of course, didn't do me any good as they all would say I'd have to suffer it out.

I was an only child, and you can imagine my mother's feelings. She would cry over me as no one expected me to live, but God pulled me through. But that was just the beginning. I had an awful time giving birth to my child, no strength, they had to just tear it out. I was torn and had to have seven stitches. My baby girl died. It was a blue baby, and it almost broke my heart for after all that suffering I lost it and it was a beautiful baby, real short, but it was pretty plump. The doctor was surprised for I ate hardly anything but a little fruit and egg nog.

Then it wasn't a couple of months until I got pregnant again, went through almost the same thing, but could eat a little better toward evening, but I could go nowhere for if I would just bend my head down I would vomit. After that baby we were never happy as I had no health and my husband was disgusted.

Eight

I have two children, a boy six years of age and a little baby girl now seven months old, and have been pregnant three times between the two. I was so sick at my stomach I could not go through with it and had to have them removed between the stages of six weeks and the three months in order that I might myself live. The last time when I carried my little girl I went through the sickest part of it in cool weather, that being in my favor, our doctor said. I was in bed the most of the time and went for five days without eating a bite or drinking a drop of water, and had to lie on the flat of my back for three weeks to keep down those fits of vomiting in which I couldn't even swallow the moisture that gathers in the mouth especially when one is sick at the stomach anyway. I had to just let it run out of my mouth.

I am not strong and robust in body either or haven't been since my first (a boy) was born, as he was a premature baby of seven months. My husband is so good and kind about those things and is willing that I do anything to prevent it or he would if it were possible. It renders me so helpless during the whole nine months. I can't do for myself and maybe another operation which is so against nature no woman can have any kind of health. It makes me afraid to risk our physician's preventive any more, and I come to you for information.

Nine

If anyone ever needed to know about Birth Control, I do. I've been married almost eight years; I have four living children and one dead. I went through with an abortion and five of the best doctors we could get thought I surely would die, but somehow with the help of God and good care I passed through. But they say I can't possibly risk becoming pregnant again. They said too much uric acid was the cause. I was swollen all over beyond description and had to remain in bed the biggest part of the seven months and then the foetus was dead, the doctors said ten days or two weeks before I was relieved, because the doctors couldn't agree on my case. Part thought I had tumor, they all said they never knew or read of a case like mine. My husband is numbered among the best and had done all he could for me, except we are both "ignorant."

Ten

I have been married since August, 1919. In June the following year I gave birth to a baby girl. I was in bed all the time before baby came. After she was born my health was so bad my milk didn't agree with her. She was sick all the time, had stomach and bowel trouble, we almost lost her. In a few months I was pregnant again, and in August, 1921, I gave birth to another girl. I was so weak and nervous this time that every little thing would drive me wild. Didn't give any milk to the baby, had to raise her on the bottle. She is a little, poor thing now. August, 1922, I gave birth to another girl, and July, 1924, I gave birth to a boy which was only six months old when I began to menstruate again. The baby is twenty months old now and I just lack two months before I will have to give birth again. I have had a terrible time with this one too.

My health is very poor, I am nervous and just faint off sometimes before I can get to lie down. My heart has almost worried me to death yesterday and today, and it looks like everything the children do or say will run me crazy.

You can see I have my hands full seeing after the children and having so much to do besides, being sick all the time. My left side is paralyzed from no circulation, and my leg is almost blue from the swollen veins, my ankle is blue and as large as two ankles ought to be. We are just poor people not able to hire help, borrowed $300 last year to make a crop, the drought caught us and we were not able to pay back a cent of it.

Eleven

I am expecting my fourth baby in about a month and I certainly have suffered from the beginning, as I have a bad heart, and about every month sometimes twice a month I have a peculiar spell. I am numb from my fingers even to my tongue. It takes from a half-hour from the time everything turns black for the numbness to start sometimes, and then I have no use of that side at all. It may be I will have four or five of them about every fifteen minutes and again I may be worse. I think they are caused from my heart. I cannot pick up the baby or do anything while I am that way and while I have them most all the time I am worse while in the family way. I have not had the first three children so close, but the last one, a boy, will not be two until a couple of months later, and I am so small my bones will not give much and I am so torn in bringing children into the world.

I don't care much whether I live or not. I am so nervous and in a rundown condition. I think when I have the fourth my family is large enough as I have a ten room house to take care of and I do all my own washing, sewing and all. I am twenty-eight years old.

Twelve

I am thirty-one years old and have been married eleven years. Shortly after marriage I had paralysis and my first baby was born dead, a boy; and then I was like that for another and was very happy but I lost that one and two years from that time I was pregnant again and was very happy as the time went on. But when the time came I found I could not bring my baby into the world without instruments, as the paralysis had left me in that condition. My little girl is now very near seven years old. Three years after that I had another little girl and last August I gave birth to another boy. I suffered worse each time. The last time I was in bed three weeks and it was sometime before I was able to walk without holding on to something.

Thirteen

Will you please listen to my plea? I am a mother of seven children, four living and three that are dead. My oldest living child is six years old, there are two dead which are older. My baby is six months old and I have been married nine years.

With my last child I suffered everything but death. I will tell you how it was. When I was just three months in family way I began to suffer when I went to bed at night. I could not get up without help and the same way when I sat down for any length of time. As the months passed I grew worse and just before he was born, I could not walk any better than a child that was just learning to walk. But when I got down, the ninth month, I could not turn in bed; could not use myself at all, and when he was born and I got out of bed, I could not walk at all for weeks and when I began to walk, I had to use a cane.

I have no health now. I have been to doctors and they tell me that I am having children too fast, but they will not tell me how to prevent it. The only thing that some say is to get rid of it when I get caught, but that is not the kind of advice I want. Will you please give me some advice as I need my health and strength to raise the four children I have. We are poor and I can't afford help, only to do the washing, but I do the rest.

Fourteen

I must write you to see if you will please tell me how I may obtain Birth Control, as I'm the mother of five children and have had five miscarriages and have suffered with epilepsy ever since my second child was born.

During pregnancy I nearly die with hard fits. Have come nearly getting burned to death three times by falling in the fire when a fit came on me. I will fall just anywhere when one strikes me. My physicians say I never will carry another child over three months. I have miscarried five times during four years and I suffer so much. I am a poor woman and have to work hard to support my little ones, as my husband is in bad health.

Fifteen

I am twenty-eight years old and my husband is forty-one and we have just been married six years. We have already got three boys, one five years old, one three years old and one two years old, and I am looking anytime now to be down again. I am in awful health, not able half the time to live myself, just to do my work. I had such an awful hard time with my last baby. I was stark blind six weeks before he was born and was blind three days and nights and did not know my way in the world. The doctor said it was some kind of a tumor in my head that caused it and it seems like the more children I have the worse I get. So I sure would welcome a relief.

I love my children, but my husband has to work for a living and I am sick so much it takes so much for doctor bills that we cannot save a dollar. Oh! If I could only find some way to stop having children so fast. I would have my health better and be so I could take care of what children I already have.

Sixteen

Am not yet thirty years old and am the mother of five children, the oldest ten years and the youngest six months. I am in poor health and very much run down; always have terrible confinements, am doubly ruptured which adds additional agony when pregnant, also have dreadful veins, which on one leg alone opens in ten places when I am pregnant and causes intense agony while doing my work, washing, etc., as I cannot afford to have help. I also take care of my invalid parents.

While pregnant with my last baby, I developed kidney trouble from which no doubt I will never be cured, and I would be frightened to death to become pregnant again as I almost lost the baby at birth and was very ill myself, and am in poor health ever since. As I am a married woman, I suppose I'll have to have more until finally I don't exist.

Seventeen

I have three children about three years apart. They are well in every respect so far, but I am of a mother whose uncles and aunts are epileptic. I have a sister who suffered epilepsy. My brother has a child suffering the same. About two months before my first child came I had an almost unbearable itching over my body. I nearly miscarried at seven months, sores on bottoms of my feet and palms of my hands, no irritation of the flesh at all. I found no rest till after baby came, then it left me. I miscarried when the first baby was thirteen months old. I know no reason, I didn't commit abortion. After that I was always in fear of a miscarriage or itching. I was all right with the second child, but with the third, not five months old, I suffered untold misery, itching day and night for three months before. This time I'm not entirely over it. I do not know what pregnancy might bring again. I think I cannot suffer what I have and fearing what the children can be under such conditions.

Eighteen

My family consists of two darling little children, a boy and a girl. My little girl is three years of age and my baby is one year. I have had the number of children I think is wise. Before my babies are born I nearly am crazy with twitching of the muscles. I jerk and twist as though I had St. Vitus dance, and of course I don't know what sleep means. I simply can't bear to think of lying down, and every morning at three o'clock finds me sitting up waiting for daylight as I cannot lie still and sleep. This, of course, makes my babies sleepless, and it is so hard and discouraging to take care of them. Now the baby is old enough where he sleeps a little better, and I hope to get a little rest myself if my back only improves and there are no more little babes to care for. I am still nursing my baby, and as I have not menstruated since his birth, I am in constant fear of becoming pregnant.

Both my husband and myself do not want any more babies. I have been left with a very weak back. The doctor tells me that the base of my spine is the cause of all my terrible backaches and suffering, as the ligaments have been torn away from the spine, all of which you undoubtedly understand. He thinks he can help me but says another baby would certainly put my case beyond cure, and it seems as though I have endured enough suffering from my back alone, saying nothing of the pain of childbirth. Also, my limbs are terrible from varicose veins and are inflamed and sore all the while.

Don't misunderstand me, I am not finding fault with my little ones, God love their baby hearts, as life would be incomplete without them. But won't you please tell me what to do and how to care for myself so as to prevent having any more? I am only twenty-seven years old, we have been married five years the 31st of this month, and now that we have our little family we want to settle down and save and have a home, and I want to help earn it.

76

Nineteen

I have borne the number of children I think should be a good family, but only one of them lived, and that is my first. In his case after I had been pregnant one month my face commenced to twitch, the left side of my body would not keep still. For two months I was not responsible and people had to nurse and take care of me. Eighteen months later I had another baby which lived only three days. That time I had an ordinary pregnant period with the average amount of discomfort. Three years later I had another baby. The last few months I suffered great pains and was ordered to bed two months before the baby was due. I had a terrible time with my kidneys and the doctor was at the house every day for over six weeks. The baby lived half a day. Last year I had another baby and it was what I always wanted—a girl, but I never saw her. I suffered hell for a year. During the whole nine months of pregnancy and several months after with little hope of having a baby in my arms, after the two previous experiences. The first week I had a trained nurse for the day and one for the night.

The doctor who assisted him at the birth told my husband, a few weeks ago, that this last birth was a case that physicians read about but seldom or never have.

Twenty

I am now in bed from a three months miscarriage which is the second one in eleven months. The doctors tell me I am not capable of bearing any more children. I am the mother of five now. When I am pregnant I lose my mind entirely for a long time and have to stay in bed three or four months before the baby comes.

Twenty-one

We have one baby now nine months old and he is a little frail white boy, has been sick since two weeks old, had to put him on the bottle and when baby was three weeks old, he lay at death's door for weeks and I sat up in a chair and held my baby all the time only for a few minutes at a time. I was so worried about him, he was so low and no one thought he would get well. Doctors say it was because I was not in a condition to have children, and I was under the doctor's care all through my pregnancy, suffered terribly, came almost to losing my life.

We had only been married ten months when baby was born to us, but we are proud of him and think he is wonderful. But he does suffer so much from being sick. I am home all the time with him. My husband works for wages. It has taken almost all his earnings for doctor bills and yet we owe him. I have been under the doctor's care since one month after we were married and when baby was three months old I was given up for an operation by three doctors and on account of baby's health I couldn't go and leave him and we didn't have a dollar in the world to have someone care for him. And the doctors say I will never be able to give birth to another child, but still they will tell me nothing to do. My trouble is all female trouble and heart trouble. At times I just faint away.

Twenty-two

Will you kindly help a poor girl of nineteen years of age whose age compares with a woman's of fifty. Before I married and after, until I got pregnant, I enjoyed the best of health, rosy cheeks, gay and happy. The world seemed so bright and friendly. I attended church, the movies and other entertainments very often because I have always lived in some little town. I never once thought how much trouble and ill health most of the women of today are going through. All the world was sunshine to me.

I married when I was seventeen years of age and lived a happy married life until I became pregnant which was not very long. Then my life seemed wrecked because I was unable to do my work most of the time. My husband was not able to hire my work done because he was only a poor working man and had just gotten up from an attack of pneumonia. When my baby was born I had a bad time. They had to have three doctors with me. I stayed in bed one month and I have been no account any more. My rosy cheeks turned to a pale face. My body frail, nervous and weak. My happy healthful days are gone never to come again unless you help me. The doctor said that I could never live to have another baby, but I am almost three months gone now and my baby is only nine months old. My God! what shall I do? Not able to work and my good husband is in bad health to. Just think: a girl of nineteen years! It is horrible to think of the life that is pictured out before me. I often tell my husband that I

79

had rather see my cold grave than to venture into child-birth again. I positively do not believe that I will live when this baby is born.

Twenty-three

Before my last child was born I would almost cry when I would walk across the floor. And when I found I was in this condition again I almost had a nervous breakdown. I have had one abortion and I don't want to try it again—unless I get beyond myself, as one has queer feelings when in this condition.

Twenty-four

When my first baby was five months old I had an operation for a tumor and appendicitis in the one operation. Weighed only eighty-two pounds at the time of the operation. Doctor said he never thought I'd come from the operating room alive. He said I was not to do a thing for a year. You can imagine my horror when in two months after this I discovered that I was already more than two months pregnant, had got that way just before I went to the hospital for the operation. I begged the doctor to do something for me, but he would not. I felt I just couldn't go through with it. But he said as long as I was cured of consumption, much as he'd like to, his hands were tied, he couldn't do anything for me. I almost died giving birth to the baby. He came coal-black. For the last six weeks of the nine months I was unable to walk or get out of bed without being lifted or carried. During these six weeks I was continually in labor, but the night he was born I was so exhausted that the pains just died down regardless of the fact that I had been dilated for two weeks, the doctor gave me three injections of pituitary fluid before he could finally establish the pains again. Baby and I were both almost dead. When I discovered I was that way with my fourth baby I was almost crazy. I asked our family doctor to do something for me but he said he couldn't risk getting caught. May God forgive me; I kept wishing I'd miscarry; I did not seem to care if I lived or died. My husband is a railroad man and was out of work, so you may understand how I felt. Eight days before baby was born I again got helpless, couldn't walk, had to be carried around; gave birth to a nine pound baby boy, but may God grant my wish that he will be the last. It seems I'm nothing but a pack of nerves, too much childbearing.

Oh! How ashamed I get of myself. I go all to pieces at the children at the least little thing, when I know afterwards the poor little kids didn't do anything, but it is just my own nervous state. I had always planned I'd be a companion to my kiddies, read and play with them, but when evening comes I'm so tired I just roll in, dead to the world.

How I long just to live for a while without being pregnant or a baby already. Surely I have done my duty having five children. I don't believe God would think it was wrong if I prevented any more from coming.

Twenty-five

I am married two years and have had two children sixteen months apart and it pretty near drives me frantic to be always worrying of more. I try and keep away from my husband but it most always leads us to a quarrel, and I am not strong. I always give way to fainting spells. I am anemic and very nervous and am so discouraged sometimes I feel like taking my life. I have trouble with my one ovary and have such distressing pains in my back. Half of the time I don't know what I'm at. I get so dizzy that if I don't sit down I fall in a faint. I nurse my baby on the breast and she gets me up three times during the night to feed her and dry her and I don't get much sleep. I must wash her every day and carry my water to the house and from the house and also have hogs and chickens to tend to and I get so discouraged and tired I just feel like dropping out. I can hardly get my legs to go for me, they seem so heavy. Have pity for me and show me a way out that I won't bring any more children in this world until I'm stronger. Another baby and then I'm done for. I have the piles so when I work too much and can't hardly rest. My last baby had eczema so awfully bad I almost died tending her. Had the grippe three times right after birth.

Twenty-six

I have had seven children, losing the first with convulsion, having seven in two days, leaving me blind for twenty-four hours. Each time I have kidney trouble which puts me on a diet for about two months, with nothing but milk. I have five children living now and three years ago I lost the seventh baby.

I can't live through again such trials as I have gone

through. My first baby was born dead. I had seven convulsions, came very near dying, had two of the best physicians in our town and was lacerated so bad the stitches they took didn't hold, and in fourteen months my second one arrived, big fine boy, weighed twelve pounds, and then I was torn worse than ever. I was sewed up again, but didn't hold this time and on the twelfth day inflammation set in. It was all the doctor could do to pull me through that time, but I couldn't enjoy my big fine baby boy. I couldn't do anything until he was a year old, and then I found myself pregnant again. Well, I was so miserable, I went to the doctor and told him about it, so he said I was in no condition to become pregnant again; he opened my womb three different times, but didn't do any good, so I thought: well, it's God's will, and I'm not going to worry one bit this time, so I came through all right and have two fine boys, one is four and the other two, but I was lacerated so badly this time, and in such a condition. I'm nothing but a nervous wreck. We are poor people. We can't clothe and feed these children as we should, and I love them so much. I don't want to become pregnant any more, so I can get well and strong and help my husband make a living. I had a nervous breakdown this last summer and lost my mind for a few days and have high blood pressure also. And I don't believe I could go through with childbirth again.

Twenty-seven

I am a young woman only twenty-two years of age and am ruined for life.

83

I was married only a little over two years when I had two children, boys, the first weighing ten pounds at birth, the second one eleven pounds. I was very sick by the first baby and lay hours and hours in pain and agony before my baby finally was born with the doctor's help. Had to be chloroformed several times and then torn so bad that I had to have several stitches, being unfortunate enough to have it all torn open again after the stitches were taken out. This baby left me in a bad shape, my womb all out of place.

I was not supposed to become pregnant any more and then I had another eleven pound boy in but a short time. This time my case was worse than ever, putting me in such a condition that I had to doctor three months straight, going to see the doctor once a week. I am torn up still more than the first time and never was stitched this time, so that's the way it stayed. The doctor says I cannot get well without a serious operation and should not under any circumstances become pregnant again and how am I, without help, for I know no way?

Twenty-eight

I have three lovely boys, the youngest three months old, the oldest will be six years old soon, and I have had one miscarriage brought on by no fault of mine, but through poor health. I have never taken any pills to bring me around, for I love children, if I had only the strength and health necessary to take proper care of them, or my husband could afford hired help.

I am only thirty-one but practically an invalid. I have

had a displacement of the uterus for seven years so my doctor tells me. He tells me this must be my last baby that I so nearly died under chloroform when he was born, and my nerves were completely shocked. I had to have an operation on my head to remove a tumor from the brain which proved successful when I was about two months in pregnancy, and nearly lost my eyesight. My nerves since are bad, that I wonder whether I ever will be better.

When the baby was seven weeks old I had to be taken to the doctor's office to take uterine treatments to relieve some of the pain in my back and after the treatment I got up and dropped to the floor; and it wasn't just fainting for when they brought me out, I couldn't move my legs, arms or talk. I was just paralyzed. I had three attacks until it began to affect my heart. I was given stimulants and finally carried into the car and taken home to bed. I have had to wean my baby for I hadn't strength enough to nurse him. The doctor tells me I must not get tired and I know what he means, and I do want to live and enjoy my boys, but oh, I am so afraid of becoming pregnant.

What shall I do? I love my husband and we enjoy sexual union. If only we knew of some good reliable contraceptives. I can't run the risk of having another baby for years, if ever, on account of my nerves. The doctor says I must live a very quiet life, lying on the couch most of the time. I am not diseased in any way, nor my husband, and my children are perfect children; but I am so run down from childbirth and operations, that it will be a long time with the best of care to get on my feet again. I never was sick before I was married, but since I have been married all I have done is pay doctor bills. I was married only six months when I had a miscarriage, then the very next month was pregnant again and eight months after the birth was pregnant again. The only way I can carry my babies through full time is to keep off my feet for weeks at a time, and this last time I was in bed or on the couch half the way. I want to live for my children's sake, for no one can take care of them like their mother, if she has good health.

Twenty-nine

I expect you get tired of someone writing you their troubles all the time but I do want your help so bad. My story is like some of the rest. I have three boys and it is just about all I can do to care for them and the other work I have to do. I work hard and I don't think I am lazy. Besides two doctors have told me I had curvature of the spine which might cause paralysis some time. I lost the use of my right arm when my second baby was born for a while and then when the last baby was born my whole right side was paralyzed for three months so I am afraid if I have to have any more babies I will finally become a cripple altogether and then I couldn't care for the three little boys.

Thirty

I have three children, the oldest three years, the second two years and a baby three months. The oldest child (a boy) is a cripple from birth on account of instruments.

He has never walked or sat entirely alone although his mind is all right and he is a normal child. Doctors say he can be cured, but what an expense we have had! Then when he was thirteen months, the first girl came, then this baby girl, and I suffered so with the second child. There was a tumor in the afterbirth and the afterbirth had grown to backbone and had to be torn loose. This time I was bothered so terribly with varicose vains I had to keep my limbs bandaged for the last two months. Then such a time at birth! She had to be turned and the afterbirth had to be torn loose in pieces. The doctor said that night that I was not built to have children. Some way my bones turn in instead of out. When baby was ten days I got up and started doing my work as I could afford help no longer as my husband only makes $100 a month. My womb is torn so I can hardly stand on my feet sometimes and I am so nervous.

Thirty-one

I have two children; first was a seven months'; I almost died. My next baby had to be taken with instruments; my hips gave way and I was not able to walk for some time, then three weeks ago I had to go to the hospital for an operation; the baby died in me and was two months dead the womb shrunk instead of opening and had to take it out through my side. I think I ought to know something now so I don't get that way for a couple of years at least. I love children and would not mind raising a few, but I think I need a little rest. I have been to the hospital three times in three and a half years.

Thirty-two

I hope you will read this and take pity on a poor suffering woman. I hate to bother you but I am desperate. I have suffered so much.

I have been married fifteen years and have six living children. All have been taken with instruments. I have suffered months before their births and the doctor works over me hours before he can take them. I have been torn with every one and the babies all have had cuts over their heads, and heads out of shape. The last one had to have its head operated on when it was a month old to let bruised blood out. For a couple of months before their birth my feet and limbs are so swollen I can hardly walk. The doctor told me when my second baby was born that no matter how many I had all would have to be taken and that I suffer enough for a hundred women. When the last one was born he worked over me eight hours and had to have another doctor to help him. I was cut and torn so they had to send me to the hospital for an operation. After the baby was a few months old they said at the hospital I had lacerations, relaxation, falling and torn womb; was there three weeks but have never felt well since. I go back often for treatment.

I begged them to fix me so I would never have to go through childbirth again. The doctor that operated said I was too young and that I would have to settle that in my own home. Just the thought of taking the chance of becoming pregnant almost sets me crazy. I love my husband and babies and don't want to break up the home.

If I could just keep from becoming pregnant I might regain my strength.

Thirty-three

I am twenty-nine years old and have been married twelve years. I have had six children and one miscarriage. I have four children living. My oldest child is eleven years old and my baby is sixteen months old. I have broken veins from my waist down and they draw sometimes until they stand out like whipcord and I simply can't stand on my feet. I have ovarian trouble and while pregnant with my last baby I was ruptured at the naval. My baby weighed twelve pounds and I was lacerated. The doctor 'repaired that but I began doing my work when baby was two weeks old and the laceration tore out again. I lived on medicine during the whole nine months.

Our physician said I ought not to become pregnant again, as my life would be endangered, but when my husband asked him for a contraceptive he said there was none. If I did not have the hope that I might some day find something that would keep me from having any more children, I know I should go crazy. I have a baby every other year and it is more than I can stand. At twenty-nine my hair is turning gray and I feel like I am fifty years old. I can't stand anyone to hardly speak or look at me when I am pregnant and noise nearly drives me insane. I do so want to give my two little boys and two little girls the care and attention they need. I am not able to hire a nurse for them, so I have to care for them myself.

Thirty-four

Before I read your book I did not care if I lived or died, for dying would surely have taken me out of my misery, but now I am only hoping that you will help me for help is what I surely need.

To begin: just a year and a half ago I gave birth to a twelve pound baby girl. I was in pain and agony for twenty-four hours. My doctor had to get another doctor as he said he could not handle the case alone. At the end of twenty-four hours' agony they took her from me with instruments, tore me all apart and put fourteen stitches in me. I nearly lose my mind now when I only think of the pain, for they could not give me ether, as I have a bad heart.

On the sixteenth day I started to develop a milk leg. Oh! the pain and suffering I went through and burning up with fever, was terrible for about seven or eight days; after that the leg was about three times its natural size. I lay there for six weeks, worried near out of my mind with bills to pay and no money coming in. (My husband at the time had been out of work about eight months.)

Just at the end of six weeks, it went to the other leg, and I had more suffering and hell to go through. I near lost my mind then. It was about three months or more before I could put my feet out of bed. Then I had to have elastic stocking on both legs from my toes all the way up, and an elastic girdle, and crutches.

I was on crutches for weeks and weeks before I could get around right. All this time my husband had to take care of the baby and me. The doctor said he hopes as long as he lives he does not have another case like mine as it was the worst he had ever witnessed. All he told me to do was douche. The city nurse told me the same thing when I asked what I should do, after she had told me not to get that way again for five years if I wanted to be cured.

Just as I began to walk around a little better I got that way again and Oh! God have mercy on me! I am to give birth to another baby in three months. I am near crazy now, even with these elastic stockings on, my legs swell twice their size and are so painful I can hardly walk on them. If it wasn't for this dear little baby of mine I would have ended all this living hell for myself long ago, but how can I leave my baby alone? I dearly love children and would have welcomed this one in five or six years from now as by then I would have been able to stand it better. I am so cranky and miserable it is a wonder my husband does not leave me as everything gets on my nerves and I can hardly do my work.

I am only twenty-two years old, but look thirty-two and feel about fifty, as every bone hurts me when I move my body. Now all I have to look forward to if you cannot help me or send me to someone who can, is a baby every year, that I cannot take care of until the good Lord takes me out of my misery.

Thirty-five

I have seven children, six living, and I am on the road again and Oh, I would rather see and know I was going to die than have to go through the awful suffering I have!

I have one child that had to be taken, and another that needles and instruments had to be used, and every one I have they all thought I was going to die. I have had child-bed fever twice, thirty days one time and two weeks next time. I am almost helpless from the time I get that way. Such awful pains in my sides. And my last child I was helped to move even my feet and was just almost paralyzed and my baby has been sick all his life.

I have cared for him enough to have raised four children and I keep away from my man all I can, but the abuse and mistreatment is awful and almost separation. Now, dear, will you just please send me the true secret that I may be free when this one is born. Please do not disappoint me. God knows I had rather see my grave than to have another child. The suffering I do go through with no one knows but me.

Thirty-six

I come from a family of fine healthy people. I am proud of their health and moral record; but we women in our family are cursed with deafness which seems to be connected with the nerves of the female organs and is caused by childbirth. I have one sister who cannot get a battery strong enough to penetrate her hearing with instruments. She has three children. Another sister, now deceased, was deaf all her life. She had a large family. We trace it back to my beautiful mother, who died young, only thirty-seven, and left ten children. She was so deaf when she died of childbirth (when I was born) that they had to write to her on a slate. The pity of it! A woman having to go on bearing and trying to rear children in that condition and leaving us such an inheritance.

I am a professional woman—my ears are failing me. It's only a matter of a few years when I must give up. I am taking a course in lip reading now. This is the reason for my writing. My daughter is beautiful and healthy as were all of us girls and has good ears and there is no reason why she and her lover should not be happily married. They might even have one or two children, but an unlimited number would repeat the curse of our women and to have to curb and fear and half enjoy the sex relation, as my husband and I have had to do, would be a sorrow.

Thirty-seven

I have seven children and am one month on the way again and would like for you to tell me what to do. It makes me not have my right mind and I would rather die than to have this one. It makes me awful sick all the way through and can't do anything and I would like for you to advise me what to do. I am only thirty-nine years old and been to the asylum once on account of childbirth and never been right since, and if you can help me I will be blessed. God knows I know what a woman has to go through with and if you can send me something to take I would be a blessed person. The doctor won't help me at all and I am a poor person and don't own the roof I live under and move around from post to pillow, and my last baby is eleven months old.

Thirty-eight

I was married nine years ago and was seventeen years and five months old at that time. My first baby, a boy, came eleven months later. A girl was born three years later. In nineteen months came another boy and it was my first unwelcome child. It died when two months. I never knew the cause as I had done nothing to cause it; then my health failed. The night I miscarried was an awful one and the good people who tried to care for me didn't think I could live and the doctor who was with us twelve hours said Providence alone saved me.

I wasted until I looked more dead than alive for weeks. And that night I fainted probably fifteen times and each time they thought I would surely go. I lived, but seemed to have something awfully wrong with my heart. I don't know but maybe you do. My heart just jumped and pounded until I thought I would go crazy. Had blind dizzy spells. Seemed the main trouble was in my head.

And here is the worst. I became pregnant again in three months. God alone knows what I endured. I was unable to do anything for the awful pounding in my whole body and I thought surely I would lose my mind, and nerves were awful. I could only lie on my bed and wish to die but I'm still here. My last baby is fifteen months old and now comes the most sorrowful part. I'm pregnant again—over two months. I shall strive to do my best as I've always done but I must learn something to prevent this happening again and I now appeal to you.

Thirty-nine

I am a mother of three children, the first was fifteen months apart. I could not nurse them on account of inverted nipples, so that set up complications and after the second child I had falling of the womb and after I would do my week's washing and ironing I had to lay in bed with my feet upon the foot of the bed the rest of the week.

Then I became pregnant again. And everything was getting fine until baby came, then I could not nurse this one either, and of course more complications came up. After he was six weeks old I started to have my menses and two days before they came I had some kind of a spell. All the blood went to my head; I was dizzy and fainted. Then sick at my stomach and was so weak for two days I wasn't able to raise my head off the pillow. The baby is now four months old and at every period I have that spell, not so bad now, but Oh! so tedious to go through and at these times I nearly have a hemorrhage.

I suppose it is as the doctor said that I had to do this as the blood was not being used for the feeding of the infant. And now if I up and have another one and can't nurse it what in this world will happen to it and would I ever live over it? It seems as if my nerves are just a ragged end. I can't go anywhere hardly, for fear of those dizzy and fainting spells. I sometimes wonder if I'll ever be strong and healthy again. When I make my husband 'tend to his business he thinks he is just killed off. Yet he knows good and well that if we have a dozen I can never nurse them at my breast and it sure is awful to have a family of runty children. The second child had meningitis. I know the indirect cause was bottle feeding and improper care and nourishment.

Forty

I married when I was nineteen years old, a good man. What we both have suffered is more than anyone can tell. I was married eleven years and am the 'mother of two living children, both girls, and two dead. I have made nine trips to the operating table for abortions.

I am only thirty years old. My hair is streaked with gray. I have had to have all my teeth out except just a few front teeth. My nerves are wrecked.

My first baby, a girl, was born when we were married fourteen months. She weighed only five pounds. She was a little, weakly, coffee-colored baby. I was sick, vomited and could eat nothing all the nine months before she came. When I got pregnant I weighed 137 pounds. After her birth I weighed only ninety pounds.

I was left with paralyzed bowels. The doctor said her head rested on the nerve cord. When she was only three months old I found I was pregnant for another baby. I had to wean my baby and put her on the bottle and we could find no milk to agree with her, and when she was eight months old, tuberculosis started in her right lung. She was five years old when her lungs got well and it took all our money and all my husband could make to pay for her treatment. She was no more than well of the tuberculosis when she got typhoid fever. Then came whooping cough, then the measles. Now she is nine years old and her mental growth is only of a child of five years. This is her second term in the first grade of school.

I had an awful time when she was born. The afterbirth started first and she came feet first. I was badly torn and never sewed and I was blind for four days. It was not a dark, it was a white blindness—just a white foamy mist which I could not see through.

When my first baby was one year old my second baby was born, a girl, and she weighed fifteen pounds. She seemed a normal mind, but she was born with three legs and three arms. The doctors gave me ether when she came, but for a week after I had the same white blindness. When she was four months old I found I was to have another baby. I weighed only eighty-eight pounds, and it was all I could do to take care of my two babies and we were too poor to hire any help for me. I was seven months for my third baby when I got awful sick, a high fever. The doctor took me to the hospital and on to the table. The afterbirth had grown fast all to the womb and the baby had died there and it all had to be cut out.

I asked the doctor what to do to avoid pregnancy, but I got no satisfaction. In ten months I was in the hospital again for another operation. It was all grown fast and had to be cut out. Then a doctor wanted to take everything out. He said he could operate and take out the ovaries, womb and all, but the law would not allow him to tell me anything to prevent pregnancy. I would never have such an operation, and in a short time I was to have another baby. We were having a time to raise the first two babies. I did not want any more babies, but I carried this one the nine months. It was a boy. I had to go to the hospital for an operation the same as before.

One doctor gave me something to use but it was no good and he would not tell me of anything else. I don't think he knew of anything else. Every baby grows fast and dies there and about the seventh or eighth month I have to go to the hospital and have it cut out, and I nearly bleed to death each time.

Just fifteen months ago I was in the hospital for an operation. They told me I have a tumor on the right ovary and if I get pregnant again I will die, and they sent me home with: "Now don't get this way again." Yet the doctor will tell me nothing to prevent it.

After this last operation fifteen months ago I lost my reason. It seemed as though the whole world was wrong side up, nothing was right, and I went to a hospital for the insane. I was there seven months before things got right again. My mother took care of my oldest girl and we put the other girl in the home while I was away. I went under another name so no one would know I was in the asylum. My husband told our friends I was away on a visit. When I came home we had no money or anything and was one year back with our rent. We got our girl out of the home and my mother sent us money to come to her place. We took our clothes but had to leave all our furniture as the landlord had an attachment on it for the rent.

We have been here all summer. We now are able to save up a little money, but although my husband and I live in the same house, we just have to keep away from each other, but this cannot continue. We don't know what to do!

There is an ill-famed house a few streets from us; it is run by two women. Last Saturday evening my husband said he was going to the next town. That evening I took my daughters and went for a walk. I saw my husband and another man go in this house. I have never let my husband know I saw him go there, but I feel heartbroken over it.

V

"The Sins of the Fathers"

WHEN we speak of the biologically "unfit," we immediately arouse the antagonism of many well-meaning theorists who denounce all eugenists and advocates of Birth Control as aiming to establish a dictatorship over the lives and families of the "common" people. God loves the common people because He made so many of them, they assert with a ringing challenge in their voices. Why then interfere in their happiness, and attempt arbitrarily to change their habits and to deprive them of the little happiness they are able to get out of life?

Such arguments and questions are totally irrelevant. They are based not upon any immediate first-hand familiarity with the lives of poor mothers, nor any experience of fact. They are inspired by an inhuman intellectualism; the suffering and agony of human beings are swept aside as non-existent or unimportant, in effort to minimize the importance of all efforts to safeguard the well-being of the race. The basic assumption is that advocates of contraception and eugenics are merely prying into human affairs which do not concern them, or are snobbishly trying to impose an "unnatural practice" upon sane, normal, and averagely intelligent members of the "lower" classes.

The group of letters included in the present chapter

indicates better than any ordinary argument the basic fallacy of these indictments. We are not seeking, from without and above, to impose any restrictive dictatorship over the reproductive powers of the less fortunate, nor to condemn as "unfit" those who do not measure up to an arbitrary and predetermined standard of intelligence or literacy.

The following documents, on the contrary, indicate a pathetic consciousness on the part of many mothers of the disastrous folly of bringing defective children into the world. The situation is not one of any self-appointed board of dictators declaring who is "fit" and who is "unfit" for the task of reproduction. Rather it is one of demonstrated unfitness—of helpless children suffering unto the third and fourth generation "the sins of the fathers."

In previous groups, our records have shown how acute economic problems among poverty-stricken families have been aggravated by the relentless drive of the uncontrolled powers of reproduction; how mothers are forced into the double bondage of toil and incessant childbearing; how the upbringing of the children is necessarily neglected. The present group emphasizes another, and an ever more tragic, aspect of motherhood in bondage. These documents expose the tragedy of the great transmissible scourges—venereal disease, epilepsy and hereditary insanity, as well as tuberculosis and other infectious diseases.

The superficial might condemn the parents of these pitiful, defective and handicapped children as thoughtless, reckless and irresponsible in their marital relations. But the careful reader will discover in these letters neither recklessness nor irresponsibility, but in practically every one of them a strong, though perhaps inarticulate, expression of loyalty to the race, an intense desire for justice to the coming generation,—a whole-hearted willingness for sexual education.

"Help me to help myself!" "Help us to help our children!" These are the reiterated cries that resound from between the lines of these pleas for deliverance.

Biologically "unfit" as the parents herein described confess themselves to be, I find a certain nobility in their recognition of the cruel realities of their lives, in their undying hope for deliverance. While society as a whole may turn a deaf ear to their pleas, and while science fails to recognize the immense value of their proffered coöperation toward safeguarding the future well-being of the race, who can condemn them alone as reckless or irresponsible?

One

I want to ask you for help. I am the mother of six living children, one dead. My oldest is ten years old and my baby one. My health is bad. I don't want to bring another baby into this world. The doctor says I need a rest. I have to take medicine before they are born. For six months I have kidney disease, had convulsions when one was born, have asthma so bad I can't lie and get my breath before my baby is born.

We are farmers and poor. Have to work for our living. Have to do all my housework and help in the field. I don't want to have any more because I want to send these to school and we can't do it if we have any more. Living is so high now I am having to diet myself. I have high blood pressure and I don't feel like I can go through childbirth any more and I would like to live to raise and care for my children that I have.

Two

A very serious misfortune befell me following the birth of my eighth child and I wish to state I have two dead, now I have a ninth child and my difficulties are greatly increased. When my eighth child was three days old my husband left the house to go to a neighbor about a mile away. We had an old bachelor neighbor living across the road from us. He had become extremely queer. Something had happened at his place and he blamed my boys for it. The truth was my boys were not on his place at all but anyhow, he started to attack myself and children with an axe. I grabbed my tiny three-day-old boy and terror stricken, I fled in my thin night gown, barefoot, weak and trembling with my little family to a neighbor who lived an eighth of a mile away. We all escaped from him and afterwards he was sent to the insane asylum. To make matters worse it was raining and I waded in mud ankle deep. It was March, a cold wet rain. That night about midnight I had a stroke, it paralyzed my whole right side. I was not able to get out of my bed for five long weeks. Since then another was born and my husband was heartbroken because he knew my life hung by a thread.

All I can do of my housework is to sew. I sit in a chair the greater share of my time and helpless like that I have to nurse and care for two babies. Before I had that stroke

I was one of the strongest and most able-bodied women in this country. Now you know that it is a crime for a woman in my predicament to be a mother of any more children. My husband asked me to write you this letter since he realizes it is the only safe way to keep me for my little children's sakes. He is kind to me and my boys and girls are considerate and helpful. Since that incident occurred I have never drawn a well breath and I never expect to. If you will be kind enough to tell me of some means whereby I can prevent conception from taking place, I wish you would do so and I will indeed be grateful.

Three

I am always getting pregnant. My husband is always careful. In fact he is a nervous wreck for that very reason; can't sit still or stay in to hear the boys crying. He is getting worse all the time and has terrible headaches. I have two boys. After the first was born we had nothing but doctor bills, born sickly and still is, besides has a fractured skull and he needs watching all the time which makes me so nervous and tired. I have had three miscarriages and two abortions; had operations for appendicitis, diseased ovary and a cyst on the other ovary. Ten months after I became pregnant again; had a hard time. Blood pressure 176 while carrying child the last month. Four days after, pressure 202, and kidney trouble and inflammation of the bladder. Had electric bakes at hospital twice a day for re-action of the kidneys. After the third week of bakes some-what better, but caught a very bad cold which settled in my throat and nose and left me with an inflamed thyroid gland and both sides of my nose ulcerated. I go to a nose doctor every week and also doctor for my kidneys and blood pressure every week for the last three months. My son is three and one-half months old. Never had a well day and am in constant fear of becoming pregnant again which would surely kill me in the condition I'm in.

But still the doctor does not tell me any safe means to avoid becoming pregnant.

Four

I have been married just a little more than two and one-half years and I have two dear little boys, the oldest twenty-two months, the youngest seven months; just fifteen months apart. I was just nine months and one week married when the first baby came and I never even had a chance from the beginning. When baby was five months old I had rheumatism for a month and just began to feel fine when I became aware of the fact there was going to be another. My children are both healthy and good but here is my trouble. Last winter before baby came I fell on the ice and my back was hurt in some way, that I just can't get up and down as I should. The doctor told me I would have to be careful or I may have to be operated on and have a bone extracted. He said avoiding pregnancy would help me but he would not tell how to avoid it. My husband is very good to the children and myself and he is also careful, but things don't seem to go as they should.

Five

I am not strong, have had kidney trouble for years and have suffered so much with my right hip and limb. Doctors say it is tuberculosis of the hip. I have been married four years. Have a little girl three years old. Have had two miscarriages, once in hospital and other at home. I didn't know I had miscarried until I was nearly dead.

I love children but realize I am not able to give them the care they should have. I now have a baby five weeks old. My children are not strong.

Doctors tell me plainly I must not have any more and I am so worried about it. I have a good husband, works hard, but makes small salary. Since my first child was born I haven't been able to do my housework and each time I get worse. Since the last baby was born I am almost helpless at times. I am ignorant and can see no relief unless you can help me or tell me something. If I were strong and the babies healthy it would not be so bad, but they come so close together. Two months after I miscarried the last time I was that way again. My doctor thought I had better go to the hospital and have an operation, but I could not stand the thoughts of that; I decided the only thing to do would be to suffer it out. I had such a hard time. I had much rather die than go through with it again. Each time it gets worse.

It is not because I do not love children that I don't want them. It is because I know so well they should not be here. If I am only spared to be with the two I have. I am afraid I love them too well.

Six

I hope the day will come soon when women can have the say if they are to be mothers or not.

I am the mother of seven living children, one set of twins boy and girl, and my little baby girl died at three weeks of age. She was a seven months' baby. When my baby before the last was born the doctors told me I shouldn't get that way again. The twins nearly broke me down and then just two years later this baby came and he weighed eleven pounds. I tried so hard not to get that way again as my back was in such an awful fix, but the doctor wouldn't tell me anything to do. I have separation of the joints in my hip and back and have to wear a brace. I was under several specialists and they said I ought not have any more children. I tried not to get that way and begged my husband not to risk it, but it didn't do any good.

When I was seven months along I was taken with the flu and pneumonia and lost the baby and I was so long getting strong. But am better now than I have been in several years, but I won't be if I get pregnant again. I have more children than I can take care of now. I have been married thirteen years and have given birth to eight children and I know it's not right for me to have any more children.

I try to keep away from my husband but that's not right. I love him very much and we are young, but I have a constant dread all the time for fear I will get pregnant. My household duties are heavy. We are rice farmers and harvest time is awful hard on the women.

Seven

I am a girl of only eighteen and have one child. It is only fourteen months old and I am in family way again. I have been married only two and a half years. I married a day laborer and can only make enough to get us a little something to eat and wear. We have no home and here I am with one poor little pitiful child and another on the road to this awful world to suffer for the want of care.

I am not able to be up half the time. I have always been bothered with something like tuberculosis and don't have the means to be cared for like I should.

My baby is so poor and pitiful. I am afraid it won't live long. Only ignorance has driven me into this awful place. I can now see that I would be better off dead than to be bringing these poor little children into poverty and sickness. I think it is awful for me to have to suffer from tuberculosis and bring these poor little children into the world, too. If I only could see a little peace while I live. Please help me if you can. If you can help me in this case maybe I can be prepared to help myself after this. Just now I am so discouraged that I believe I could die.

Eight

If only the knowledge you advocate were mine it would no doubt save my life. And you, who are a mother yourself, know how precious life is for the sake of the little ones. I have been married but three years and have two baby boys. My first child came the first year; and as I had always worked hard in factories previous to my marriage I hadn't the strength or vitality to stand it. The result was that I got the flu and for six of the nine months I carried him I was a complete invalid, causing untold worries and dreadful expense.

No sooner had I barely struggled back to anything resembling health, than I again faced motherhood. The next nine months were filled with terror, as my first little boy was so sickly and difficult to care for. At the second birth I went through a twenty-four hour labor that seems as if it will never fade from my mind. And because I nursed the baby eleven months, he has a most pronounced case of rickets and is a constant care. It is not morbidness that makes me feel sure I could not live through another child birth; it's simply that I am at the end of my strength and nerves.

Please, I beg of you, if it is any way in your power, please help me. My husband is only a boy and all the life and hope is being crushed out of us both. Oh! if only there could be help and hope for me. Oh! if there is anything I can do please let me know, and to help others too. All around me there are so many dying and living in hell through ignorance.

Nine

I am a mother of three little girls, the oldest three years old, the baby is three months and the other one is two years old and a cripple. She can't sit up and can't bring her hands to her mouth and can't talk. So I have to handle two babies all day long, and sometimes I can't do my housework. Now I ask you to do me a favor and advise me what to do to be free from babies for a while. I would be very thankful to you.

Ten

Have been married for nine years and have six children, the oldest seven and a half years and the youngest a few weeks. I have had lots of trouble bringing them up; the oldest had infantile paralysis when he was eighteen months old. Of course he is lame but he can walk. He is paralyzed in the spinal cord and the knees. It makes it very hard for me. Besides this they all had eczema. I do not know what this comes from but it really is very discouraging to put children in misery of that kind. I married when I was sixteen and a half years,—very ignorant of what marriage was. Am now twenty-six years old and as you see have six children. Really I am discouraged. I try to keep away from my husband as much as possible, but this always brings us to quarrels and his saying that he will go elsewhere.

Eleven

I am the mother of six children ranging in age from one year to eleven years and am very much afraid that I am pregnant again. This is discouraging to me to the point of despair, for with the one year old baby and a two and a half year old girl who has tuberculosis of the knee joint and has worn a cast for fifteen months, I have my hands full. Then there are the four other children, three in school. My husband is a painter and makes good wages, but he is not strong and should have rest but that is impossible with six little ones to feed and clothe. My health is unusually good, but how can it last if I am to bear a child every year or so?

Twelve

I am a mother of seven living childern and am only twenty-nine years old. My oldest is eleven and baby two months. My two youngest children have eczema and the baby is going to have it the same,—it has started on its face the same way. My little girl twenty-two months old had eczema so bad last winter she had it all over her body and her head was nothing but a scab all over, and the doctors can't do anything for it. They are so hard to take care of. I have to do all my work, my husband is only a laborer and we can't afford to have our work done. My eleven year old girl is not very healthy because she works so hard at home, and I am so weak sometimes I can't hear my children play or talk. I am so afraid of having any more I can't sleep at night for worrying. Please help me somehow. My friends only make fun of me when I ask them about this.

I have a lot to write, but I am so nervous my hands tremble. Please excuse me for not writing very good.

Thirteen

I have a little girl fifteen months old. I have eczema on my hands and arms so I can hardly do my work half of the time. It is very hard for me to do my washing and housework and take care of my baby. The baby breaks out with it behind the ears. It cracks until it is a raw sore for her most of the time. I certainly don't know what I would do if I should have another one that way. My husband helps with the washing, scrubbing and washes most of the dishes because of my hands, and that keeps him from his work. My husband's father, being old, lives with us and that makes more work. So I am writing to ask if you will help me in some way from getting any more babies.

You certainly are working for a worthy cause. The rich don't seem to have so many children, why should the poor people who can't afford to?

Fourteen

I am a young wife nineteen years old. I have a baby eight months old. This baby has had eczema ever since she was one month old. I have had all kinds of doctors for her and she is not cured yet. Her face is just one mass of rawness. I put in the most sleepless nights with her because she scratches in the night till her face bleeds and oh! the misery I am in each night to see that little body suffer so and now my great fear is that I shall get in family way again. I do not want another baby for at least two more years. What will become of my baby if I have to wean her right away. Her stomach is so delicate that she cannot eat anything. I have tried feeding her with cow's milk but she vomited so that I quit. The doctor knows all this still he won't help me. I don't know what to do so please, for my sick baby's sake, help me.

Fifteen

I have thought time and time again that I would write you a letter to see if you would help a poor woman that is in need of help. Now I want to tell you about my thirteen and a half years of married life. When I was married a year and a half, there came a girl baby, and she is afflicted with St. Vitus dance, which the doctor calls it. She did not walk until she was seven years old and at this writing she is twelve years old and she still don't talk. In the meanwhile I have given birth to five other children, four of them were living and the other one was dead when it was born. Have miscarried six times and am in family way again. We are poor folks and have not a home even, and it seems that we will hardly make a living for them sometimes. But husband and I both work as hard as we can to keep them from starving, but that is about all I can say.

I feel like if there was ever a woman under the sun that needs your help, I sure do. There is sure no one that would appreciate help any more than I. I feel sometimes like putting an end to my life and again I think what would become of my little ones that are unable to take care of themselves, but if I have to go one having children it won't be long until I will be unable to care for them for I have been in awful poor health for five years and every term gets worse.

Sixteen

I am only thirty-eight years old and have had nine children. Two are dead. My youngest living is three years old and has never sat alone or cannot feed himself. He is awful sweet but will never walk and I have to handle him like a new born baby. I am so nervous I can't write fit for any one to read. I was confined in November. It was born at eight months and only lived one day. I am almost crazy for fear I will become pregnant again. I can never carry one to time again. I haven't the strength. I will only bring it here to die and maybe die myself. My other little ones need me and I don't need any more babies. It hurts me to write this way but it is true. We are poor and no one to work but my husband. My oldest girl should be in high school but we are not able to send her. Can you tell me how I can keep from becoming pregnant again? I do not want to miscarry, for that would be murder. I want to know some harmless way that will not injure any one.

Seventeen

I have reasons enough for wanting Birth Control information. The first is because I am not strong and the second is: my oldest daughter has convulsions and can't talk. She was in the hospital two months and came out worse than before. She is six years old now and can't talk yet, and we have lots of sickness. My husband is not very healthy and has to work, but by day wages.

We are living in a new country where there's no land cleared yet. I am sick myself this winter and I'm laying around most the time and ain't able to do my work and we can't afford a hired girl either. I am losing my eyesight too. I don't want to bring blind children to this world. When my last baby was born I was pretty sick and was afraid I was going to die. We couldn't get the doctor right away and I was out of my head for some time.

Can you help me so not to have any more babies? The doctor said it would be worse every time I would have a baby, so will you help a poor soul? A man don't know what a poor woman has to suffer. I cannot see why it's always the poor that's got to suffer.

Eighteen

I am the mother of eight living children, only three of which can take care of themselves. My oldest is fifteen and the baby six months. I am afraid he will be crippled too. They seem to have a weakness of the back and legs. The doctor says nothing can be done and they will die before reaching a teen age. I have a terrible time during confinement and have thought I would surely die the last three times. I wish I had, for then some of these poor cripples would not be here to suffer and die before my eyes. My husband works by the day and we do not own a roof over our heads. I live in dread and fear that I may have yet more children which I will, unless you tell me what to do, as I am only thirty five years old.

Nineteen

My husband has pulmonary tuberculosis of the lungs and out of my nine children only two are any way healthy looking and as they are only six and nine years it's no telling about them yet. I've been married just eighteen years so you see my children are only two years apart and as I have bladder and kidney trouble pretty bad I sometimes have a dangerous time at confinement. It makes me afraid of the next as each time the doctor says "Don't let this happen again."

Out of my nine children six are living. The first was a puny four-pound boy, who only had one lung and he died at three months with his first cold. The next was a boy,— died at eleven months with meningitis. The rest lived till just three years ago I lost a girl with tuberculosis of the lungs just such as her father has. Her father was at the hospital three years ago and they told him he was bad and wouldn't live nine months but he seems to keep on his feet so far but is poorly. I think it is a crime to bring any more poor little puny babies in the world as my husband's disease may be bad for them.

Twenty

I am a farmer's wife and I have five children. The oldest is eleven and the youngest is one and one half years old and I am worried for fear I will have another baby and I can't take care of the ones I have. My husband and I run a dairy of thirty cows all the year and we can't afford to hire any help so you see I have to work very hard. My last baby was only an eight months baby and was very weak. She weighed three pounds when born and we kept her with hot water bottles around her for five months and the doctors said that all that caused it was my working so hard.

As for myself, I am almost a wreck ever since she was born and I know I can't stand it to have any more.

My husband has throat trouble of some kind. I don't know what it is, he has had it operated on three times and he gets worse every year and last week he was so miserable, I went to our family doctor to get him more medicine and he told me not to be surprised if it turned into consumption of the throat. He said I had better try and not have any more children, but he would not tell me anything to do. If that is so what will become of me and my children if I can't find someone to help me?

Twenty-one

I married young and am a mother of four children, all living, the oldest seven and baby fifteen months. Both are frail and undernourished. The baby has been sick all his life and is such a care.

Now I didn't want these children,—the last three, although they are sweet dear children. Of course, I love them as dear as any mother could, but their father hasn't any health, has been operated on for rupture and stomach trouble and has had ten inches of his intestines taken out, and isn't able to work regular. He is a molder which is awfully hard work and don't pay very much and you see it is impossible for me to work out, even if my health would permit as it takes all of my time to do my work and look after my children and then they are neglected.

Now I fear my husband has T. B., he is so frail, he or the doctor won't tell me, they both say I have enough to worry about as I worry lots. Now he or I don't want any more children and we live in constant fear of my getting pregnant again. Now will you tell me how to keep from having any more.

I am afraid I'm pregnant again, which if I was sure, I would commit suicide for I have nothing to live for if I have to keep bringing children in this sinful world and nothing to promise them but suffering and to become a public burden. My health has been gone since my second child was born who is five years old and suffer with my back day and night and have cried myself to sleep hundreds of times, also washed many a day and cried over the tub. Could not afford to hire it done or hire any help as he wouldn't be able to work only part of the time. Now is there a hope for me or have I got to leave my babies on the mercy of the world and go to city hospital and have my female organs out to keep from bearing more?

Twenty-two

I am twenty-six years old. I was nineteen years old when I was married. I am a mother of four living children: the oldest is six years old and the baby is five months old. I do not feel good when I carry my children and after my child is born I am awful weak, and have to get up when my baby is four or five days old and get around and do what I can. We are poor and can't afford to keep any one to take care of me and the children.

My husband is a hard working man and brings small pay home. It is hard for me to make ends meet. I do not get much things as I can't afford to get them things that I really need. My husband is more sick than well, but of course, he goes to work. Sometimes he should stay at home and rest and be in bed but he has to go out and make his living and the family. My husband asked the boss to give him a better work that he is more sick than well so he could work and the boss won't change his work. Boss tells him if you are sick, stay home. My husband was operated on just before my baby was born, for stomach trouble. The operation don't seem to do him no good yet. I just think the reason because he started work soon. The doctor said it would take a while for him to get well. I keep away from my husband and he is very careful with me but still it does no good. I am asking you to help me to prevent having more children.

Twenty-three

I am just another poor unfortunate woman not able to raise children and I think the greatest sin of this world is to bring children in this world without any means of support, no chance to educate or give them a chance. I just want to give you a few pointers as to the conditions under which I live. I was a strong healthy girl, done man's work before I was married. I was married at eighteen. Eleven months later I had a frail little boy which has been sickly most all the time. My worrying about him has almost drove me crazy and my fears of getting pregnant again.

My husband has had the syphilis and he also give it to me. So the last four years of my life has been hell through pain and punishment. I have managed to keep from having any more children. Number of times I have had to have operations and only last Spring I almost lost my life over one. For months I was confined to my bed. I didn't dare put my foot on the floor.

The doctor said to me one day, "Do you think you will try it again?"

Dear, I am telling you just what I told him. "I had rather die and leave the one I have than to bring another into this world to suffer."

I stay away from my husband as much as possible. We have serious quarrels and have almost separated over it.

Is there anything you can do that will enable me to keep from getting pregnant any more? I am a nervous wreck. God only knows how much it will be appreciated.

Twenty-four

I am a poor woman with two children, one thirteen months the other three years and will you please tell me how I can avoid having any more. I have such a hard time when they are five and six months old, they suffer so much with abscesses all the time. My baby can't even crawl and is so puny. And I have a hard time birthing them. I have to be put under chloroform and have shoots and I suffer with an awful itch all the time before they are born. My husband can't make enough to support them and I can't care for them like they should and will you please help a poor needy one like me. I can't begin to tell you my condition. My husband is a heavy drinker and he suffers all the time with abscesses and he is awful weak himself, and the children never walk until they are about two years old.

Twenty-five

I have four children the oldest just past six years. The second four years in April, she was born disfigured and while I was in bed I very near lost my mind. She has had five operations from a surgeon here but she is not yet finished. Then I have two babies, both boys, the first boy two years last Oct., the baby six months. The first two are girls. I went to town when the baby four months old and took the little girl most four years to see if I could have her finished by a specialist that did this kind of work. By caring for the baby and carrying him different places in search for the right doctor, my milk left me and baby cried so much I took him to a doctor and he said baby was going underweight, as I started him on a bottle. I took my little girl to the Dr. as he had had several cases like her. She has hare lip and double cleft palate. He performed the operation.

We have all we can do to care for the four and have the little girl operated on as the doctor said about three more operations before she would be finished and they cost so much and living so high. I am trying to bring them up clean and send them to school as I believe every child should be given the best schooling, but my husband is a mill man, not earning very much as the way everything costs. I think it a sin and crime to bring little ones into the world and not be able to take care of them. I would rather see my girls dead than know they would be like some others in large families.

Twenty-six

I have been married four years this June. When we were first married I became pregnant in the fourth month, and in the second month of pregnancy, my body broke out in purple spots. Not having the least idea what could cause it I consulted a doctor immediately. He took a blood test of both my husband and me. When I went back for my answer, it was "syphilis" and in the worst form. It nearly tore my heart out, and my mother's as well, for I had always had such a horror of the very sound of the word. Then my husband told me he had got it from his first wife. So I had to be operated upon—it was not quite the same as abortion and yet a whole lot worse.

Then we started taking blood treatments, three times a week. I could scarcely stand the inoculations. I had to keep an ice pack on it all night in order to sleep, the pain was so dreadful. My husband had no trouble.

The doctor said we could not risk having children for they would be afflicted. For a year we took those treatments, and during that time I was operated on three times. I used every available preventive that other people used, but I had no results from them. The doctor said I could not stand another operation—that it would kill me. So it remained for my husband to protect me. After much persuasion I got him to use precautions, but it was a constant nagging, for he hated to do it. Yet he claimed to love me dearly, and I told him there was one way of proving it.

We went to Arizona. The climate was better there and I felt better right away. We had blood tests there and both were negative. Soon I was pregnant again. I had the baby, and he was perfect so far as we could see. But the disease is in his blood. I have had several symptoms since, and there is little doubt that it is dragging me down —I am a nervous wreck. The baby is fifteen months old;

I am six months with another. Because we are poor, we cannot stand the operation so often, and it can only mean for me to go on having on right after another. I cannot nurse my babies, for my milk is poison.

And now my husband and I quarrel whenever I remind him that he could prevent it if he would. My affection for him is waning, and he looks elsewhere for pleasure. It is no wonder I cannot hold him. But if I did not have children, I could make myself as attractive as any girl, and then his attention would revert to me.

There must surely be some means of prevention, and no one would be more thankful to hear of it than I. It is not because I do not love children. I love my baby so much that it drives me crazy to think that his blood is diseased. We went to a clinic for awhile, and I saw other babies there taking treatments. It made my heart ache to see them jam those needles into the tender little bodies. Poor little helpless creatures, who are not to blame, yet they must suffer from others' follies!

Twenty-seven

I grope in the dark for the knowledge for which I am searching. I am a young woman, twenty-six this month, and a high school graduate. Before I married in 1922 I was employed as assistant post-master at a small mining town. Soon after my marriage, I noticed that my husband had terrible sores, which, even though he doctored them persistently, refused to heal. I suggested that he go to a doctor and have his blood tested, which he quite readily did. The test was sent to the State Board of Health, and a report came back, 4-plus—syphilis. My husband became enraged, and refused to take treatment, all the while denying the report.

At this time I was pregnant three months. What could I do but go through with it to the end? When the baby came, the doctor refused to speak to me about syphilis, and we have had to doctor the little fellow ever since. I determined not to have another child, but three months after my confinement, I was again pregnant. I can't stoop to abortion, and must I go on bringing these little deformed, defenceless creatures into the world?

Twenty-eight

I am today the mother of six living children, and have had two miscarriages. My oldest son is now twelve years old, and he has been helpless from his birth. The rest of my children are very pale, and I have to take them to the doctor quite often. One of my daughters has her left eye blind.

I have tried to keep myself away from my husband since my last baby was born, but it causes quarrels and once he left me saying I wasn't doing my duty as a wife.

My husband, I have learned lately, had syphilis before we were married, and on account of that loathsome disease he is never in good health. I do work for other people besides taking care of my family and the house. Please help me if there is a way.

Twenty-nine

I am writing you for help. I know you can and will help. You have such a big heart in you. I cannot go to our doctor for he believes in every woman having all of the children they can and if you are not pregnant he will help you get that way. I don't want any more children. I have borne six, one dead. I inherit syphilis. One sister has T.B., one brother nearly blind, one brother deformed and my brother had twins grown together. I believe it would be all right for you to tell me something. I don't think I can stand having any more. I almost lost my mind for nine months after my last baby was born.

Thirty

I am 25 years old, have been married seven years and I am the mother of five children. When my first child was a year and six months old I had another, when that was a year and five months old I had another, when that was a year and four months old I had another, when it was six months old I started with another but miscarried at three months and three months from then I started with another and miscarried that at eight months, so by right I am the mother of six. My husband had the clap before we married and I don't think he was cured at all. That lasted about six weeks then he got better. When my first child was three months old my husband had what they call Bubose. I took sick and stayed sick unable to do anything for two months. I had womb trouble, but I didn't know it then, so I tried to stay on my feet and work. After I was sick one month dark spots came on my leg and the flesh got soft and I couldn't walk for one month. And ever since then I have been suffering with womb and ovary trouble, but I continue to have children.

Thirty-one

I am a weak, run-down, sickly woman; been married five years. This tells the story—a radiant bride at twenty; at twenty-five—what? If you could see me you would not have to guess.

My first child was still born. I had an awful time. My next was a miscarriage at six months. In two months I was pregnant again, and by staying in bed for seven long months, I went full time. But my baby was almost blind. I spent three months praying night and day for my baby's sight, and God heard and answered my cries, for at twenty-two months he has pretty blue eyes. But I would rather die than have another one, for my husband is a sufferer from gonorrhea. I have begged him to leave me. I would rather be separated than have any more. Please help me. I think the law is hideous. There ought to be a law against diseased men to marry pure, clean girls, to bring sickly children into the world to suffer, and oh! the suffering the poor women have to endure!

Thirty-two

My husband wrote for your book, when it arrived I was in the family way so put it away and hoped and prayed that the child would be born perfect. I suffered more than can be imagined. Once I felt faint, then got something like a stroke on one side so I fell on the floor, still remained conscious. I always have indigestion and palpitation of the heart. Two years before this I had the horrible experience of having a monstrous birth and the next one was just like it. The doctors could tell me nothing of any value. Said I may have fifty more children and none would be like the last, or there may be more like it. Since I had two already now this leaves me in a very uncomfortable position as you can plainly see. These two little ones had no head just a face, no skin or scalp on. The first was a seven months' baby but the other went nine months and was just exactly like it. My father is insane. Could this have anything to do with it? Our first three children are all right. I have three married sisters; their little ones are all right.

Thirty-three

I am the mother of three children, the oldest five years, the youngest one year. I feel like lots of others, I would rather die than have another as we cannot afford the three we have. Besides I have another reason. Within the past four years, two of my husband's sisters have been sent to the insane asylum. One is better and is home again, but the other sister died there about six months ago. So you see that worries me a lot besides caring for the children and not much to get along on.

Thirty-four

I am a mother only thirty years old and have only been married five years and have had three babies and two miscarriages. My first baby was a healthy boy although I had to raise him on the bottle part time. I was left with fairly good health, then in five months I had a miscarriage and sixteen months later I had a tiny baby girl who was very delicate until one year old. We took her to a baby specialist. She was almost dead but with all perseverance this doctor saved her and now she is fairly strong but we have to be very careful what she eats yet.

My health continued about the same and just fourteen months and one day from her birth I had another tiny baby girl who was sickly and never grew scarcely any until she was ten months old. She died very sudden. Two doctors did not know what was the cause of her death.

I had milk leg following her birth and my health has been bad ever since and just sixteen months after her birth I had another miscarriage and I have never seen a well day since. Some days I can scarcely be up at all. My husband has Bright's disease of the kidneys and has been under the doctors care for nearly three years and shows very little improvement. We are deeply in debt with doctor bills and all we have is our hard earnings. I keep roomers and boarders part the time and take in sewing to help get along and live in constant dread that another conception will take place. I would not care if I could have strong healthy babies and had good health myself and Mr. —— had better health. We could find means to keep them but when our health is bad it is hard to make a living much less to pay such terrible doctor bills and taking a chance on bringing more delicate babies to our home.

Thirty-five

I am coming to you personally, and when you see the urgency of my case I do not think you will fail me.

I am forty-two years old. When I was fifteen I married a man who contracted tuberculosis shortly afterward. We had five children in eight years, *all of whom died* except the first one—a girl. She is married and expecting to become a mother soon.

After the death of my first husband I married a young farmer. He owns a small farm, but it is only by the very hardest work that we can make both ends meet. By him I have six children, including twins, and have miscarried three times. Two years ago he became insane and was taken to the asylum. While he was away my children and I suffered from want, as one of my babies was born shortly after he left, and of course I was not strong enough to do any work. My health is broken, and I can hardly do my own work.

My husband stayed eight months, and was then sent home as well. I have investigated his family and find that imbecility has run in it for generations. One of his sisters has a perfect idiot. (All of mine are all right except the baby. She does not develop.)

My husband will not practice continence. It really does seem to make his mind worse when he does. He says he has only a little while left in which to enjoy life and he doesn't intend to miss any of it. He doesn't seem to be right in his mind yet. At times he is completely "off," and yet if he should leave me I could not support my children and myself to save my life.

I believe if I can keep from bearing children for the next few years I can pass the change of life, and gain some health and strength with which to rear my children in my old age. I have taken some courses by correspondence, and have a very fair education, although I have never lived anywhere but out here in the country. I am hoping to leave the farm in the near future, and try to get a position in some office.

Thirty-six

I have four children. My oldest girl is deaf and dumb and my baby is only three weeks old and I feel just as bad today as the first day I got up. We are poor and could not get no one to give me proper care, only the deaf girl took care of me and my other girl of ten years old. Since I am upon my feet we all have been sick. We are not all better yet, even the little baby is sick and my husband and I am so discouraged at times I don't know what to do, and I am so weak I have to do my own washing and all my work, so like that it is very hard for me to get better. When I am carrying my babies I have a tooth that bleeds all the time and the gum comes right away from my teeth. I am up all nights with it. It bleeds so much and I had a very hard sickness. If you could please tell me what I could do to keep out of it. I have a good husband but I am afraid he will get discouraged also. We are having such a time with sickness.

Thirty-seven

I am a young married woman but do not feel young, I have always had so much trouble. I am the youngest of eleven children and have always had to work so hard and had such poor health that I feel like an old woman.

None of us are strong. My mother has very bad kidney and stomach disease which I contracted when I was born and just in the last year since I married erysipelas has broken out on her, or at least that is what the doctors seem to think that it is.

The doctors don't seem to know just what to think of our family. I have a married brother who has a boy whose mind is not right. Another sister whose children are poor, weakly little things. Before I married I worried a lot because I knew that we are not a strong healthy family.

I told my husband-to-be, but he did not want to give me up. I kept on putting our wedding off and was under the doctors' treatment for over a year. They helped me to a certain extent, and I loved my husband so much and loved a home so much I finally consented to be married, but I almost regret it now.

Oh! the awful worry of getting pregnant. If I was a strong healthy woman I would not mind but when I think of the little weakly bodies I would bring into the world I just feel like screaming. You may think I should have thought of this before I married and I did, but I thought I could keep from having children, and then I was young and didn't realize that it could worry me as it does now. There were so many remedies to keep from having children that I had heard women using, that I thought if I could keep from having children I would be all right. And I do believe that our family would be all right if we would not have children. It just seems like it is the generation running down and getting weaker and weaker all the time.

Thirty-eight

I married when only seventeen years and have been married ten years. Have gave birth to five children and have had two miscarriages and my health has been very poor most of the time.

You don't know the agony I have to suffer and if my children could be alright when they come it wouldn't be quite so bad but their father I believe is going insane by his actions at times it acts like epilepsy fits by what I read in the doctor books. My two last children died when in infancy—one had convulsions and my last little baby had fits. It is terrible to see our dear little ones suffer that way.

I have watched over them till death came and if only we could do some way to keep from having more it would be much better for us all. But they keep us poor women in ignorance but I must do something because I don't want to bring any more children in this world to suffer.

Thirty-nine

I've been married a year and four months, have been to the doctor twice, got rid of one each time. We don't wish to have children for the reason my husband has been diseased and our doctor told us it was for the best not to have any. He decided that drugs should be taken after conception, which I have been using since and fear it will kill me for I am getting weaker every day. My husband has no desire for children but he takes the privilege of married life at will. If I had an absolute contraceptive I should be a very happy woman. At the age of nineteen I married the dearest of all men and very thankful to have a little home to call our own.

I did not know my husband had been diseased but I love him just the same.

Forty

I married when I was only sixteen years of age, not knowing what trouble I was getting into. I thought I couldn't be no worse off as I had only one brother fourteen years old to support my mother and four children. I was only trying to lighten his burden. His wages were only $12 a week and you can imagine how we had to live to get by and everything so high.

I married a poor boy only twenty years old. We lived for one year in a 9 by 12 room. While we lived there I had two miscarried children. No one but me knew the pain I suffered. My husband worked by day and we wasn't able to hire help. I stayed by myself in bed from morning till night and husband doing the work at night. I wouldn't have been living today but we found two rooms for $1.25 a week, and we moved there and in ten months a little baby girl was born, weighing seven and one half pounds.

We were two of the happiest people on earth. She is three months old now and I cry half of the time about her. She has been sick all of her life and nothing we do seems to help her.

My husband has T. B. and heart trouble. My prayer

every night is for God to let my dear baby live and not let no more come. If my husband was healthy and his salary was enough to care for them I would like two more but it doesn't seem right to bring the little innocent things to this world just to suffer.

VI

Wasted Efforts

THE process of maternity is the most exhaustive of all vital functions. The whole modern program of maternal welfare and prenatal care is based upon a recognition of the great demands exacted from the constitution of the woman during the long period of pregnancy. If undertaken by girls who have not yet passed the period of adolescence, their full physical development may be rendered forever impossible of attainment. From the vital forces of even the most richly endowed constitution pregnancy imposes a heavy tax. A careful régime of peace, quiet, and proper nourishment is essential during the nine months preceding the birth of any child. A sufficient period of recuperation is an absolute necessity following it.

As many of the letters presented in the preceding chapters have sufficiently indicated, the ordeal of pregnancy places an added strain upon all the vital organs of the mother-to-be. If any predisposition to constitutional weakness exists, this increasing strain often produces a crisis and breakdown. Maternal mortality is one of the great dangers. We are not dealing with those innumerable deaths brought about by pregnancy—that is another tragedy which may be verified by the statistics concerning maternal mortality in both the United States and England.

In this group we are concerned with the records of women condemned to one fruitless pregnancy after another. One unfortunate mother confesses that nine out of the eleven pregnancies she has begun have been fruitless; another that eight out of the twelve children she has attempted to bring into the world are dead.

The mothers who so briefly and laconically recite their woes in these letters seem to be of the very opposite type of those whom we have characterized as "breeders." Constitutionally they are not strong enough to bear the burden of successive and almost uninterrupted pregnancies. Nature, however, refuses to release these women from such endless servitude. At the cost of their frail health and battered bodies, often at the cost of their lives, they must go through the long Golgotha of pain and suffering.

In these painful narrations miscarriage follows miscarriage. Still-births seem the rule rather than the exception. Only those who have time after time proved their inability to carry the embryo in their wombs to its full development are given the brief and temporary relief of therapeutic abortion.

These letters reveal a composite picture of the unending procession of little lives making fitful apparitions in this world—just long enough to kindle a spark of hope in the breast of the mother—and then being carried lifeless fill tiny graves. "There are four little graves in our churchyard," writes one mother. Yet always the mother must take up her burden again, since she knows no way of avoiding pregnancy. She endures miscarriage; her babies are again born dead; or to save her life, she submits to therapeutic abortion. Her doctor has told her she is unfitted for maternity, yet finding herself pregnant again, she is forced to live through months of nightmare suspense, terror and anxiety.

These cases, moreover, demonstrate that a small family of one or two surviving children does not necessarily mean that any conscious control of the reproductive powers has been exercised. A small family does not necessarily imply the practice of Birth Control, any more than a larger family of four or five or six healthy children implies that Birth Control has not successfully been practiced. Behind the so-called "small family," of the type described in the following cases, there may be secreted the unuttered tragedy of a mother's life—of repeated pregnancies, of miscarriages and expensive operations; of doctors' and hospital bills continually draining the limited financial resources of the family, even depriving the surviving children of food, clothing and the advantages that should be their birthright.

Such cases as these make us wonder why, in an age which has developed science and industry and economic efficiency to their highest points, so little thought has been given to the development of a science of parenthood, a science of maternity which could prevent this appalling and unestimated waste of womankind and maternal effort.

Succinctly yet graphically the letters which now follow depict these wasted energies.

One

Left an orphan at birth I am now a woman twenty-six years of age and just been married now seven years. I must say seven years of misery as I am just about broken down now to a point where I cannot go much further in life. I have just recently had another miscarriage. It is only three months followed by typhoid fever. This is the sixth time it has occurred and it generally comes on when I am pregnant on or about sixth and seventh months and they are all badly deformed babies.

I am very fond of babies and I have prayed and prayed to the good Lord over and over again for one until now I pray just for the opposite that I shall never bring any crippled children into the world to suffer, as that I think is the greatest sin I can ever commit. We are not wealthy people as my husband is a farmer and he has spent so much money for doctors and other things that were needed to try and bring me back to health that we are almost paupers now and must sell the farm at an early date.

All we ever got from the doctors was pills and the advice that I could never bring normal babies into the world and that the best thing to do is to keep from getting pregnant.

God help me, nature is stronger than anything in this world so how is a man healthy and strong to be kept from nature's doings? If it could be done I would gladly see that it was done.

The thought of you gives me a faint hope, a hope that I don't dare to lean on too heavy and it seems to me at this moment that it gives me strength such as I never have felt in the past three years just to feel that here is a faint hope that I can get around again and take care of myself if you will help me. I don't dare say happy as I don't know what that means; from a child on I had

to work very hard for a living and never was taught anything, as my mother died giving birth to me and my
father died when I was six but after that I was from one
relative to another and none were very kind. God grant
that you can and will be my uplift and save me from so
much misery as I would rather die than go through what
I have in the past few years.

Two

I thought I would drop you a few lines to ask you if
you would not be so kind and advise me something that
would sure be certain and not disappoint a person. I am
thirty-three years old a mother of three living children,
two died for me and had about eight miscarriages. Have
made up my mind that I would not have any more children if it would kill me. When I have a terrible time
and after the birth I get the hemorrhage. To tell the truth
I don't wish no dog to go through what I have to stand,
let alone a human being. My husband is a miner and does
not as much as make a miserable living. Please excuse my
writing as I'm a Bohemian.

Three

I am twenty-seven years of age, have been married almost ten years. In the last eight of these I have given
birth to two stillborn children, one living one, and have
miscarried four times, making seven times in the eight
years I have been pregnant. We have only a limited means
and don't know how we would have taken care of them

had they all been in full term and lived. Will close trusting that you can in some way help us.

Four

I was married at seventeen and quite ignorant. I had a child and he was born with deformed eyelids. He died at the age of five years. I had another one which was a premature and also deformed but only lived a few hours. I had two more miscarriages within eleven months after my second. I now have two more children and an adopted one. Each time I get weaker and before my last one I suffered from hysteria. I now have another one only one month old and feel myself going into a nervous decline. My husband has chronic asthma and I feel as though we are not able to provide for any more and also my health isn't what it should be.

Five

I am a young woman age twenty years old. Have been married four years and my husband is only a laboring man. I was married only six months and I had a three months miscarriage and in five months after I had another miscarriage and then in a year and a half I had a fine ten pound boy which is awful sweet. I am expecting in a week or two for another baby and when I am pregnant I am in the awful shape, can hardly go. Most things are wrong with me in my body I look like not able to do my work and I have broken veins on my legs. Can hardly go and I fell the other day and hurt one of my legs can hardly walk and now expecting to birth a child any time. What on earth am I going to do? It is death to birth a child, let alone the other things after the child comes.

Six

I am twenty-two years old. I am in bad health, am not able to do any house work much and I had a six months miscarriage with my first baby and in fifteen months I had eight pound girl and in three years a nine pound boy. In sixteen months I had a three months miscarriage and in three months I had a two months miscarriage. In seven months I had another two months miscarriage and I almost died the last time which the doctor says I can't stand it many more times and he says I can't carry a nine months baby any more because I am too weak.

Seven

I am married fourteen years and I have been pregnant fifteen times. I only have four living children. I am getting weaker these last few years. I have buried two full time babies, one only lived five weeks and the little girl at three months with waste of flesh, and my little boy now that is living he had that too but he overcame it, but he aint well. I carried to seven months and lost them and the rest at two and three months and lost them and I expect to be confined in August and when I get over this if I only would know what to do I certainly would prevent myself from getting that way. My last full-time baby living is eighteen months old this month.

My husband is an awful moonshine drinker and I should not have children; but what am I going to do, drive him away from home? My heart is broken the way I get just one after the other. I am only thirty-three years old and I am not like I used to be, so if you please, help me out.

Eight

We are only a poor family, four girls, my husband and myself, but my husband has made small money and we just struggle along. I have had ten miscarriages and four children, so a woman told me to write to you before I'll be in my grave, I am only thirty-one years old. I was married young and had a child every eighteen months or two years at the most. You may not believe I have had ten miscarriages but it is true and can be proved as I have been in the hospital not so long ago.

Nine

I am a poor farmer's wife. I sure do appreciate what I have learned in your book. My husband says he sure did enjoy reading it himself. I hope you will pardon me if I ask you anything I had not ought to. I am a mother of eight children and five mishaps. I had a mishap two weeks ago and it cost my husband about fifty dollars before I got over it. I had to have a serious operation. We had to have two doctors to wait on me, besides the deaths I did suffer. I have not got a round vein from hip down to the bottom of my feet, they are all broken veins. And I have bronchial asthma so bad until I can't hardly live some times, I just feel like I would give the rest of my life to only know or to have the Birth Control knowledge. I am only thirty-eight years old but I feel like I am fifty years old. I am not able to do any house work half the time. There is no tongue that can tell my hardships and suffering. I don't know any of the pleasures of life but that don't keep me from hoping for them some day.

Ten

The first time I was pregnant I was in an accident and got hurt so badly that I cannot carry any through the full time. I have had seven miscarriages in eight years. Have nearly died each time. I have had hemorrhages and infections almost getting blood poisoning as the result. I have had different doctors but they all say they cannot do anything for me. They always warn me at the hospital not to let it happen again but do not tell me what I need to know. If only I knew of something that was harmless to the health and yet positively reliable I could regain my health to some degree which has been ruined by my ignorance of such things. My uterus is badly torn, dropped and fallen backwards against my rectum so I get pregnant very easily.

Eleven

Please picture a mite of a woman not quite four feet nine inches tall, weight just last week ninety-seven pounds (with suit and top coat on), crippled physically by a heart lesion, the outcome of inflammatory rheumatism, dreading from one month to another the chances of accidental pregnancy.

Why? I am thirty-four years old, married eleven years; was married most two years when my first came. I was wild for my baby during my period of waiting—it was one of dreams. I had good care because we prepared for this only baby of ours. In nine days less than a year a baby girl arrived. That doctor attending me through a difficult dry-birth later, called in to quiet an over-worked heart, had no other solution to offer than to be "more careful." Being careful didn't help any and in seven months I was pregnant again, though the baby wasn't walking or talking.

Well, I carried on till I broke, my heart couldn't stand up to it's load, they put me to bed and for five long months I laid waiting my time—heart too weak to be up. God alone knows of that awful time, two babies, cared for by any one we could get, when the wee laddie came, —a poor under-nourished babe, he only stayed with us five months. Every minute he lived reflected on his parents for bringing him here. He needed a mother's nourishment and care. I laid too sick and weak to even care about him and I thanked God for taking him. Could I but add that was all—no, I was just getting around again when I was right back in the same condition not quite six months grace to recuperate. Then, it was decided, abortion was the only relief, after the third month. I was put to bed and the usual method of dilatation was used but not successfully. My womb refused to empty and at extreme I was relieved forcibly. My heart condition did not allow me to take anything to ease the pain, it was terrible, a three months child torn from the womb. I laid for twenty-four hours at that time not daring to move to prevent flooding, my bed not changed, truly it seemed like slaughter to me. Just three years ago this month I went through my second abortion, a six weeks child. This last time was a hospital case, the surgeon who operated on me said my only hope lay in having the cords cut but I run more than the ordinary person's risk taking ether.

Can you wonder at my fear from month to month? I have a comfortable home, two splendid children and the only drawback to my happiness, despite my poor health is the fact that the horror of what I have gone through and the chance it may happen again is always with me.

Twelve

I was married when only fourteen years old. My first baby came, died at birth. I was torn so badly. In eleven months another baby came. Then the third one came. I went to the hospital to have the laceration repaired. This was three months after the baby came. Then I got that way again so when baby came these parts had not got strong so it was torn again. The baby died. All my babies are instrument cases. Then I had another baby and since then I was that way again but had a miscarriage. I was not strong enough to carry it. The doctor told me I could not have living babies so I let him open the womb and he had done it four or five times but I would rather not have to again, but I want to get well. You know I cannot keep on having abortions.

Thirteen

I am a married woman living with a man eight years. I have a boy six years old and between him I've had three children taken away from me—three months, four months and two months. I've went through abortion to have them taken from me. I cannot have children because I am partly helpless. I have fallen from the trolley car five years ago and have hurt the whole right side which is kept partly paralized. I can get around and do my work but not without the aid of my crutch. Now this is very hard for me you see, to have children. I would like you to advise me what to do to prevent from having any more as I would rather die than have children.

Fourteen

I have been married eight years and have had four babies in the last six and lost them all. The first one lived three and one half months, the second one four and one half months, the third one seven months and my last little one born last May only lived two days. In the case of the first three we had two different doctors, and our own doctor is an up-to-date, well-read and studied doctor. They both admitted that they were completely "floored" as to the cause of their deaths, all three being taken sick completely from a clear sky. Convulsions and death and no reason for same at all.

When my last baby died our doctor wanted to take her to the state medical school and my husband accompanied the body of my little girl there. The doctor in charge of the autopsy talked to my husband later. It seems that death in this case and presumably in the other three, was caused by an enlargement of the thymus gland causing asphyxiation. The specialist advised my husband that we have no more children for at least five or six years.

Since then I have lived in a state of suspense from one month to the next. I loved my babies and wanted them too, even before they were born, hoping each time that this one would be spared to us. But now I live in terror. I don't believe I could keep my reason and go through nine months of worry for fear I might lose the next even before I could hold it in my arms.

The death of my last baby at two days of age was the cruelest of all. Every one said, "What a blessing, if it had to go, that it should go so soon." But oh! it was the hardest of all for me. I had planned on my baby so much and made such pretty things for her, trimmed the little basket she was to lie in so pretty and I never got to see her in it and held her in my arms only a few times. The disappointment was almost more than I could bear and the time I had to spend in bed with no baby to cheer me was the worst I ever spent in my life. If you could only find it possible in your heart to tell me how I can use preventive measures until such time as the doctor thinks I may risk having another child I will be grateful all my life. Although I am only a poor farmer's wife I would love to have a houseful of happy healthy children.

Fifteen

I am a woman of twenty-three years. I was married when I was sixteen years old and in thirteen months after,

I had a baby boy of seven pounds who died five days after, and I was torn inside and outside so bad that four months later I went to the hospital to be all sewed and after I came home in nine months I had a miscarriage of three months and flowed every month while I was in family way. Then in fifteen months I had another baby boy weighing three pounds and is living, is three years old. I flowed for two months with him while I was in the family way. Then in twenty-two months I had another boy born weighing five and one half pounds, flowing for two months until the doctor gave me medicine to stop flowing. He was born with a ruptured naval and died when he was five and one half months old.

In eleven months after had another baby boy weighing four pounds; flowing for two months until the doctor gave me medicine to stop while I was in the family way. He died when he was six weeks old and if the doctor wouldn't give me medicine while I am in the family way to stop flowing, I would have nothing but miscarriages.

So I have only one growing and the doctor says I am too weak to have more children for at least four or five years, and I am torn now just the way I was torn with my first baby. The doctor says when I won't have any more children I will have to go to the hospital and get all sewed again.

My husband is thirteen years older than I am and my last baby was only an eight months old baby because it didn't cry or nurse for three weeks, fed it from a teaspoon every two hours. The doctor said it was not fully developed.

Sixteen

I am only twenty-one years of age yet I have had two babies in less than three years. I was married when I was eighteen years old and my first baby was a premature birth, it was born dead and I had a bad time for I had a hemorrhage. Then septic poison set in and I lost all power of my legs. I went to a hospital and could not walk for five months. Shortly after I became pregnant again, and I worried a lot for fear I would be the same way as before, but when my second baby was born it was paralyzed and had septic poison, and the doctor said it would not live long. It lived for three months, and I now live in constant dread for fear I will have more.

Seventeen

I married when I was eighteen years of age and was ignorant of life and the mysteries it holds. In about eight months after my marriage a seven months' baby came, and it lived only about six weeks. In a year to a day another baby came which I also had to give up at five or six weeks. I've always loved babies and looked forward joyously to the coming of each of them, and my heart was almost broken when they were both taken away. I felt that I would rather die than suffer to bring them into the world and give they up so soon. In about eleven months a little girl was born and she is the idol of our hearts. Then in about a year there was another that lived only a few hours, still another came and lived only a few minutes.

There are four little graves in our churchyard. Next came a miscarriage and the next year I became pregnant again. The physician told me I could never carry one the full nine months, but by taking treatments and using an invalid's chair I gave birth to a boy who is eighteen months old now. My life is wrecked by all this, and my health almost ruined. During the period of pregnancy I am unable to do any work, and as we are only poor farmers it is almost impossible to get work done. I don't want more children at the price I have to pay. I love my babies, but I don't want more if my health is so impared that I can't be a real mother. I have asked doctors' advice but they only think I am foolish.

Eighteen

I am the mother of four children, only one living, and he is poor and sickly. My last baby lived to be six months and twenty-two days old and died with a stomach trouble. She suffered four weeks before she died. All of my babies have been taken by the doctors and I nearly die every time. I am broken-down and nervous and not able to give birth to children and only twenty-three years old. I was poor and didn't have any education. My husband is a poor man, only makes $2.00 a day and you know we are not able to care for one child, much less a large family. I married when I was fifteen and my baby was born eleven months after I was married, I've done my part of suffering in this world.

I never know nothing when my babies are born and lose them after all my suffering. I realize you are a friend of humanity and want you to tell me what to do to prevent having any more as I would rather die than bring babies in this world to suffer and die. Will you please help me be free from suffering? I nearly lose my mind worrying and wondering what to do. Is there any answer for women like me?

Nineteen

I was married in June, 1913, and the next year in July I had a girl, that lived two months and seventeen days. And the next year, in January, I had a boy who lived eight months and four days. And the next year in January I had a girl, she is now seven years old, a lovely girl going to school every day. Eighteen months from that time I had another girl which lived two months and seventeen days. In 1920 I had a boy who lived five months and one day, and the next year in June I had a girl which died an hour after it was born. In 1923 I had a boy in June and he died on the 17th of November, and in January I had a miscarriage of three months.

So you see we have had pretty hard luck and a lot of expense. It leaves me nothing but a wreck. A friend of mine gave me your address and my husband told me to write to you for he was tired of seeing them come and go all the time.

Twenty

What I want to know is how to keep from getting in the family way. I have been the mother of seven children. I have three living and four dead. The youngest one was born dead just one month ago. I always think I never can live to birth another, and I surely wanted to die this time. I was sick five weeks before I got down. I could not rest when I would lie down. I would almost lose my breath. I could not rest up or down and when I got sick, sure enough I was sick thirty-one hours and had two doctors with me and they say I will never stand such a thing again. So I wish you to tell me what I must do to keep that off. We are very poor and I have to work so hard to help my husband make a living. We have so much sickness and so many doctor bills to pay. It takes all we can do to live.

I am now only twenty-eight years old. I have been married twelve years. I married when I was only sixteen. That was entirely too young but I did not know at that time, but I love my husband and my children and all of God's people. I always try to help everybody in every way I can, and so now please won't you help me. I haven't gained my strength yet like I should so if you will help me I surely will help you.

Twenty-one

I was asked sometime ago to write you for some information as you could give it. I have been married ten years six months and had misfortune to loose eight and sometimes two in one year. I can go alright up until between the third and fourth month and that's when the trouble begins. I have one little girl five years old.

Twenty-two

I have two children the oldest is five the other two.
Have been married nine years. When the first was born, I
had convulsions. It died at birth. Just a year there was
another one. It was dead a week before it was born. Just
thirteen months there was another one, He is living but
was sick all the time till he was three years old; in eighteen months another one. It died before it was born. Then
a four months miscarriage. Just a year till another one
came. He is still living, I had a miscarriage last October.
The children were all boys but the last one. We are poor.
We haven't a roof of our own. My husband has to work
by day work for a living, hasn't got a steady job. Don't
believe I can stand it any more. Please help me so I can
help raise my children.

Twenty-three

I live in a small mining town. Even in this small town
there are many families it is a tragedy to see,—many who
would be glad to not have any more children for a few
years as they have three and four so small they cannot
take proper care of them. All are poor people. I married
in April, 1921, at the age of seventeen. In April, 1922, I
had an eight pound boy born to me. At this was in labor
thirty-eight hours and had to be put to sleep and the child
taken. It was not developed right inside. The doctor
did not think it would have had any mind or ever walked

153

it died in 24 hours after birth, all due to misconception. In May 1923 I had an eight pound girl who has never been well and has to be weaned young because my milk isn't good. In Nov. 1924 I had three and a half months' miscarriage, and now four months pregnant again, I am so uneasy I don't know what to do. I am afraid it will be like my first one. I feel some times as if I would rather die than suffer again as I did then. So please help me as I do not want any more children for a while after this one and always I will be your grateful friend.

Twenty-four

I thought I would drop you a few lines to find a real friend that would help me of my distress. I am a woman at the age of thirty-four at the present and have had twelve children up to the present time I had a child just two weeks ago it was born dead and inside of ten years I have had six children and none of them was born alive. I have my three children that are living but the rest of them all are dead. When they do come they are all born dead. I sometimes feel like committing suicide if it was not for the children that I have.

VII

Double Slavery

THE life of the mother who must toil to support her
growing family is less dramatic perhaps than some of the
cases we have considered in previous chapters, but no less
poignant.

We have now to consider the confessions of a number
of those mothers upon whom falls the economic burden
in the maintenance of the family. Due to the disabilities
or the dereliction of their husbands, some of them have
become its sole support. Others, and these are mainly
women of the farm, actually labor harder than their husbands in keeping the wolf from the door. A third group
toil as teammates with the hard-driven man, with a cour-
ageous and unswerving resignation. Heavy farm-work is
the lot of most. In addition to the relentless routine of
cooking, sewing, washing, ironing, and the care of the
children, they are driven like beasts of burden.

Vainly we might hope that once the heavy task of maternity had been accomplished, the double slavery to which
these mothers are condemned by Nature and custom might
be brought to an end. These letters demonstrate that
such relief is seldom attained.

Despite the lash of economic necessity, there is no cessation, according to the present records (which I have se-

lected from hundreds of similar confessions), from the heavy drain of pregnancy and childbearing.

"I dread thinking of my husband coming to me, for fear of more children coming to press us harder, as we are sorely pressed now," writes one mother who has been forced out to work to support her children, because the "head of the family" has failed miserably to do so. Another writes that she is the main support of a family of nine. A mother of six living children goes to work in a brass factory, the husband's only competence apparently lying in his ability to increase the number of hungry mouths in the poverty-stricken family. (The shiftless father seems indeed to be quite an ordinary phenomenon. The careful reader will note that it is the carefree happy-go-lucky father who is as a rule most violently opposed to contraceptive methods.)

"I weigh ninety pounds, do all my housework, care for the children and go to the field," another worn out woman succinctly sums up her life. "I have to work out with him, just like a Mexican, and also have to find time to do the necessary work for the family," writes another toiler in the sunburnt fields of the Southwest. "I get up at three o'clock and go to bed at nine," wearily writes another victim of this double slavery. . . . "I seem to have lost all interest in life and I would be glad to die sooner than to have more children."

Indeed, in each of these letters there is tragedy expressed or hidden beneath the suffering—the tragedy of a whole life, often of a whole family. A novel of American motherhood might be developed out of the naïve confession of one woman: "I long to feel well one more time, just so my children might know their mother as she would be if she was only well and had the strength to be a mother." Doesn't the whole tragedy of family relation, of family misunderstanding lie buried in this simple ingenuous confession. The mother of this type is too crushed by her double slavery ever to know her children. The children know as their mother only a beaten, mutilated, hopeless drudge they cannot comprehend, nor (in how many unrecorded cases?) truly love. "I try to force my feelings below the surface and grin," confides the mother of one of the most heartbreaking letters in this book,"—grin, smile and go ahead, but Lord, I can't, my body goes to pieces, I break down, and can't help it. . . . If only I had a little health I might be different, and I might be spared to raise my darling little children."

When food is scarce, always is it the mother who deprives herself, who suffers most from the lack of nourishment. Hence in addition to the heavy toil exacted of her frail body, she often suffers from lack of sufficient sustenance.

Children must be fed at any cost! The "breadwinner," who is often that in name only, must keep up his strength. Mother gets only what remains for herself and for the coming infant she is carrying in her womb. Hence her physical depletion, her threatened breakdown, her susceptibility to neurasthenia and maladies of every character, as well as her inability to equip the infant with sufficient motor force to carry it through the first year existence.

One

I am a married woman, have one boy five years old. My husband is a cripple. He sits in a wheel-chair and will have to as long as he lives. I have to lift him into bed at night and again in the morning I have to lift him into his chair. He weighs 180 pounds so you see I have my share of hard work together with housework and making a living. We are poor. Only have what we make but that's not very much. I am afraid I might become a mother again if I do not get some good simple safe and reliable way to prevent it. What should we do if I get in this condition? I couldn't lift my husband and there is no one that we can hire to do it because we haven't the money. Won't you please give me the information I need?

Two

I have often heard people speak of you and also of the good you do for people who are overburdened with children and have been wondering if you would help me. I am a woman with seven children and the eighth one coming. My husband is crippled with rheumatism, so I have to earn a living for them and have to earn it by working beets in summer and taking in washings in winter as that is the only work there is to get here. My oldest child is eleven years old so can't get much help from him and you know as well as I do that it is hard to make a living for such a family.

158

Three

I am a mother of four babies and I have to go out and work for my living. My husband has been sick about eighteen months and isn't able to work so I go and do people's washing and in the evening I do my own. Every night I come I just sit and cry many times I wish I was dead sometimes I get home and can't hardly stand on my feet.

Four

I was married when I was seventeen and seven months. After nine months married I had a miscarriage eight months. After fourteen months I had a baby boy and he is living and is now seven years old. After three years I had another boy. He was born with consumption in the bones and would shake his head one side and another, but doctors did not know what that was. Now I have them nervous spells myself. All through my marriage life I have been working in factories. I took my children to the day nursery. Two months before the birth of my last child my husband deserted me with my children. He had left home eleven times before that but always came back, but that night his mother gave him money to go out of town. I was then married five years to him. After four years I could not get no trace of him I got the divorce. I had to work hard to keep my furniture and pay the rent as I did not want to go boarding. Now as I was twenty-six and as I had no one to depend on I married again. He is a good young man of twenty-five and he is not a lazy gambler like the other, but even with that I fear having any more children as they will not be healthy. We were married a few months ago and neither of us had any money and he is only a laborer and makes twenty-five dollars a week, so you see I have struggled with the first husband and I wish I will not struggle with this one, so please if you can help me.

Five

Please tell me what to do to keep from having any more babies. I am only twenty-six years old and the mother of five children the oldest eight years and the others six, four and two, and I have four living. The last time I had a six month's miscarriage and I have been weak ever since. It happened this past August. My husband is gone to try to find work and I have to support my children myself. I have to work so hard until I feel like it would kill me to give birth to another. I am nervous. My back and side give me a lot of trouble. I am not able to give my children the attention that I desire. I take in washing to support my children. I suffered this last time from the time I got that way until I lost it and am yet weak in my back. Please! for my sake tell me what to do to keep from having another. I don't want another child. Five is enough for me.

Six

I work in a cotton mill and I have three children, and I feel as though I don't want to bring any more into the world under the conditions. I always have to go right back to work after childbirth and leave my children for someone else to care for.

Seven

I don't care to bear any more children for the man I got he is most all the time drunk and not working and gone for days and nights and leave me alone most of the time. I'm sewing for support me and my baby that is two years old and one dead born so I know you don't blame me for not wanting any more children and he is always talking about leaving me he might as well for what he is doing but I am worried that I may get in wrong.

Eight

I am thirty-eight years old, have a family of six living children, also lost two in infancy. Our baby now is just past two years. Our lives and home is happy, husband does everything to avoid more family. But there is always fear and nothing sure except what is injurious to him. I am not one that would die before I would have more babies, but we are not able to raise any more family. I have to work hard every day to keep the family going. Husband has not been able to work now for eighteen months. He has back trouble, has doctored all this time for it but gets no better. He does a little about the house and takes care of the baby. He can be on his feet only a short time and doctor don't give him much encouragement of being any better.

Nine

I am forty-five years old, have a blind husband and one little daughter of nine and as I have earned our living for nearly fifteen years with a constant mental distress as to my physical condition I feel I must have something to prevent further trouble if it is possible. Have nearly died at childbirth several times always being badly torn from use of instruments in every case and then not always saving my babes, so I am too old now to take any further chance, so I hope you will be willing to send me the desired information.

Ten

Here I must come to you in a very distressing time. Please, dear one, hear my plea and help me. I am going to tell you my condition. We have nine children. I am the stepmother of three who I do for as I do my own. I am the mother of six, my oldest one being only twelve years, No. two only ten years and No. three are twins only eight years, No. four twins again only four years, where I came very near dying when they were born. For three months was in bed. We are very poor. My husband has been in poor health for over a year. He has not been able to work regular at all. We have nothing only what he can make. I have been forced to leave my home and babies, go to work to try to help clothe and send the children to school. I am very much afraid of becoming pregnant. Oh, me! I don't know what we will do it I do. I am thirty-nine years old.

Eleven

While at a neighbor's house working, saw one of your books and read it, and seeing there are others think as I do makes me feel we can have friends instead of being sneered at by all, as so many of us poor hard working women are because we have to work for a mere existence. I want to tell you I have six children and have always had poor health so you might guess how I felt before bringing each one into the world while we were poor and nothing to support these children as they should be. We finally took up a homestead seventy-five miles from town thinking we might prosper but every time a little one came it pressed us harder. Then as there was no school and the children being brought up like animals I decided to bring them to town and work to support them, as he does not and could not support them alone. I find my health is breaking and fear I can't stand this strain much longer. I dread thinking of my husband coming to me for fear of more children coming to press us harder, as we are sorely pressed now. God only knows how thankful I would feel if you would only help me by telling me how to prevent child birth. Hope your good work goes on and I think it is the only sure road to the upbuilding of our country and race.

Twelve

I am thirty-four and have had seven children, six of them living, but I have never been what one would call

163

healthy, and was hoping I would find out some way to keep from having any more. We can hardly make a living. I hired my little one's keeping last winter and the rest went to school, and I worked in a brass factory. It was awful hard on me but we couldn't make a living without. I'm not working now but I guess I will have to again as the children are getting out of clothes and we are getting behind. My husband is terribly mean whenever I get that way. The day I was sick for my last baby he went away and left me alone he was so mad to think I had to have it. I sent my little boy after my mother so I wouldn't have to be alone. I know I hadn't ought to live with a man that way, but what can a woman do with a lot of little ones, who hates to part with any of them, so I am hoping and praying I can find out a way to keep from it. My youngest is three years old and just getting so he isn't so much to care for, but enough at that, but one loves them just the same, and he is an awful loving child, thinks there is no one like his mother.

Thirteen

I am a mother of seven children. My oldest thirteen, youngest seventeen months and I have a very hard life of it. My husband ain't a very good worker and we have such a hard time to get along. I work some but I have a bad heart. I can't stand to work too hard and as soon as I wean my babies I get in the family way right away and from the time I feel life I can't do nothing. I suffer so bad with one side that I just pray to die and suffer so much at the time my baby is born and I don't want no more. Please help me. My baby is so cross. Cries all the time for me, three of them, that sometimes I think I will go crazy. Then I do washing and ironing besides my own housework, so I would die before I would want another baby for the way I suffer to have them and live the way I have to live. I am just a nervous wreck. My husband goes out with a bunch to drink and I worry so much till the next day I am sick, for he is so mean when drinking. Oh! I hope you will be so good and kind and help me. I am just a poor broken-down mother. It is a shame if I bring more babies into this world to live like we must live. I do think it is a sin to have them and can't bring the darlings up right.

Fourteen

I have been married eleven years and have five children, the oldest nine years and the baby eight months old. I weigh about ninety pounds, do all my housework, care for the children and go to the field. I have also taught school three years since my marriage. I have had this to do on account of my husband being in ill health and last fall he had to undergo a very serious operation which left us heavily in debt and him unable to work. And in justice to the children I have I do not want to have any more children for a few years, but I know of no way to keep from it so I come to you for help. I will greatly appreciate any help you will send me as I cannot do my work now without neglecting my children. I cannot instruct and care for them properly. I cannot even bathe them and feed them as often as they should be.

Fifteen

I am a dressmaker and I married a clerk seven years ago. He drinks some, and I have been sickly all my life through. The doctor told us to be more careful as I have a sore on my left lung, but in a few months I will again be a mother. I am dreadfully sick throughout the entire confinement, but I still have to work or we would not have bread enough to eat. Even as hard as I work I have to neglect my children and my housework because it takes so much money to keep the wolf from the door. It is terrible to think of bringing these poor little babies into the world without means or strength to care for them. I am weaker every time I have a baby, and every one I have I think it will be the last, it would be best too as I have nothing to invite them to.

Sixteen

I have three children all fairly healthy except they are nervous, but then how can they help that when their mother and father are nervous, all, I think, from overwork. My husband is at his work bench 6 A. M. until 5:45 P. M., then we do extra work in the evening until 10 P. M. It is poor pay but every little bit helps. I do all my own housework including the washing and ironing and sewing and a little extra. Is it any wonder we are nervous, and the worst of it is we are not holding out. We want to try to give our children a fair chance which I think every child should have. I expect to go to the shop when my children are a little older to help out, if we don't have any more and right here is where you can help me if you will.

Seventeen

I am a young mother of twenty-seven and have five children the oldest only eight and the baby one year. I married a farmer when I was seventeen years old and have had to work hard ever since to live. I have worked out in the fields every summer taking the children with me to save money on hired help. I've sat on a mower two weeks before my baby was born. It seems no use cause we are no better off now than when we started. I would die before I'd have another child. I am just a nervous wreck. I am so nervous I almost go out of my head when I am in the family way. My husband feels sorry for me but he can't do anything to help me. I weigh about ninety-five pounds and am always tired and worried sick for fear I will have another one. We are poor and I have to make over old clothes the neighbors give to clothe them and they never get no care cause I am always sick. I have heart trouble caused from tonsils but we cannot afford to have them taken out. It really is a sin to neglect my babies like I do, but it can't be helped. I am not fit to do any better. I only hope you can help me. Oh how happy I would be. My heart is just sick now I can hardly write.

Eighteen

I am dropping you a letter. I am twenty-seven years old and my husband is twenty-eight years. We have been

married nine years my oldest child is eight years and I
have had six children. The last were twins, two girls.
One died at two days old and the other is five months yesterday only weighs nine pounds but is improving in looks.
My husband is very good to me but his health is poor.
And I am so dragged down by the children that some
mornings I think I can't get up and start another day's
work. We own a farm but we are just getting started and
it goes hard when you have to buy one little thing at
a time. For four years my husband rode eight miles to
work on the railroad—every day horse back and home at
night and done his farm work beside. I have milked all
the way from one to three cows summers and sometimes in
the winter and raised over one hundred chicks in the summer, besides my children's care and garden. I am nearly
to my end. I tell my husband if I have to go through what
I did again this second of last October I never will live.
I worked myself to death and nearly had my twin babies
at seven months but as I couldn't stand up to it why I
quit for a couple of weeks on doing so much until they
were born. One had convulsions and a broken hip. It was
born double. I don't see how I can ever stand to have any
more children right away again. If I do I know it means
death, for I nearly died when they were born. This fall
my husband has worked like a slave to support us and
I have joined in with all the help I could give him. I have
to drive myself to keep up with every day's work.

Nineteen

I am the mother of five children, three boys and two
girls, the youngest a baby boy twenty-two months old. I

have just weaned him and I nursed him so long for just the reason that I should not get caught. I never menstruate while the baby nurses, but I was getting so weak and nervous I just couldn't stand it any longer. Now I worry for fear I'll get pregnant again. We are putting in cotton this year so I'll have to chop and pick cotton and raise chickens and care for the kiddies. What care can I give them as we have no money to hire anything as we can scarcely buy enough to eat. If you could please help me to stay well a few years anyway till my health gets better. I love babies but we have our share and more than we can keep comfortable.

Twenty

I married when I was not quite seventeen a man I thought no one could love as I did. Have three children, one girl nine years, another girl four years, a boy two years. I have worked very hard. We truck for market and I have to help my husband. I have had rheumatism of the nerves twice and had it so bad. Once my husband had to carry me back and forth to the bed. I been right good so far this last time till here last week I got my menses for the first time since the baby was born. Hoeing, I feel so tired all the time. I don't suppose all women are alike. I don't know as I could get in family way as I always worry and I think of consumption but my husband has a head of his own and won't listen till it is too late, then he gets mad and tells me it's no fault but mine and still I have to work with it all. Some people tell me they don't see how I can do my work and tend to my children and still help outside like I do. I tell you I have to have some grit and then my little children don't get looked after like they should. I am writing to you for help like many others. My husband is very hearty person but I cannot help it, I am not.

Twenty-one

I married when twenty-eight and after eleven months had a splendid little boy who is now eleven months old and I am expecting another at any minute now. Father who lives with us is eighty-five and beginning to be quite a care. My husband is just a splendid fellow, ten years older than I, a carpenter by trade but he had nothing to do all winter and not much so far this summer, so our funds are getting pretty low. We live on a small place in the country and I try to do all I can to make ends meet. We have quite a patch of asparagrass and I bunch it all and take it to market. I also do all my own work including washing and ironing, and most of the time I hardly feel able to get around but of course have to. I get so tired at night I can't sleep. It isn't that we don't want children for we both love them, but we don't want more than we are able to care for financially and physically. I certainly don't want another in eleven months again for I am afraid I couldn't stand it. If I could only wait three or four years I would be so glad.

Twenty-two

I am one of the many thousands who dread sexual intercourse simply because my husband is not able to provide a home for the child we now have. We live on a ranch, in just a shack, with no conveniences whatever and as we cannot afford to hire help I have to work out with him, just like a Mexican, and also have to find time to do the necessary work for the family. When my first baby was born eighteen months after I was married, we had planted ten acres in tomatoes and it was necessary for me to work at the picking, packing and lifting full boxes, until the time the baby was born. As I was not reared to this kind of work it injured my health very much and I've never got back to my former self, especially as the proper nourishing food was not obtainable. It is a continual struggle to meet the bills and interests due. I have since had to undergo the terrible ordeal of abortion, and now live in continual dread. Our one little boy seems fairly robust; but my husband's mother informed me that my husband was tubercular and this is a constant nightmare to me.

Twenty-three

I have four children and I think I got all I can take care of as I run a small grocery and meat market and as I work and my husband in it from five in the morning till late at night and as I cannot afford to keep a maid or anyone to help me I must work days and nights till I am almost dead with work as no matter how I watch myself I am always in trouble and just last month I went to someone and it almost killed me so I cannot keep this up as I cannot afford it and cannot stand it as it would kill me in time.

Twenty-four

I was married three years ago and have two children one two years old and the other almost a year. Before I was married there was no other girl in the community that was stronger or healthier than I—I did not know what it was to be sick. We rented a house and my husband intended working in the mill but then the mill shut down and he could get no work anywhere. I was in the family way and of course we tried to live as cheap as we possibly could, having no work I worried all day and couldn't sleep at nights. I would worry all the time. When my baby was born it only weighed three and a half pounds and cried lots. Then my husband still had no work. When baby was three months old we got a chance to work on a farm. I to keep house and him to work on the farm. I got up at four o'clock and went to bed at ten o'clock. I was in the family way again. Then last spring we came up to my father's house I to keep house and husband to work in the mill. I had lots of work, I get up at three o'clock and go to bed at nine; there is father and six brothers and sisters, myself and two children now. I don't want any more children. If I get in the family way again I don't know what I will do. When I am not in the family way my periods are every two and a half to three weeks apart and then a whole week at a time, and the terrible pains I have all that time is enough to set one crazy. I never used to be that way only since my first baby, and when I am in the family way I am sick enough for bed instead of working like I have to. I weigh one hundred eight pounds now, before I was married I weighed one hundred thirty-five to one hundred thirty-eight pounds and felt good all the time, now I seem to have lost all interest in life, I sometimes feel that I would be glad to die sooner than to have more children.

Twenty-five

I was thirty-nine years old October 28th and have four children, my oldest is ten years old and I had a terrible time and the doctor didn't think I would have any more but in January 1921 I had a nice baby boy and in April 1923 I had a baby girl, and the doctor said I shouldn't have any more, but in February 1925 I gave birth to a baby girl and the doctor said I must not have any more but they won't help you out. Of the four children I had one natural birth, but I am so miserable all the time I carry a child I can hardly walk only with the use of a cane, and then at times I can't walk at all. My husband will have to carry me up and down the stairs so I can watch the children while he is at work as he can't afford to keep help only while I am in bed. It seems like as soon as I would wean one baby I would get that way right away again. I have nursed all my babies so far and as my girl will be a year old the sixteenth of this month it is time to wean her and I am so afraid I will get that way again. Now we love children and wouldn't take anything for those we have but my husband is past forty-two years old and works every day as a railroad switch man. We want to raise our babies right and give them a good education, but it is almost impossible on our wages. I do all my own work and we are trying to pay for our home and besides the care of my house and babies, I have a brother who is almost an invalid that I take care of, I am so tired at night and the nights are so short as I do a lot of work after the Mr. comes home to take care of the babies it seems like I never get rested. I am five feet two inches tall and weigh one hundred forty pounds, short and stout and seems like I get caught so easy. Now I don't want to burden you with my trouble but there are so many things I could tell you that is hard to write. I surely would be grateful if you will help me as we have more than we can take care of properly and don't want any more as we are both getting along in years. Sometimes I feel like I am about a hundred; everybody says I look so much older than my husband but I can't help it. I try to keep neat and clean, but I never get out to get away from the cares of the house, and it surely makes me look and feel old.

Twenty-six

I am young and have three small children and an old invalid woman to take care of besides all of my housework and help on the farm. I certainly have my hands and heart full and I am sure if I can't learn some means of prevention the children will continue to come. I do not want to do anything wrong. I want to do my duty to my God and my country, but when you are burdened down with more than you can get through with you cannot be a homemaker or a mother to what children you already have.

Twenty-seven

I am twenty-five years of age and a mother of three children and in less than five years. I had the three of them and it's very hard for me. I do be very sick and I have to take chloroform and roar like a lion with pains. So please help me, give me some good advice what to do to take care of myself as my dear mother is died and I didn't know any better so I married young and a poor man just like myself and so his mother was died also. So we went housekeeping for his father. Now there is five of them, who are all boys and a father-in-law and five of us: now there's eleven of us and only myself to take care of all those people and my three poor little ones are neglected and my baby one seventeen months old and a very very mean father-in-law. He says throw the kid down on the floor and you do this and that and hurry up. So I would not want any more children for I can't give the care they ought to have and I have tried to do all the washing, ironing, cooking, baking bread and yet beside sewing for my children and myself as we can't afford to buy things ready made. Just think the work for eleven people! It is very hard for me and when evening comes I'm in and out all tired. Why when I go to bed I can't turn round and can't stand it any more and I work all day and cry beside and when they get home from work I don't even hear a kind word from any one. Oh, I cried hard when I was writing this letter to you. My heart is broken. No one ever takes pity on me and I'm just tired of living and bringing those children into this world to suffer.

Twenty-eight

Please tell me some way of preventing childbirth. I have given birth to ten children and eight are living and I have done all I knew to prevent it. I have all my work to do and my stepmother to care for and her mind gone and she is a lot of trouble. I am failed down all the time until I feel like death would relieve me and an insane sister-in-law also and feel like I can't bear any more. I have all girls but one and I am not able to care for them as I wish to. The oldest seventeen, the youngest eleven months. Please tell me why some women have so many children and others just a few. I never wanted but two children.

Twenty-nine

I have had four children and not over sixteen months between each birth. My baby is four years old and ever since her birth my health has been a total wreck. I am so nervous and over-worked I can't be the mother I want to be and do justice to my family. My husband thinks I don't try to be pleasant, but how can I be when I am unfit for anything but a hospital. My health is like this, tired, nervous and were it not necessary, I would never move. I bore children and now I get pregnant every two or three months and in a few weeks miscarry. I realize it is killing me, soon I'll be gone and then who will see to my little children? I don't know how to prevent miscarriage. The doctors say go to bed, etc. but how can I as I have my babies to see after and no help and no money to hire your work done? One doctor said an operation might relieve me, but we have no money for that. Still another said guard against conception. I can't, for I do not know how. It is one thing certain, my husband won't give up his right as a husband, for I've pleaded for it as my very life seemed to hang on it, each intercourse is very painful, at times almost deathlike. What can I do? Is there any remedy? If there is, why not send it out to one who's very life depends on it? There is nothing I can expect of my husband or doctors. I long to feel well one more time, just so my children might know their mother as she would be if she was only well and had strength to be a mother. As things are I can't last long unless things are changed and their remembrance of me will be a worn, tired out nervous woman who never had time for anything, not even strength to do their washing and sewing as it should be done. I do all my housework, live in a cellar on a homestead. For wood and water I go outside; there are six steps to climb to get outside. I take care of milk and chickens, also have a garden, besides I have to do most of the work of running a small grocery store and postoffice which takes hours of time from my work every day. My work is always behind, nothing can be done on a schedule, just have to snatch a minute now and then washing, ironing, sewing and all never done when it should be. I know I am not pleasant. People talk about it. I know none never seem to realize why I can't always be pleasant. I try to force my feeling below the surface and grin, smile and go ahead, but Lord, I can't, my body goes to pieces, I break down and can't help it.

If only I had a little health I might be different and I might be spared to raise my darling little children.

Thirty

I am the mother of five children four living and one died at the age of a year and five months and I had one miscarriage and lay in the hospital seven weeks over it. I have had to work six years at night to help support my children as I have a husband who drinks and does not care if we live or not. Every month I'm in dread of being pregnant I have only a year and eight months between two of my children and I think I would rather die than ever have any more, not that I don't love them but it is so hard not to be able to give them the things they should have and have to go out to work so that they can have something to eat.

Thirty-one

My husband is a laborer, his wages is not enough for us to live on and pay rent which is very high. We have two little children and a miscarriage. My health is weak. I am doing washing for the rich people. While I work I must leave my little ones uncared for at home only to come home all tired out and hear my neighbors scolding me for leaving my children uncared for at home, but what can I do to prevent some more like these. I already have to suffer the hardship and bitterness of a wicked world and now I have turned to you for help. It is my only and last hope.

VIII

Voices of the Children

So far we have been listening to the voices of the
mothers—the accumulated reiterations of the same story
of enslaved and compulsory maternity. The elements
vary, the circumstances differ, but fundamentally these
confessions repeat the same chorus of despair, voice the
same cry for deliverance.

Let us listen now to the voices of the children—to those
daughters who have been born in the midst of these large
and growing families, who at the tenderest age have been
brought into immediate contact with the dire realities of
life as they are so starkly depicted in the earlier chapters.

Have these mothers told the truth? Out of self-pity
have they not been led into exaggeration? Perhaps life is
not as hopeless as it has seemed to them. These questions
may be brought up by the sceptical.

In the present group is presented the testimony of the
second generation, most often of women who have been
left upon the death of worn-out mothers with the responsibility of taking charge of the bereft brood. A certain number of the accompanying letters are from that
large class of women who have been "child mothers." The
child-mother is an easily recognizable type. Often the

eldest daughter in a large brood of children, she is called upon by the death of the mother to take over heavy household duties, to bring up younger sisters and brothers. Not infrequently a helpless infant a few days, a few weeks, or a few months old, is left for the child-mother to tend. Young enough to feel keenly the deprivation of the joys of childhood, this girl is to face precociously the harsh biological realities of life. She grows into early womanhood disillusioned of all ideas of romance or of any possible happiness in marriage.

Beforehand she knows what to expect of matrimony. Ahead of her she sees only the meaningless repetition of the slavery of her mother's life. This she seeks to avoid at any cost, no matter how expensive, or what temporary happiness she may be called upon to give up. Several eloquent letters of this type are included in the present group.

A quality of almost irresistible appeal is revealed by certain letters from young girls standing at the threshold of marriage, girls who hesitate before taking that fatal step which would inevitably plunge them into a needless repetition of their mothers' lives.

Another set is from mothers who realize that if they bring more children into the world, they will perforce swell the ranks of child-labor, infants predestined to the factory at an early age. Such mothers are conscious of the injustice done to the children of the second generation and the cost to their own bodies and souls.

Perhaps the most eloquent letter in the present group is the briefest: "I am going to be married soon and I don't want any children for awhile. My mother died at childbirth and I had to take care of them. She had fifteen children. I don't want any for awhile." There is another letter of great dignity from an unmarried woman of sixty-two, who has been forced to work for her living since the age of eleven. She had been one of many children born into a poor family.

Cheated as most of these mothers have been of the roseate romances of adolescence, one finds in their sobriety a dignity and a spartan recognition of the harsh realities of family life. In their case, concealment of biological laws had been futile. Between the lines we may read of the close companionship that exists between the enslaved mother and the growing daughter who helps to lighten the heavy burden placed on the mother—even to the extent of taking her place in the factory when the breakdown of the elder woman is imminent. We may imagine the warnings whispered by the mother to the eldest daughter—beseeching her at any cost to avoid entering that destructive maze of maternity which has enslaved them all.

These letters possess an authenticity, a crudity, a tang of the soil, that makes them, despite their illiteracy and stammering expression, far more impressive than the more elaborate feats of imaginative fiction.

One

I have six living children and God! the suffering and torture I have went through getting rid of unwelcome ones. I love children and wouldn't take a fortune for any I have but I have had more than my share, more than I can dress and feed these awful times. Had to take one of them from school at the tender age of fourteen and place him in a factory doing a man's work for half the pay a man got and now I see the results before me all the time. He is tall and thin, the color of death and is always ailing. He is now eighteen, been working steady since the vacation of his thirteenth birthday. Poor child! Half educated; and the second had to do the same and God, it will keep up and always more, more, more till I have just took death in my own hands and faced it and I will die before I have another to suffer.

Just two years ago I got rid of one and almost myself. . . . Had blood poison and had to doctor up until about four months ago. It almost killed me but it ain't the first time. It is the only sure thing I know and the doctor told me it was sure death if I continue doing it. Now I don't want to die and leave my babies. But God! I don't want any more as we cannot support them!

Two

I must try and get some help from some one before it is too late, for I am not well yet nor strong. I just gave birth to a baby. It was only a seven and one-half months! It lived one month and died. I was almost dead when it was born. The doctor had to give me chloroform and take the baby. I have a weak heart and the doctor had poor hopes of me pulling through. I would be more than pleased if I could keep from having any more babies. My health is bad and I have a family enough, all the children I want and can take care of.

I have to depend on my two little girls to help with

the work and it is too much on them. The oldest is only eight and the other six; and one four and a boy only twenty-two months old. I have only been married ten years and have had seven babies, and only four living.

Also while I am writing as it is no use being ashamed to tell it, my husband is not being very good to me, he is one of them mean men and likes to keep me tied down with a little baby all the time. I have been sitting home ever since we were married. I am twenty-seven years old and would like to see a little pleasure. He goes to ball games and has his good time alone and when I can get to go I have to take all the children and see to them.

Three

I have six living children and they go to work early in life. I brought on several abortions and almost died. I was in bed three months at a time, one a hemorrhage and the other matrutis or something like that; and the last blood poison it was the nearest call but still I wouldn't hesitate. Were I to become pregnant again I would use it and die before I would have another running around half clothed. Now if you possibly can, please, oh, please tell me something to do, as I dread to see my husband come home. Always that awful fear of another little one. Life as us poor women have to live it is only a misery. My little ones are only twenty months apart but I have died dozen of times in between to make them farther apart. But no one knows but us poor overburdened women the drudgery and misery of too many children.

Four

I am the mother of eight children, oldest fifteen, youngest fourteen months. Now I don't want any more children for we are too poor to provide for them and besides my husband has T.B. and has not worked at all in over six years and almost blind too. Still we have babies every two years or less. Nearly all of my children are underweight and some are weak-eyed. My baby girl only weighs seventeen pounds at fourteen months. My two young sons and myself have to make our own living.

I have to work just the same when carrying a child as when I am well. The tears I have shed would almost make an angel weep.

I had rather die than become pregnant again. I am thirty-seven years old and my health is giving way. If I had not been extra strong we would have starved long ago. His old father has had to furnish us a home ever since we married as he was always frail. We are farm folks. I think you are doing one of the noblest works on earth, for the pitifullest sight on this earth is more children than can be cared for.

Five

My mother died when I was sixteen years old leaving four younger children for me to raise. I worked like a slave for these brothers and sisters for five years until they were old enough to take care of themselves with my younger sister their boss. I thought when I should marry

I should have a chance to rest awhile and pick up a little strength and weight. I weighed ninety-eight pounds.

All my dreams are a misery now. I had a son nine months after I was married. When he was sixteen months old I had another; in thirteen months another, fourteen months later a daughter. I had hemorrhages a week before the last baby was born. I try my best to keep my lads clean. Sometimes I almost go insane taking care of them. Many a time have I prayed to God to kill me before I have another one. How changed the world would be if I knew I would not have to have any for awhile! I am slowly turning into human waste from worrying over that.

Six

Kind friend: I do want you to be a friend to me for I feel that I have not one that can do as much for me as you can. I want you to tell me how to keep from having more children. I have a girl two years old and a boy eight months old and would rather die than to have any more. My mother died when I was only two years old and I had to work as soon as I was big enough to stand on a chair and wash dishes and never had any one to tell me much. So I married at seventeen and am only twenty now, and I haven't very good health and I had a hard time with both of my children. I just worry from one month to the next. I try to keep away from my husband but that causes quarrels.

Won't you please write and tell me what to do or what to get to keep from having any more. I am sure the two we have now shall never get the education I would like for them to have for I never had any and I would like to put them through school. We live in the country on a rented farm and my husband works every day but there isn't anything made on the farm. I pray for you to help me and anything I can do to help further your good work I will do.

Seven

Would you kindly tell me how I could learn the safe way to prevent childbirth. I have one little boy but I wouldn't want to have any more till we can afford to keep them and then I do not want as many as my mother had, and also my mother-in-law. My mother had eleven at the age of thirty-six and that is the last for she died giving birth to the eleventh. That was ten years ago. I was thirteen years old and had to take care of seven and myself. There was a brother older than me but I was the oldest girl and had to "quit school" to take care of the home and children from one just born the others was only one and one-half years apart. . . . That is no life at all. It is always work and never play.

Eight

I am a young woman twenty years old, have one baby she will be three years old in May. I was the oldest of a family of seven. My mother died of child-birth when I was thirteen years old and my smallest brother is a crip-ple. I kept house for my father and six children. I know what it is to care for a big family. I was just a child myself, but I sent them all to school and done the washing and housework and also the sewing for all of them. My father was a poor man and couldn't afford anyone to help, so I could not go to school. My crippled brother was as helpless as a baby, when mother died. He was born crippled, his back was paralyzed. He is ten years old now and one side of him has never developed. I know my poor mother suffered having so many children and I would like to know of a way to prevent having one right after another like my mother. I'm afraid all the time and will be awful glad if you can help me.

Nine

I was married a year and a half ago and have a little baby girl that I think is in perfect health, but would not care to have any more for a few years as I feel I am all out of strength. Now I guess you will wonder why a young woman of twenty-one years should say such a thing, but it is true.

See my mother died at childbirth from paralysis and left eight children on my hands besides an infant of one week when I was sixteen years old. I worked so hard for them trying to raise them that I feel that I am sapped of all my strength. I guess you know what it means to raise nine children besides my father and myself. I did this for four years. I try to take care as much as I can and so does my husband but I am constantly worried and worrying alone kills me, as I know in my heart and soul that I have no strength to care for another.

I do not want to do what my mother did.

Ten

I was the oldest of nine children at home—eight girls one boy,—my dear mother never well and still broken in health. As soon as we were fourteen we went to the factory to help out at home. My whole desire was to graduate at high school and be a nurse, but I had no other way but work. My husband also came from a family of eight. He also could not follow the course in life he wished to take, having to quit school and go to work. I married at twenty-three and am the mother of one girl and two boys. Now my aim is to try and keep them from going to the factory. We would like to see them get some education and amount to more than an ordinary laborer.

But as it is, when one baby is six or seven months old, then I am pregnant again and unless I resort to some means we will have more than we can care for properly and I spoke to my doctor on the subject since reading your book. He told me I might as well have my share now as when I am older. His wife don't want any though.

Eleven

I have your book "Woman and the New Race." If everybody could see woman's sufferings as you do and a few others, this world would be a different place for a lot of women. I am one of them that would be in a different world. I don't want any more children for I have got all we can take care of. I have a boy nearly twelve years old and a girl nine years old and my little sister, ten years, lives with me, and it seems like I could not wait on any more children for I have to do all of my work and about half of the time I am not able to do my washing and such as that. But it don't make any difference. I have just got to drag on and do any way, somehow, for we are not able to have it done. The children are in school nine months out of a year and they can't help me but a mity little for they have to walk a mile to school. I guess you think it is strange I am writing to you for information and I have not had a child for nine years, but I have miscarried several times and will surely times more if it don't kill me if I don't find out some way to keep from getting that way.

For I don't intend for my children to suffer from a too large family like I had to when I was a child. I had to work hard and did not get all my schooling and had no good clothes and fun like other girls, but because it was too big a family.

My mother had fourteen children and raised seven of them. I said raised seven, it was seven when she and papa died leaving three of them very small, and us grown ones has had to take care of them and me being the oldest one in the family it has most all of the care for them been on me. My life has been a hard one ever since I can remember and if you don't give me some information I guess it will still be the same old thing.

I live at a big saw-mill and I see poor women suffer every day and the men going around as happy as June bugs and I think why did the Good Lord put it all on the poor old weak women?

Twelve

My mother was thirty-six years old when she died and left six children, a pair of twins not two months old. I was the oldest of the six. But my mother never knew a sick day in her life until she had me and she had it very hard then and with every child thereafter had internal hemorrhages which left her very weak. We could not afford anything to build her up and she was too far gone, she died with consumption two months after giving birth to a pair of twins. I was the oldest, so I had to keep house and help look after the children. A year after mother died, one of the twins died with the same disease, and four years after another brother. My father was a heavy drinker so we did not get the right care. He would come home and beat me up for nothing at all.

At twelve years old, I went to work to help look after my sisters and brother. I stood that for a year but I could see no headway so I broke up the home and took my two sisters and brother and put them in a home. And I went to work at bookbinding and at night I did a lady's housework so I would not have to pay board and the money I got paid for my sister's and brother's board. I never was out to play and I never saw a moving picture till I got married, and that was when I was seventeen years old. I knew nothing about married life.

My husband was a young fellow nineteen years old and made $12.00 a week, but I lived with his parents and was happy till I had my first baby. I carried it seven months and lost it. Had another seven-months boy and suffered awful. He is now nine years old and is a very sickly child and one of his lungs is very bad. Two years after I had another, that was five months when I lost that. I cannot tell you how bad I was. I got operated but it was no different. I had to go away and my husband enlisted in the Navy and stayed until after the war ended, thinking I would pick up.

When he came back I had three more miscarriages, and two years ago I gave birth to a little girl and four months ago to another little girl and I can't stand it any longer for I am all dragged out and between washing and sewing and the housework and looking after the children, I have no pleasures.

Thirteen

I'm a mother of two living children and two dead, only married six years this coming July. I'm a nervous wreck at times. I have a good husband but he is attacked with rheumatism often, that keeps him from his work most of the time. I wouldn't want another child for it brings my health down more with the more children I have and wouldn't want any more for there isn't hardly anything to raise them on. My mother had eleven children, five of the oldest died, six of us are living. She went insane with the last baby boy she had. Was taken to the hospital where she died four years later. Father was killed six months after mother died, leaving six of us children without money. I raised my youngest brother and he is with me ever since. He is a boy of seventeen years. I was forced to go to the silk mill after both of my people died. I worked eleven years to raise my brothers and sisters. I married when I was twenty-four years old and have the same thing over again, a baby year after year. I wouldn't like to follow the same steps my mother did to bring a big family out to this world for suffering.

Fourteen

I am a girl of a large family. My mother raised eleven children, six girls and five boys. All have large families and every one of us have to raise them on a bottle. What use are poor run-down mothers? I am raising mine on one. Yes, I just cry and think, and cry and think, what will become of the poor working race of people, with no one to help them?

When I was a girl I worked in the field and wasted my life and made myself sick trying to take care of my mother and tend the children for her, when I could not be in the field.

I know father will go to town and tell people what he has done, "raised eleven children," when he ought to be at home under the bed with his head hung down. He never done no such of a thing; mother did, and cared for him besides. Sometimes I can hardly keep from hitting him to save my neck. Now that I am married myself we have five and my husband is like myself, did not want more than we could take care of. Well it may seem strange to you, but not to me. I told a bunch Sunday I would be glad and willing to give my children away to someone who could care for them. They said I was a fool. I am thirty years old and a wreck. Think of it, when I ought to be in the prime of life. What are we to do? Can you do something to help us?

Fifteen

It fills my heart with grief to read of the thousands of poor suffering women. And how sad it makes me feel when I think of my dear angel mother. How she suffered! How I wish she had known of you, that she might have gotten some help. She gave birth to eight of us, seven of whom are living. The last two that came she didn't want them, but how could she prevent it? She tried many means to, but it only helped to ruin her health. She worked hard all the time, for we live on a farm. There is always so much to do and we just have two small rooms and it has been so hard. And we children all work hard too, but don't seem to get very far. She said she would rather die than give birth to any more. She was expecting another then, and she did die, the dear suffering mother. How hard it was for us to see her go, leave us seven to look after ourselves! It makes me grieve to write all this.

Well, as I was the oldest, just sixteen, I had to take her place. I had just started high school. I was more than willing to quit and do my best for my dear brothers and sisters. The baby was left, which was a year and a half old, to look after, and all the rest of the family, the house work, baking, cooking, washing and sewing was for me to do. It was hard indeed. I work just awful hard all the time until I am almost worn out now. I am going to get married soon, yet I dread it when I think of my dear mother's life. She said many times she just hated to think of any of us girls, which was five of us, getting married for she hated to see any of us have the life she had, to bring to the world so many unwanted babies.

I am twenty years old now. How I wish you could tell me how I should take care of myself, when I get married to prevent all these hardships before it is too late! And then I remember again how my mother and father used to quarrel and almost separate, just on account of that. But how could they then, there was so many of us to look after? I dearly love children, but I wouldn't want more than two. I feel like my dear angel mother did. I would rather die than have any more than that, for I know what it is to raise a large family. Am not so strong as I was anymore now. I know of so many poor women that died just because there were more children than there should have been. If they didn't need help I don't know who did. How I wish over and over again that my dear mother could have reached your help.

Sixteen

I am going to be married soon and I don't want any children for awhile. My mother died at childbirth and I had to take care of them. She had fifteen children. I don't want any for awhile.

Seventeen

I guess you would think I was married, but I'm not, and here are some of the reasons why I'm not. My mother is the mother of ten children. I am the oldest and have always had a very hard time, as mother has put the responsibilities of home life on me. I've been almost a mother to the children, as there were so many of us, until there had to be someone to help do the hard work. I've had to sit up nearly all night at times, get up in the morning, cook breakfast and dinner, get the children off to school and then wait on mamma, her not being able to work, and go to school myself. I have done this many, many times and even harder things; but now I've been teaching for several years. I have now become tired of teaching.

Here is my case. The boy to whom I'm engaged has as good a name as anybody I suppose. He served in France for thirteen months and I've known him all my life, and we have been going together since he came back from France. My parents like him and we have been engaged for about five months. He now has a position with the railroad company and is boarding, as it is too far away for him to stay at home. I teach school about half a mile from the section where he boards. I also have to board. I have to leave home about four o'clock, when I go home, and go about a mile before light in the morning. You see this is very bad. He can't see why I won't consent to marry, as we could easily live on the board we have to pay, but it seems like I just can't agree to it before my school is out, as I'm afraid I might become pregnant and have to resign my school. If you could only help me to solve my case, the praise would be all yours. What is your advice? Can you tell me any sure preventives?

It seems hard for him to beg me so much, and me to

refuse just on this account; but my grandmothers—one had ten children the other twelve, so you see I can never bear the idea of marrying, if I think I've got to do that; because I know that's too many for any woman to care for properly, and that is the greatest of all sins I think—having children you can't care for properly. I only teach eight hours and he works only eight hours, and I feel that if I knew Birth Control was sure for us, there would be no happier couple anywhere than we would be. I know you could tell me a remedy and give me advice. Why not? I must stop as I know I've written too long. The ruin of our country today is too many unwanted children.

Eighteen

I've sent for and read your most wonderful book "Woman and the New Race." I think it's the most wonderful book I've ever read and I'm sure if more would read it this would be a better world. I'm a young girl of twenty-one, of a family of fifteen, have had to keep my younger sisters and do the house work when I was but eleven years old, when my mother had to work in the factory doing her best for all of our sakes. At fourteen I went to work in the factory, so mother could stay at home, but it was too late. She had overworked herself, and shortly afterward she was taken sick, and when my younger sister was only thirteen, she had to give up school and stay home with mother as she wasn't able to do a thing, and hasn't been able to since. We had no chance for an education, it was always working to get along the best we could.

My mother is a wreck from having such a large family. We've had no chance for an education on account of it, it's always been one discouragement after another, so have always been afraid of married life. Have kept company with a young man for about three years, I think the world of him, but whenever he'd speak of getting married, my experience at home of seeing my poor old mother as far as I can remember, always having such a hard time, and always working like a slave, I could never make up my mind to that kind of a life. And my father, like all fathers of a large family turn out to be with all their worries and troubles, was awfully cranky, and thought it was terrible to keep company with a young man so long and finally didn't trust me, so it was one argument after another. Oh! its' always been so hard, all around ever since I can remember, when we were at the age that we should have gone to school, play and enjoy ourselves we always had to work.

But the reading of your most precious book a few months ago has given me new hopes, new views of the future, of a happy husband and wife in a real home, with the few children that they can give the proper care and education, bring them up in a love home and be their companions as every father and mother should be.

Oh! you'll never know what a happy girl you've made me, because I feel so sure of your kindness, I just know that you'll help make my life as a wife one of happiness.

I'm to be married in a few weeks, and am writing to you now because I love children and think no home is complete without them, that many which you can take care of in the proper way, but before they come I want to work and help my husband, to get a place we can call home for them when they come. . . .

I will close now very happy in the thought that someone is to help make my married life one of happiness, instead of a burden of unwanted children, and working like a slave as my poor dear mother did. So please oh please don't disappoint me.

Nineteen

I have for many years admired your brave courage in advocating Birth Control. I am an unmarried woman of sixty-two years old. I too was a child of poverty owing to a large family, which merely existed. I never knew what the word happiness was in my life. Since I was a child of eleven years old, I had to work for a living, as my father never earned enough to support us. He was a very good noble man, but luck was always against him. My parents both lived to be very old, my father reaching the age of ninety-two years old, and were dependent upon me for support, as the older children got married, and left me with the cares of parents and home.

I am still compelled to go to work every day for a living, as I have no one to care for me, or support me, as I always had to paddle my own canoe. I suppose my fate will be, when I cannot work anymore, to wind up in some old home. My aim had been to become a schoolteacher when I was young, but though I worked night and day to earn a few extra dollars, there was always rent to pay, and doctor bills, and living expenses. I never knew what it was to have a vacation the last forty years, for it was always a hand-to-mouth living, and no chance of getting ahead. Were I not a first-class hand at my work, I doubt whether I would have work, for no one wishes to employ greyheaded people.

Therefore I feel so very bad when I see young boys and girls, especially the girls, hardly out of the cradle, being forced to work, because the family is so large. Oh! I do not like to have any child go through life, as I was forced to go through it. Therefore go on with your noble work, for the world needs quality, not quantity, and a poor overtired overworked mother cannot bear a healthy child.

Twenty

I'm writing you as last resort—in a search for happiness. I've loved and been engaged to a man for five years but have been unable to marry him because of the fear of having babies before I'm able. I am the wage earner for my family (a widowed mother and young sisters and brothers). After my marriage, it will still be my duty and obligation to support them. My fiancé is now coming to my town to again plead his cause. I need him and a home—but to have babies means suffering for my family. I am laying my cause before you—is it possible for you to send me any information on safe preventives?

Twenty-one

I am a girl one year out of high school and rather alone in the world. My mother was taken when I was five years old, and my stepmother last winter, the latter leaving me with five small children to care for and no near relative in a position to take them. She left a baby three weeks old, two boys three, and four years, and two girls six and seven years. Besides these I have three full brothers and three step-brothers, but they are all out in the world for themselves. I am left in a hard position being the only girl of any size. As you say, it is a sheer pity to the country and a bad thing to have stairsteps made of children when a woman works herself to death caring for them, and to know there are more coming.

I was utterly disgusted and left home, but forced to return for there was no one to look after the little ones after her death. I have ambitions too numerous to mention and a high school education for a basis to work on but I am home now only to live on the scenes of my wrecked hopes. I have always been tied down at home, week-ends during school months and summers.

One month and twelve days after I had returned home, I awakened one morning only to find the baby boy that she had left in my care dead in the bed beside me. I nearly went crazy, for I had already responsibilities too great for a mother, let alone a girl of nineteen. She had a weak constitution and a weak heart undoubtedly leaving the baby likewise. To further prove to you I have ambitions mainly in music and art, I am carrying on a course in mechanical drawing and next fall I hope to put my training to practical use providing I can locate someplace where I can hire a housekeeper to look after the children during the day. After I have this branch of work established, my next hopes are to master a musical instrument for I am wild about them. I'd walk twenty miles to hear one played. I have mastered the piano, but my musical ambitions and longings seem yet so undeveloped. I have for two years been engaged to a young man four years my senior, and had planned to be married this last spring, but the death of my stepmother put a quietus on things for I refused to ever give up the two youngest ones. My friend was willing to proceed with the wedding ceremony and take any I refused to give up, but I hated to start our married life with a family, and then probably have some of my own flesh and blood. Then the death of the baby took the starch all out of me and I don't ever want any more babies in my care until I fully recover from the effects which I assure you will take time. Now my friend says we must marry next Christmas for he is getting tired waiting. I am twenty this coming Saturday, and he is twenty-four, but he knows not how I have suffered, and he wants children of his own. I'd give anything to have a home for two years or three, minus children, for I have had to care for a baby incessantly ever since I was twelve years old.

Twenty-two

My wife is one of twelve children and spent her young days like most of the working class. As soon as she could earn a dollar she had to go out and earn it. The father did not work. The mother had her hands full holding a janitress position and between some working and the others not working they lived from hand to mouth.

IX

The Two Generations

HERE is a correspondingly pathetic type of letter. These letters are written by elderly women broken in health and spirit. They have finally been released from the long, indeterminate sentence of child bearing. Their tired eyes cannot avoid the spectacle all around them of the renewal of that meaningless cycle of procreation— they appeal to save daughters and their grandchildren. They who have been "through the mill" shudder as they think that generation after generation must repeat their own suffering.

"I have been a wife. I am a mother and a grandmother now," begins the starkly simple account of her own life and those of her daughters. "I have several granddaughters I want to help out," writes a woman past seventy, "that they may not have to suffer the anxiety and hardships I have gone through. It was easier in many ways to raise a family in my time than it is now. . . ."

There are also the daughters, as we have seen, young in years but experienced in the spectacle of the suffering and useless sacrifice of their own mothers. Often they write not only to save themselves but to spare the still prolific mother from the burden of future pregnancies.

Then there are the fathers and even the sons, schooled

in the misery and poverty created by excessively large families, turning to Birth Control as a solution of future troubles.

A father of five, the son himself of a large family, and the progenitor of another, sees his own sons starting, at an early age, in the path of uncontrolled procreation—this father hopes to make them see the error of leaving children to chance and suffering the penalty of poverty. Another father appeals to save the happiness of his own daughter, the offspring of an epileptic mother.

"Poor mother!" exclaims a daughter who is herself a mother, reviving memories of her unhappy childhood. "No wonder that she is a mental and physical wreck today when only in her early forties. . . . I understand now why she had so many faults to find and scoldings to give us children, but as a sensitive oldest child I was very unhappy because of mother's shattered nerves and broken spirit and body." Her mother had "commenced having children right away and kept on having them until father's death."

The importance of these records lies in the earnest realization of the problem by those who write, and the hopelessness of their efforts to find a satisfactory and dependable remedy for those who are dearest to them. Their situation is comparable to that of the bystander who witnesses a disaster and yet finds himself powerless to avert catastrophe.

One

I have been a wife. I am a mother and a grandmother now. My first child was a daughter who was crippled and

203

diseased from infancy by a diseased father. She lived to womanhood and then died in an effort to give birth to a child. This after her husband had been repeatedly told by our physician that she could not give birth to a child and live. By a later marriage I had two daughters, one of whom is now married to a man of no means and little ability and who I fear has tuberculosis. They have been married six years during which time they have had four children, two of whom are already dead. During this time also the husband has disposed of a nice little estate left his wife by her father and they are at this time dependent on his small wage, and she lives in constant fear of having more children. For her sake and mine and for the sake of the unborn little ones can you not tell me what method to use and tell us so that we can understand.

Two

I am a mother of a daughter who never intended to marry for she knew she could not stand too many children as she has always been a very nervous child. But in spite of all she could do, it seemed she has become so attached to her friend who she has kept company with for five years, never going with anyone else in her life, that they are so devoted to each other that it seems impossible for them to give one other up. For he thinks he would like to be married as he has no home, but has means to have a very comfortable home. But she is going to be very unhappy if she marries and she has children fast. She is such a nervous girl and the constant worry day after day will cause derangement of her mind.

Three

I am begging you to help me. My two daughters who are just from the hospital from operations caused from childbirth, and the doctor says that if they have another child they just as well say good-bye to themselves. Could you tell me where and how to get a preventive against having more children? Just to see how my daughters suffered wants me to help the dear mothers of our land.

Four

I have had two children, raised one. The one living is married and very sickly, always puny, will soon be married three years, has had one miscarriage, one seven month baby and is almost seven months with the next and as puny as ever. Is doing everything she can to keep this baby but I don't see how she can.

If she lives over this I would like to know something for her to keep out of the family way. You know doubt think it funny for me to ask you this as I have been married twenty-two years and had two children but I have a very good man. My son-in-law surely don't care what my daughter has to go through with, and it seems the larger she gets in the family way the less he thinks of her. It's very hard on me as she was the best child I ever saw.

Five

It is not for myself I am writing but for my daughter who is only twenty-three but looks thirty years old and has three children, all born within less than four years. With her second one when the baby was ten days old she was stricken with uremic poisoning and lay for six weeks in the hospital hovering between life and death. As we had to put the baby on the bottle it was just a short time till she was pregnant again. At two months she had to be operated on for appendicitis so she still carried on till her third baby was born. At three days old she went into convulsion with uremic poisoning again and had to be taken to the hospital to battle for her life again. As it is near the danger stage again I am writing you with all the pleadings and prayer of a mother's heart. If anyone needs the knowledge of Birth Control it is my daughter. Will you please send me for her a word to prevent this. Her husband is more of a beast than man, he doesn't have any consideration for her whatever. It is only his own satisfaction he is looking for. He doesn't have any care for the children after they are here. It is up to her to do the best for them she can. She wants to do something if she can only learn what as she says she had rather be dead than go through what she does again. He is against her doing anything but she means to anyway. He is very cruel to her and abusive; so I am telling you this that you can know how very bad she needs help—it is the cost of her life to not know. I have asked the doctor but he has refused to tell me knowing her condition, but he still says to not get that way again.

Six

I am forty-four years of age and the mother of fourteen living children. My baby is five months old. I am anxious to know what you can tell me. Please send me the information at once for I am still thinking that my age won't interfere with me continuing to become a mother yet awhile, then I have one daughter, the mother of five at twenty-five, another the mother of twins at twenty.

Seven

I have had a very large family, mostly girls and I know all the pangs of sorrow that a poor mother suffers. At these times it's a shame to bring a large family into the world. If us mothers who have gone through the mill would only educate our daughters all we can in a way which would not be hurtful to them many a poor home would be made a happy one. Now I have eight girls, three of them married, the others young ladies, the youngest sixteen and I am only forty-four. Think of that now, one of my girls has three little children and she is not very strong and her husband is very mean to her when she is in the family way and they are poor folks and he has to work by days work for a living and I am writing to ask you if you will kindly help me to see she gets a preventive which will not injure her health and which she can depend on. Also the other married girls do not wish to have a large family and they will be very glad to learn something of your good work. You sure are a Godsend to humanity. Birth Control is the uplifting of a nation while large families is only pulling it down. I have had the experience and know. My daughters are all fine young women but I have had to pay hard for it, but I do not wish to see a one of them go through what I their mother has had to go through.

Eight

I have a dear sweet girl who is soon to be married and while I am glad that she is to have a mate and sometime children, I have had many a cry when I have thought of what may be ahead of her. I was married at nineteen and in ten months I had a little girl. I had five children and I loved them all, but we did have a hard time to raise them, for my husband is only a working man and I know if we had only had one or two children we could have done better for them. As it was we were never able to do anything for them in the way of educating them. I am fifty-five and past having any more family, but I have prayed that my children might escape some of the hardships that I have had. I know that one thing that does make hardships is bringing more babies in the family than a man's wages can support, but what is a woman to do? If she refuses her husband there is usually a fuss or he will go elsewhere. Not knowing how to prevent we have gone on bringing child after child into the world that we neither had means or strength to properly care for. I am asking you can you show me how I may help my child to escape some of the worries (the biggest worry) of what may be a happy married life. My daughter loves children but she says she hopes she will not have to have a big family.

Friend I am an uneducated woman and it is very hard for me to express my thoughts in writing to you, but please answer this and show me the way to help some other dear to me. I hope I may hear from you soon and thank you for putting such a book as "Woman and the New

Race" in the way of thinking people and that I have had
the privilege of reading it.

Nine

I am married twenty-one years. I have four living children, two eight-months' and two seven-weeks' abortions.
I will soon be forty-four years of age. The doctors have
been telling me for ten years that I am in the change of
life, but I have had three conceptions during that time.
My last living child, a boy of seven years, is so delicate
I can't keep him in school, he just complains of being
tired all the time.

The abortions were not criminal. I do not believe in
murder. I am not so concerned about myself as I know
there are only a few more years at the longest, and my
husband is willing to let me alone, as he knows that another conception would mean death. But I have two girls,
one nineteen, the other fifteen. The older one is betrothed
now and she has never been strong, was in a hospital at
one time for ten months, with abscess on the right lung,
and had to be operated on which left an open sore on her
side for eighteen months. The younger girl has sugar
diabetis, so you see they are neither one really physically
fit to become mothers as often as I have so if there is a
sure contraceptive will you please tell me so I can help
them. I have a son eighteen years old who will marry
some time and I don't want his wife to go through what
I have.

Ten

I am, as to years, rather old, just having past my seventieth birthday the 25th of June. I am the mother of eight children, four of whom have preceded me to the Great Beyond, perhaps because I could not give them proper strength and care raised under the old time way. I just went along and took what come, but long ago I came to the conclusion that there was a better way, or should be. Of course I knew what rich people could do, but that didn't help out.

I have several granddaughters I want to help out that they may not have to suffer the anxiety and hardships I have gone through. It was easier in many ways to raise a family in my time than it is now for I think people were stouter.

Eleven

I saw in paper how a college professor was running you down. You will be remembered long after he is dead, as a benefactor to the world and what you advocate will come to pass before long. Wish I could help you, for I know to my cost what a wrong it is to have a very large family.

I am fifty years old. We have had nine children, eight boys living. Have only two going to school now but as I was only working for wages, I never had enough to do as much as I would have liked to for them, and of course though expert at my business, could not save a cent to go in business. Have worked hard for forty years and have not a cent—some life insurance and that's all. I married very young, as I was alone. My parents died while I was a baby. Now my boys are following me, marrying young, one of twenty has a wife and now a daughter last week. His wife is not sixteen. Her mother is thirty-six and has ten. The boy has a good start in an office, gets $75.00 monthly, but he will be severely handicapped if there is another birth every year, spoil his life as it has mine.

Don't get the idea I dislike children. I don't. I care too much for them to bring them into this hard old world. Its a crime against the parents, the children and the world, to have large families. My youngest boy has just recovered from six week illness—scarlet fever—nearly lost him, it will take me rest of year to pay off nurses and doctor's bills, though that is first real serious illness any of my children have had.

If we had, say, two, we could have done more for them and I might have had a business of my own instead of having to work for someone else at fifty, in fact, fifty-one, in June. Even now we can't save anything.

Well, I must stop and come to the point. Won't you be so good as to send me by mail or express, information on Birth Control, so my wife can tell the boys' wives what to do so their lives won't be spoilt.

Another one got married in March, another goes off in June.

It makes me boiling hot to read the stuff—we must increase the birth rate to have soldiers (to be killed)! Like raising cattle to be slaughtered. Too many people in Germany is partly cause of this horrible war.

The women of the world ought to band together and say "We won't have any more children till all armies are abolished."

I hope this reaches you and that you realize I am only anxious to save my boys from the hard time I have had, and of course if you are good enough to answer you need not fear that it will do you harm.

Twelve

I am sending to you for a favor for my daughter. I want to know what to do to prevent childbirth. I will tell you why I want to know. I married a girl twenty years of age and after I had been married a short time I discovered that she had epileptic fits and she got in a family way. I wanted the doctor to give her something to prevent childbirth and he would not. When she was four months along I had to send her to the city asylum.

There my daughter was born and in three years my wife died. I am afraid if my daughter gets in a family way she may go in the same way and maybe leave another to follow in the same way. I am now a man forty-nine years old. She is my only child and I have done everything in my power to save her and if I can do anything to prevent childbirth I may save her, but I think that is all will save her, for she takes after her mother in looks and action.

Thirteen

I live among the poor mothers you so truly picture. I am one of them. To begin with, ever since I can remember all round me has been the constant dread and fear of being caught, and there has been grounds for such fears. We were very poor and mother's health very bad. She was married such a long time—she married at fourteen to a widower who already had two babies—a twelve months old and a two year old.

She commenced having children of her own right away and kept on having them until father's death. And this despite the fact that in her desperation, she resorted at times to such drastic means of getting rid of it as she managed to procure.

Poor mother! No wonder that she is a mental and physical wreck today when only in her early forties. For the past twenty years she has suffered the torture of a falling womb and even in this pitiful condition she has carried children, though only four of us are living of all. I understand now why she had so many faults to find and scoldings to give us children, but as a sensitive oldest child I was very unhappy because of mother's shattered nerves and broken spirit and body.

I remember seriously contemplating suicide in my unhappy childhood. And, oh, I don't want my children to ever feel that way on my account! I want to have the health and strength to bring about the time and the means to give them all the mother there is within me. Please, please help me before it is too late.

Fourteen

I am married just a few months to just a poor hard working-man and I am working to help him along to get a little home together and I don't know who to go to for advice as to avoid children at the present time. I feel very much that we can't afford a child just now, and I would also love to get information for my mother. She is a mother of sixteen children living in a small country place and when I look back on what my mother has gone through I want to make sure we will have a little more than what we do have before we have any children. With all these children my poor mother has had nothing in life and before that I would sooner not have any. I am the oldest of our family. I am twenty-six years of age and the youngest is two years old and I feel it has been a crime to put all these children into the world for we have known but poverty.

Fifteen

I was married when I was only eighteen and knew very little about married life. I was only married eleven months when I had a little girl baby. She is just eighteen months old and I am expecting to be confined again in two months. Don't know what I will do if I have to keep this up for I am not very stout and had a terrible time before. Would be so thankful if you would tell me some harmless way to keep from having any more for a while at least, as I have no home to take them to.

I would be so glad for my mother also as she has been in very poor health for six years. She can't walk a step though she has had two babies since she has been sick, the youngest a girl one year old. They are neither one healthy children. Surely some one could tell her some way to keep

THE TWO GENERATIONS

from having any more as she has got nine in all and now
broke down and can't care for any of them. She has been
to the hospital though the doctor wouldn't operate on her
on account of her lungs. They said she had symptoms of
T.B.

Sixteen

I am twenty-three years of age and the oldest of nine
children (besides seven miscarrages). I have often heard
Mother say that married life was nothing but a living
death. She always works in a cotton-mill as long as possible before her babies come, and as soon as they are two
or three months old they are left with the other children,
and she goes to work again. She is not able to hire cook,
nurse, or even a washwoman, she does her washing on
Saturday afternoons, and house work at night. The children are always put to work as soon as they are old
enough. I went to work at the age of twelve years so you
see I had hardly started my education.

My sister just younger than I married at fifteen and
died seven months later with a three months' miscarriage.

Seventeen

I am writing in behalf of my mother who has had
fourteen children (miscarriages included) and fears becoming pregnant at any time again. She was married at
seventeen and is now forty-four. I cannot explain to
you the condition of her health which is very frail and
weak. Our family physician says she could hardly ex-

pect to pull through another case. If mother passes away I will need to be at home to keep house. Then we will lose our home as at present I am teaching, thereby supporting the family. Our doctor did not seem to be able to name a relief for her. Eight of us have lived. One died from epilepsy at the age of eighteen. We are now six children.

Eighteen

I am twenty years old and the mother of three living children, and one miscarriage. I come from a large family which consists of eleven living children, two dead and one miscarriage. A total of fourteen. My mother is fifty-two years old and still living with a brood of five small children to raise, the youngest six years old. Father is also living.

He is not good to mother nor the children. He claims they are not his, that one man cannot be the father of so many children. He often beats mother, and she goes away and neglects her children, leaving them to care for themselves. I am writing you this to let you know what sort of living I had, in hell all my life with my brothers and sisters. I am young and know that I will have more children if I do not find a way to prevent them. I do not want to have as much as mother had, poor mother. How she had suffered bringing us mortals in this world to suffer as she had suffered. I know she did not want us all but could not prevent us coming and cannot give us no advice. I think you will know what I mean when you read this.

Nineteen

I have a little girl a year old and would not want any more children as we could hardly afford to care for them. It surely would be a crime to bring them in the world and not give them the care they should have. My mother had eight children and died when I was just six years old. My father died four years after.

My mother died of too many abortions, as I later found out from my relatives. Now I never did that because I think the same thing might happen to me. I wouldn't want anything to happen in that way and leave my little one motherless to be put in someone else's care and neglected like we were, pushed from one home to another. My brother lived up in —— since he was three or four years old (since my parents died) with strange people, and was neglected so and worked so hard in the shipyard that it soon pulled him down to nothing but sickness and he died a year ago and was just sixteen years old. I hope you will pardon my writing as I never had much schooling. What could I expect, hardly ever going to school and always working? That is why I am interested in birth control so I could give my baby the education she should have that I didn't have.

Twenty

My mother was telling me last week about herself, that she had twenty-five children. This is something to say. Five of us are left, all the rest are dead. She had lots of miscarriages and today she is very sick and she wants to know from you for help. She has a fallen womb.

Is there anything to be done? A good many friends of mine have from nine to fourteen children, which I just hate to see. Could you tell me which way I can help them? It's a pity, half-unclothed, not much to eat. Their fathers don't earn much. I myself have got six and another coming. I'm so disgusted and I tried everything I could know, nothing done good. I would like the truth to help myself and lots of women. Please help which way for myself mother and friends. Excuse my writing, read carefully so you'll understand what I mean because I'm not excellent a good writer. I went to school until the third grade and I got married at twelve years of age and now I'm twenty-three years old with six children.

X

Solitary Confinement

ANOTHER aspect of maternity, usually neglected by those who expound the theory of unrestricted fertility, is here illustrated. To most of these mothers pregnancy comes as a sentence to nine months' imprisonment, and often longer. Rapid repetition makes this an indeterminate sentence. In a great number of cases it is a sentence to solitary confinement.

This confinement is aggravated because it is prolonged by the arrival of the helpless and ailing baby. In the majority of cases, any prospect of a bit of intermittent freedom vanishes with the discovery that conception has again occurred.

With additional burdens of caring for the infants who have already arrived, heavy household duties, this strain of pregnancy upon the undernourished constitution of the prospective mother makes itself felt at an early stage. Adolescent mothers, who have been deprived of all the youthful pleasures to which they consider themselves legitimately entitled, cannot suppress a smouldering rebellion against the bondage into which they have been thrust by the harsh realities of life.

But as pregnancy succeeds pregnancy, and as these slave mothers approach their thirties, this spirit becomes feebler and feebler. They are forced to recognize the futility of their efforts to escape from the indeterminate sentence of compulsory pregnancies to which they have been condemned. Despair and obsession take the place of rebellion. The utter loneliness of their solitary confinement becomes more and more bitter. To them the only possible escape seems death. In several of the letters included in the present group suicide or death in childbed seems preferable to any future repetition of their suffering.

There is a group of older mothers—discouraged and utterly hopeless. Their loneliness is complete. During their long periods of illness and confinements some have been deserted by their husbands. No illusion is left concerning the unwelcome advent of the unfortunate child on its way. One of the bitterest ironies of human psychology is that the blame for its conception is placed by the lord and master upon the wife! Deprived, as a number of the present records indicate, of the sympathy of the father, who has tired of the unending series of pregnancies, the mother's confinement becomes, literally as well as figuratively, a solitary one.

One desperate mother, only thirty-one years of age, complains not so much of the straitened economic condition of her family as of "the terrible agony through which I have to go, not alone at the time of delivery, but for the continual period—agony and suffering of which I dare not tell anyone, not even my doctor, who says there is nothing he can tell me to keep from having babies. . . ."

"My people have turned against me because of my condition," writes another, confessing further that "sometimes it seems that the grave is awful inviting, a cool place to rest. . . . I have no one in the world to turn to for sympathy or advice. My husband has no understanding or does not care . . . and tells me that my condition is all my own fault."

Another writes: "My days and nights are one string of terror. Have dreams or nightmares that I am going or about to go through the grind again and wake up in a cold sweat."

Modern science has been making interesting revelations concerning the bodily changes due to long protracted fears. Experiments prove that there are definite chemical changes in the composition of the blood, brought about by the action of fear or continued obsessions. Quite apart from the human tragedy involved in these cases of mothers condemned to "solitary confinement," and protesting with every atom of their body and soul against the injustice of their fate, it requires no prolonged scientific analysis to realize that babies born under the conditions herein described are burdened with a terrific and heavy handicap in their feeble struggle for a foothold in life. Small wonder that so many of them die at an early age.

Out of such environments, biological and social, do we desire to recruit the American citizens of the future?

One

How can one control the size of a family? I am the mother of four children, thirty years old. Our first child died of pneumonia in infancy. Since I've had three others, —six, three years and nine months old they now are, and it's a continual worry for fear I shall be having more soon as we would be unable to care for them. My husband is a barber, earning, besides tips, $26.00 a week. Out of this we are trying to pay for a home, as it's cheaper than renting with three children. The baby requires certified milk because I am so overworked I am unable to nurse her. If it were not for my mother we could never get along. I do all my own work, make over all my own clothing and my relatives' for the children, even all our coats and hats, as I learned to do this before I was married. You can easily see there is no recreation or rest. I do nearly all of my sewing nights after the baby's 9 o'clock feeding, and really I am so tired and run-down it seems I could never have another child. I had one miscarriage at three months as I did not have the vitality to carry it.

Please don't think I dislike children; I love mine dearly, but trying to care for them and bring them up properly wears one's patience all away as I have to make every minute count to keep things going. I can't afford any improvements to help me in my work. I must wash every day in order to get the washing done and keep the children clean as I have neither the time or strength to do it all at once. With a baby one cannot anyway. I can't bear to be a cranky, cross mother to my children. I haven't been to a place of amusement, even a picture show, in over seven years. The last time I was away from home for a few hours visit was Christmas 1924. The only way I can get downtown to shop for an hour is when my husband takes the time off to stay with the children. Don't you think I am doing all I can without having more children.

What help is there for a woman? Must she separate from her husband and break up the home?

Two

I have been married six years, at the age of seventeen. Am twenty-three now. It seems I can't keep out of the family way. Have had six children, four living and two dead. One I lost in a tornado, the other about a week ago, which was eight months, born dead. My husband only makes $25.00 per week, and pays $32.00 per month rent and all other household expenses, we never have anything left. The children are such an expense and after they go to school it will be much harder. Charities have helped out at times when my husband was sick one whole winter and every year there is another arrival. I don't have any enjoyment out of life, staying at home all the while. I will not have anything out of life but worry, children and cares.

Three

I have had five children, my oldest died when ten months old. I expect my sixth next month and this in eleven and one half years in which I haven't enjoyed no life at all. When my children are small I can't go nowhere, and as soon as I think I have a little rest from a baby I'm getting another. I am thirty years old and I feel older than my mother which only had two of us. My father would not bring more into the world than he could bring up decent; but my husband is different. He does not want any children, and still he is not careful, but brings them into the world.

When he knows it's coming he treats me in the worst way because I don't get rid of it. I have always tried drugs the first couple of weeks but they don't do me any good. I get them just the same. I am just wishing I would die giving birth to this child if I can't stop having any more, but I feel sorry for those children that I have. If they were treated the right way by their father for every little thing he scolds them and hits them instead of teaching them.

I can't see why in the world God gives children to such a man.

Four

I was married when I was seventeen and am now twenty-eight. I have four living children and had two miscarriages. My last child is nine months old. I had no doctor for two hours after she was born and only the assistance of a neighbor; I laid on the bathroom floor until they could get a doctor and nearly got blood poison and am still suffering from milk leg as the result of my last baby's birth. I had to get up and start right to work as my husband doesn't make enough money to hire help and keep a family of six.

It is so hard in the winter time with so much coal to buy and winter clothing. I get heart-sick.

There is no joy in living. I am only twenty-eight and am penned up till I can't have half an hour to myself. Please, please help poor people like us.

If we have any more I don't know what we will do. We don't even own our own home and it seems like we never have a cent left. I don't know what a new dress or box of powder is like any more.

Is there much use, dear Margaret Sanger, in living for people like me? I have the fear of pregnancy on my mind all the time. If I try to stay away from my husband, he is terrible mean to me and says awful things to me. He doesn't seem to think what I have suffered, having my babies and what a terrible worry it is when they are sick and how hard it is to make over old clothing and I don't know what else. I could go on with my troubles and fill a book, but for God's sake please help me with your knowledge so I need not have any more as I have heart trouble and I would like to be here and raise these four than to have more and maybe die.

Five

I have four children now and would of had two more only for circumstances preventing it. My oldest child is a boy. He is nine years old and four months before he was born I fell and crippled one of my legs. Of course a good doctor could of cured it but I did not have the money to pay for the treatments. When my little boy was two years I had a little girl in November. Then in the following February a year later, I had a little boy and I was very sick at the time with the flu. When the little boy was born he cried for eight months night and day, then in a year I would of had another one only for a mishap, then another one again a year from that. Now my baby is seventeen months old and I have a very bad leg. Sometimes when I am walking it turns and throws me down. The doctor tells me not to have any more children but what can I do when they won't tell me nothing to prevent.

My man makes $60 and $70 if he works every day, but almost every pay there is a few days out for sickness and my man says if we only knew something so we would not have no more children. That makes six to keep. We can feed them alright but we can't clothe them because when we pay rent, store, gas, doctor bills, there is nothing left for us. I am only thirty-three but I feel like I am sixty-three. I get so tired because we can't afford nothing life craves for.

We don't have any water where we live unless it rains. We have to carry water from the river to do our washing.

Six

I am a mother of six children all under eight years old. There was one born every year for four years and now I am almost a nervous wreck being confined so close. I am almost a prisoner. I have very little recreation. I go to a picture show about once a month not to church at all, because I have nothing fit to wear.

Now I am not complaining about the children being born. I love them and want them, but I don't want them to come into the world without a fair chance to live because they are not healthy. My youngest baby is two and a half months, and one sixteen months old and not walking. Am taking him to a hospital each week. We are poor and are not able to give them the things they should have. Will you advise me please.

Isn't there something that can be done for me that I may not bring any more handicapped babies into the world?

Seven

I am an overburdened mother of six living children, the oldest ten years of age the youngest one year old. I married at twenty-one years of age. I am thirty-two now. Was strong and healthy when I got married but now I am an overworked and nervous wreck, not able to care decent for my family, and they all suffer because of my state of health. I think it is not fair to the children in having more and more and not be able to give them their care.

We live on a rented farm in a small unmodern four-room house, where one cannot get or keep help if one could manage to pay for it, so I am compelled to do all my housework, sewing, gardening and all the worries that go with raising a family.

I am so tired of being always so tied down, never getting any place at all, because I am always alone to take care of the babies, never get any rest or recreation even when I am sick. Sometimes I think I can't stand it any longer. So I take courage and come to you for advice and ask you if you will help me get a contraceptive, as I am as ignorant as a child in those things, and would like to get a few years' rest, which I am not able to get without your help. As soon as I quit nursing a baby I find myself in the family way again. Keeping away from my husband as much as possible don't seem to do much good either.

Eight

I am a young woman twenty-five years old and I have four children. Three living and one dead. I wish to God that you would give me some information how to prevent from having any more children. My husband is sickly and half-times we haven't anything to eat, and I have two of the children that must go through an operation. One has a running neck since he was one year old,—gland trouble, and he is going on five years now. It looks like it will never heal and I can't get the money to have him operated on. He is a pretty child, and the baby is five months. He is ruptured. I am almost crazy. My sleep is all broke up at nights as the baby suffers with the rupture.

I am a slave. I don't know what it is to get out. If it hadn't been for people giving me cast-off clothes I don't know what I would do. If you would only help me and tell me how to prevent from having any more I would be more than thankful. I don't think I could stand it to have any more. I am all run down.

Nine

I am a woman thirty-one years of age and the mother of four children, three girls and one boy. The oldest child is nine years and youngest five months. I am small in stature, weighing only ninety-two pounds while my husband is large, weighing 192 pounds at present time. We feel we simply cannot afford to have any more children. Am sure if we raise and educate our four children we are doing our share. It costs a great deal to feed and clothe and educate children. I think it a great sin to bring them into the world to just grow up any old way, as so many children do. I feel that I cannot train and mould more than four little lives as I do all my own work, washing, ironing, etc. I do not have much extra time to be with my children. As you see we are poor people.

The question is worrying me how to keep from becoming pregnant.

When my first three children were born I got along very well in confinement but five months ago when my last baby came I had a horrible time. The baby was so large I could not give enough and it came very near being the end of us both; as it is he is partially paralyzed in his left shoulder caused from the doctor pulling so hard on his neck and stretching the nerve in his shoulder from the pressure.

It seems to me I cannot risk going through it again. I cannot afford to go to the hospital at such times and am afraid it will sooner or later kill me. As you know there are harmless remedies how much better it would be for me to know how to care for myself so that I might live to see my children grown. Can't you tell me what to do to keep from becoming pregnant?

Ten

I am the mother of two small children. During my whole time of pregnancy that is for nine months while I must carry the child, I suffer so dreadfully that I'd rather be dead than alive. I can't find words to describe the sufferings I must undergo. It's so terrible. Oh, I am awful discouraged and sick at heart with married life, don't know what to do with myself sometimes. Have so much work to do at all times and can't do it properly, as I am a very frail person since my babies came. I know I could pick up strength and be my normal self again if you could only help me in this hour of need. I would appreciate your kind advice so much and could be happy.

Eleven

Can you help me any way from suffering to bring children into the world to suffer and die? I am twenty-two years of age. Married when only seventeen. I was married only seven months when I became pregnant and lost it at three months, and in eleven months more I had a tiny girl baby born to me and until this day she looks like death and in one year and eight months I had a little boy born and now am expecting to be confined every day. I have done everything in this world that I know to do and nothing seems to help in any way.

My husband and I are both discouraged. I never wanted any babies until I had a home for them and now I have the babies and no home yet for them. My husband and I have both worked just as hard as we could ever since we married and it seems like we never get anything ahead, but a doctor bill from one birth to another. I would rather die than to have the fourth one, but I did not know all this trouble until it was too late.

Twelve

I have three children and expecting another shortly, and the oldest was just three years old last month, so you can see my plight. If there is something very sure that can prevent the coming of another child for many years I'd surely be thankful to you.

I'd like a rest. To tell the truth I'm only twenty-one years old and I'd like to enjoy myself a little while I'm young. Also be a playmate to my children instead of just a cranky impatient nervous tired mother (if such a person can be called a mother). I don't feel that I could call my mother that if she felt and acted like I feel.

Thirteen

I am eighteen years old and was married exactly nine months when my baby was born. Of course I adore my baby boy, but what did I get out of life in my eighteen years? I was seventeen when I married, and now I long to go around with the crowd but on account of the baby I have to stay home. And now worse than all I fear that I am going to have another one when my first baby is only one year old. I am frantic from thinking that such a thing might happen.

Fourteen

I have two small children twenty months apart, the baby now seven weeks old and am twenty-one years myself. You might know what this means to me to care for two babies at this age when it simply stopped my being with my friends who can still be free to go, although I would do anything for my two children to help them go through a decent life. I am constantly living in fear of becoming pregnant again so soon. Mother gave birth to twelve children.

Fifteen

When I was a girl my mother begged me not to marry, for she thought my freedom was the most precious thing in the world and she told me that after I was married I would have no holidays nor pastimes nor anything, only just baby after baby, and that when I didn't have one I would be worried to death expecting to become pregnant any time. But I was twenty-four years old; I had no special talent; and was not, I think, especially adapted to the work I was doing and I did not care to follow in the steps of others so-called "old maids" in our office; moreover I was in love and I have never regretted the step I took and the loss of my "freedom."

My first baby was born eleven months after marriage. When my first baby was sixteen months old the second was born and died. He was a little "blue baby" and lived just three weeks and I believe that his heart was probably affected.

About three months after he was born I became pregnant again and I expect my third baby to be born in a few months and I have been married but a little more than three years. So far, I think I have no organic disease but ever since I became pregnant the second time I I have been so lifeless with absolutely no pep or ambition and sometimes I am so weak that I can't lift my little son on to my lap to dress him. Besides this weakness I have no interest for anything. I can't concentrate my thoughts long enough to think of something that would be nice for supper tonight and I am always just this way. Then too, I have another great worry. I know my husband loves me but he likes recreation. Sometimes I think he is unusually restless and pleasure-loving. We used to visit other young couples and have them in for supper and cards and go to a show occasionally even up to the time for me to be confined, but this last year he never asks me to go with him anywhere and he goes out with some of the men almost every night. Besides I never feel like entertaining or dressing to go and I am always tired enough for bed by 9 o'clock. Of course, his pleasures are absolutely harmless now but I'm so afraid they will become more dangerous unless I can arouse myself and become more of a companion after the baby is born. And what chance have I?

Sixteen

I am only eighteen years old and have one child a year old and am expecting another. I did not want another child for three or four years at least, but now I feel that two children will be all that I can take care of. I feel that there is no joy in married life unless I can have a few years of freedom while I am still young.

Seventeen

I, like many women, am interested in Birth Control, although I am young yet; but that is exactly the reason I want you to help me. Honestly, please help me if you can. I am a young girl-wife, as you can say, eighteen years old. And just imagine I'm not married three years yet and have two children, or babies rather. Oh, I do not think I want any more children, but what can I do? I suppose next year I'll have another baby—of course I'm not in a family way just now but I may be any time. How I would love to enjoy myself still! My heart is just craving for good times, like going to dances and parties. But getting babies every year, why, life will be an utter misery. Kindly help me. I pray to you like to my God.

Eighteen

I have three little girls, one eight, one five and one three. Now I am delicate, nervous and anemic, and suffer from a severe valvular leakage of the heart. My three children have all been delicate, the last baby could not sit up until she was eighteen months old, and was two years, three months, before she walked at all. Though they are all bright and intelligent girls, they are a continual worry. Now my last baby was only five months old when I became pregnant again, but at the second month I had a miscarriage, due, I believe, to weakness. I can only say I was glad when it happened, but I was so afraid of another conception, that at the time I refused to have a doctor called, for I was anxious to die rather than recover to go through the same thing.

Well, my husband loves me and we both love children, but he is only a working man and I don't think we should have any more children for I am not able to properly care for these, except as I know I am shortening my own life, by neglecting to have the care and attention I need. The doctor who was with me when my last baby was born said he would be sorry if I had any more, but that is all, he'd give no advice on how to prevent the same thing happening. My husband has prevented it since, but by continual continence. I know that is impossible if a couple lives together and loves each other.

Nineteen

If I could only speak to you personally,—but to write everything I have to say takes too long. The children make me too terribly nervous. I am a woman of a lot of trouble, twenty-four years old, married six years and four children, boys, the oldest is five, the baby five months. I am always sick since my first childbirth. Now I have been missing my times three months and took sick with cramps every month was up, so I went to a lady doctor to be examined. She says my bladder is out of shape, my womb is clear tipped over, heart trouble and I can't tell all what else. I am so weak, just ready to fall over, so I wanted her to doctor me up and sew me up just what she thought I would need. No, by God, she would not touch me. She was afraid I'd be in the family way and might get a miscarriage. I told her if I should really be I sure would like to have a miscarriage but she would not.

Now I have tried all kinds of other pills and stuff for monthly periods but no success. I am scared to death that I really am in that way and if I do not get any help it will be born before the other is a year old. Now tell me what is there no mercy for me. I just sit down for hours and weep away. I can't go no place, I can't walk with all my pain, bad large legs. I carry the baby on my arms, no baby buggie, poor clothes and seems everybody despises children nowadays.

Well, I don't want to lose what I have got but oh, God, I do not want any more. We are poor,—hardly any furniture and not our own place.

If I do give birth to any more I will have to give them away, the poor things and who wants children, and if I keep them to mother them myself they will have to starve, where the world is so full. When my third baby was born I got heartbroken. I was sick in bed, as sick as a person can be.

I had to stay all alone in the house in bed and the two bigger ones crying without my help. My man run off to the show till midnight. When my fourth one was born I was awful sick again. He came crossways without a doctor. There was none in town. The next day my husband run seventy miles to go fishing with other men and how I was wishing I were dead. But no, I had to live to be this way again, so I do not know what to do. If I take my life, what will become of my beloved ones I got already?

Twenty

I am thirty-one years of age, have had six children. Married at the age of eighteen. My husband is twenty-eight, drinks habitually, don't think women are for anything else only to cook, wash, work in the field and have children. I don't get stout from one time till I am that way again. I have the care of the whole family. He doesn't ever seem in a good humor. I have tried everything I have heard of but doesn't do any good.

I am sad, downcast, ashamed to go out in company because I have so many children and cannot fix them like other children.

I have refused sexual relation, but this causes awful quarrels, grouches and everything else. If there is anything you can do to help me I would be glad to hear from you at once. My baby is four months old so I must get busy in time or I'll be gone again without remedy. My family physician says I have fallen womb caused by lifting things too heavy. I wish I could see you face to face and tell you all I want to. I am in despair. Can you help me? Will you help me?

Twenty-one

I am in great need of help and I am sure you can help me as you have done others who cried "What can I do?"

What shall I do to prevent forever and always being in that condition? I am married almost six years. Have had three children, two girls are living aged four and two years. Had my first born not been born and died premature, I would not be living today. How many times I have wished I could have gone instead and escaped all this suffering. And had I not taken medicines a few times since my last baby I might have one or two more. Don't think that I don't like my children. I surely do. I would give my life for one of them if need be but I know that we (my husband and I) have all we can care for and dare not have more but just the same they keep coming and I am desperate and will suffer anything rather than bring more into the world.

My days and nights are one string of terror. Have dreams or nightmares that I am going or about to go through the grind again and wake up in a cold sweat.

I know enough not to have any more, but not how not to. That is why I am writing to you baring my very soul, for your help, for you have the knowledge and I want and need it. I have tried almost everything and keep my husband away for months, all to no purpose. As soon as I have intercourse again I find myself in that condition. Have even threatened my husband to keep him away forever but how can you when two small children depend on his wages for bread and bed? How could I live with him then? Is it wrong for a married woman to have and want to have intercourse without having children? I was brought up to believe that was wicked, that such things were only to produce children. "How can I have intercourse without children and constant dread of it?" That is my one earthly fear. I must have more knowledge on the subject. I must be sure and will you please write and help me to overcome my fear. If I can't overcome it there is no telling what I might come to yet as I am determined not to have any more children. Please accept these statements as true and because of them I know you will help me and answer my fears.

Twenty-two

I believe I have found in you what I have craved for and that is relief from the suffering that I have gone through. My husband is just as interested in my writing you as I am myself. I have gotten to the place that sometimes I wish I was dead. I would even rather die than go through with it again. Oh, won't you please help me just this one time and may God in the Heavens above bless you forever.

We have three children: the youngest is six months and the oldest is three years and we haven't got anything and for me I am only eighteen years old and my health is gone against me. I am only a frame and a doctor bill. My husband and children seem to hate me. I can't go on bringing children in this world without a roof to shelter them.

Please help me before I go insane. The thoughts of more children make me hate all men. My children seem to be feeble-minded. For God's sake please help me. My life and happiness have been wrecked for the lack of knowing what to do. Help me and I will by the help of God help you too. I am ignorant to everything pertaining to married life.

Twenty-three

Can it be possible that there is any way to keep from having children? It would seem too good to be true. I have six children, my youngest two months old and I am just scared to death for fear I will get that way again for I never can live to go through with it again. I came near dying this time. For three months before my baby was born I could not get any shoes on my feet and I could hardly get my eyes open to see. I was bloated up so bad. The doctor wanted to take the baby away when I was eight months, but I said no, I did not care if I lived or died and I did not have the least idea of living, but the Lord spared me probably so I could go through with it again. But I live on the banks of Lake —— and just as sure as I get in the family way again I will end my troubles and be at rest.

Twenty-four

I am writing you an earnest letter. I have a child every year and I am so weak and rundown and nervous I can hardly care for my other five children, who are sickly all the time. At night when I go to bed I always pray that I'll never wake up again for I hate the dawn of a new day. Life is miserable for me and when you live through the days of torture like that you may as well be dead. I have six children, the oldest one is seven years old, and had one miscarriage.

I get that way every year and when I know I am that

way I take everything so I don't have to bring another unwanted sickly babe that cannot be taken care of properly nor fed properly, in the home. But it seems nothing helps only hurts my health. So I make a last and final plea to see if you can give me any information telling me how to keep from getting any children. I would gladly do without a loaf of bread so I could get this help.

Twenty-five

I am sure that you have never seen anyone living under the conditions that we have to live. My confinement is only one month off and I will need some medical attention then and do now, but will not get any.

It is nothing but work, work. Sometimes I feel as if I just can't go on, sometimes it seems that the grave is awful inviting, a cool place to rest,—just so tired, tired.

My people have turned against me because of my condition. I have no one in the world to turn to for sympathy or advice. My husband has no understanding or does not care, or something, and tells me that my condition is all my own fault. So, dear, please send any instructions that I can carry out. We live miles and miles from any drug store. If I cannot get help from you I don't know what I will do.

Twenty-six

I am thirty-eight years old and my husband sixty-five, and we have seven children. Cannot find clothes and food for them and now I am five and a half months in family way again. I have went and seen doctors here and asked if they could do anything so that I would not bring another living child in the world to suffer and they said no, and there are no midwives here, so what am I to do?

I pray night and day hoping that it might come in the world dead so it will not suffer hunger and for want of clothes to keep warm. I have lung trouble and heart trouble and some of the children have the same, so if there are any medicines I could take so that I would lose it at seven months I would be sure pleased. I do not think that I would be doing a crime so if there are I would sure be glad if you would let me know and if there would be anything that I could do to keep from the family way I would as soon die as bring children in the world without food and clothes and not able to take care of them.

Twenty-seven

My baby is only two months old. I am the mother of six children, and had one miscarriage. I married a day laborer, so you see it takes all we both can make to keep in bread as they all are so very small. The oldest is five years.

Sometimes I think I am done here on earth. They run me about crazy. Will you please tell me some way that I may get a rest. I hardly ever get to church. Nothing in the world but work and worries. Will you please send me something that will help me at once. If any one need help it is me because we have nothing, no home, no money and a very poor way of making anything. No work to do. Now is there an answer for a woman like me? When with a baby I drag one hip all the time. I was unjointed for about seven months. Well I prayed and prayed last year, after I got that way, to the good Lord for some way to be helped out, and I do believe that he heard me pray for he always do if I ask in faith that he will do as I am so easy to turn back again. Please hear me at once, please a safe and sure way. Hurry to me before it is too late. I am so tired and sleepy. I can hardly write. I don't have time in day time to write. Do excuse all mistakes please, also bad writing. Baby will be three months old now.

Twenty-eight

We are only a young couple working by the month and haven't the means to care for more. Even if we did I will never go through the living hell that I went through with my first boy (unless it be to save him). If I must shake hands with Death there are plenty of shorter routes than listening to an owl hoot over your roof for nine months.

Then there is my husband. He is so considerate, but you know the discord that comes with trouble of this kind. Yet I feel sure he would do something desperate if he found he was the cause of my going through this untold suffering again.

Twenty-nine

I am just past thirty-one, and am again pregnant for my fifth baby. My husband is nearly thirty-six. We have been married ten years. The first year we lived on a farm which "supported" his widowed mother, his sister and us, during which time we also had to prepare for our first. The last nine years he has made from $12.50 to $25.00 a week (his present wage). It is almost impossible to get along although we manage splendidly by my doing everything that a woman can do to get along and economize.

But I do not complain of that.

It is of the terrible agony through which I have to go, not alone at the time of delivery, but for the continual period, agony and suffering of which I dare not tell anyone, not even my doctor, who says there is nothing he can tell me to keep from having babies, so I am turning to you for help which I pray God you can and will give me.

Do not think, dear woman, that I do not love my babies. I most sincerely do and there is nothing I would not do for them, and not one of them would I willingly give up, but surely there can be no harm in trying to keep from having babies which we cannot properly care for on $25.00 a week and for whom I have almost to give up my life every time one comes. I am nearly desperate, and if it were not for my babies who need my care so badly, I do not think I would even go through what I know I will have to suffer until October.

Thirty

I am a young wife twenty-two years old and the mother of two children, one and two years old, and am expecting the third in a month and a half. I know we can't support it, as my husband is a laborer in the brass foundry and only gets $3.20 a day and he can never make a full pay, as he isn't very healthy. I have undergone two operations, one for appendicitis and the other at birth which left me two incisions. I also have a hard time at each birth. I have to take ether each time. These incisions bother me terribly during each pregnancy. Ofttimes I think the child is going to come out through these incisions as they hadn't the time to heal up right since the operations as I am constantly in family way. It is about two months apart from the last births that I get in family way again.

I would rather die than suffer like this and bringing these unwanted babies into this world. I have been hunting this blessing for two years. Even my special doctor won't tell me and he knows that the hard time I have giving birth and during pregnancy as he is my only doctor. I am paralized in my right side which leaves half of my work for my husband to do when he comes from his work. It isn't healthy for him to do two jobs. It is breaking him down terribly in health. I am afraid he will fall into consumption from worry if I don't find a way to stop having any more children. I have suicide in my mind if I don't find a way out of this and I don't care to live. I want to die. I will be better off dead than live through more of this hell that I have gone through, and I see no relief of this unless you give it to me or tell me where I can get it.

XI

The Husband's Own Story

WHILE the evidence presented in the last chapter tends to emphasize the selfishness, the ignorance and the thoughtlessness of a certain type of husband and father, counterbalancing evidence is offered in letters I have received from another type of husband—thoughtful, loving, modest and intelligent. In the increasing prevalence of this attitude, of a new generation of men who enter marriage with a full realization of their responsibilities toward their wives and the children-to-be there is certainly hope for the future.

Apart from their sobriety, their honesty and their earnestness, and despite the sympathy sincerely expressed for the suffering of their wives, these letters cannot fail to indicate a vast contrast between the psychology of fatherhood and motherhood. It is a truism to point out that the actual agony, the physical suffering, the descent into the valley of the shadow of death, can never be, in the very nature of things, experienced by the father. His is an experience fundamentally vicarious in character, never at closest grip with the great biological drama of reproduction.

One important fact is to be noted: it is the husband deeply in love with his wife who appeals for aid in contraceptive measures. It is the husband who is in love with his wife who is ready and willing to restrain his own impulses, to make sacrifices for her protection. How serious this problem becomes in the lives of young husbands and wives is indicated by the number of self-imposed separations, the efforts toward continence, which are usually unsuccessful, and which of course offer no adequate solution toward intelligent control.

Impressive is the statement of that man who has suffered the loss of two wives in childbirth, and who in marrying again is now anxious to avoid a repetition of the same disasters. Then there is the type of intelligent observer who has been able to draw the logical conclusions from the lives of his own immediate family and relatives. Another example is that of a young man on the threshold of matrimony who is firmly resolved that his own little family shall be established on the firm foundation of prudence and intelligence. The attitude expressed in such testimonials is certainly a hopeful sign toward a coming régime of sane procreation.

Careful perusal of these records in which the husband tells his own story indicates that this problem confronts every man and woman reaching maturity who wishes to fulfill his or her life through marriage. Each must seek an intelligent practical solution, or drift into the chaos created by irresponsibility and selfishness. To certain young men, born and educated in the more enlightened levels of society, freed by birth from the cruel grind of poverty, city-bred and familiar with all the sophisticated refinements of civilization, the solution is close at hand. It is theirs for the asking. But let us not therefore erroneously conclude that the technique of contraception is available to all. These letters from distant outposts, from frontiers, from deserted countrysides, from factory-towns and congested slums, all exemplify the seriousness of the problem.

Many find themselves standing almost alone. They are confronted by the prejudices of the primitive social organism in which they happen to be placed; they are surrounded by the ignorance and indifference of neighbors; they are often faced by the cruel cupidity of druggists, the narrow legalism and limitations of country doctors, and above all they are oppressed by that vast conspiracy of silence which still envelops the whole subject of sexual hygiene in all but the most liberated strata of human society. It requires courage to confront custom, prejudice, and ignorance, confident in the certainty of your own conviction.

One

In May, 1919, my wife gave birth to a baby boy before she had recuperated from a previous birth; before time for her to get up she was taken down by childbed fever and a severe case, as it got worse and she grew weaker it developed typhoid, and she was bedfast until the following September, she then was able to get up only a few days when she was again taken bed fast and remained there until the following November. She got so bad that we no longer was able to keep her in our home as we were unable to give her necessary treatment even with a nurse, so on Nov. 29th, 1919, she was taken to a hospital where she remained until September 11th, 1920, at this time she was able to be brought home and for a year was hardly able to walk by herself. Today she is able to take care of herself but that is all, her former health has gone forever, no doubt her death will be advanced by this fate. During this siege of trouble I sold my home, spent what money I had, borrowed what I could, and all in all cost me approximately $3000.00 though I have only missed five days work since Feb. 20th, 1920 including Sundays and holidays which I also have to work I am yet in debt and with my invalid wife and six children to clothe, feed and if I don't miss another days work for two years it will take me that length of time to pay out. Why all of this? just because my wife conceived when she was in no condition to be so, just because no doctor would reveal a preventive or relieve her from her condition. Now, who, that is fair minded would say that it was right to go ahead and let nature take its course? Wouldn't it be nice to have three or four more in like manner. Just keep on landing them in this world I suppose take them out of school to help make a living, half clothed and half fed, that's just what will happen to me if I get sick and have to lose some work. Had Birth Control been given in my case years ago I would, the chances are favorable, still have my home, probably two or three children, a little money in the bank for their schooling. I could at least have a vacation of two or three weeks a year and last but not least my wife's health would be like it used to be, strong, healthy and able to take care of her home and family.

Two

I am a young married man thirty years of age and have one child and that is enough. Especially for a man such as me that can only earn forty cents per hour and only get seasonable work at that. The best people in this country are as a rule well enough off financially so they can support large families, but they only raise one or two or not at all. When a forty cent per hour working man raises several children it certainly means poverty even if he goes without a Ford car, and I have no car. If I did my outgo would be greater than my income.

Three

I am forty-six years old and my wife is forty-four. Have been married twenty-seven years and have raised ten living children and my wife expects another. Have had no deaths and no sickness worth mentioning. Our sex relations are just as enjoyable and seem just as necessary as twenty-seven years ago. The only thing that ever marred our happiness was the fear of conception and that fear done no good as our record shows. We were always glad and willing to bring up our share of babies and are proud of the record, but we think eleven is really more than our share, and there is perhaps several years yet of the bearing period. All the books and all the doctors I have ever consulted have never offered a workable remedy. Must this go to the end? We have not now nor ever had any desire to avoid my duty but we think we have done our share.

Four

I am now thirty-five years old and am one of a family of twelve children, I therefore know something of the handicaps of a large family. Because of a lack in opportunities that should be every child's heritage I am at this time of life still doing school work that I should have fifteen years ago. My wife is also studying to make her capable of earning enough money to give our two children the opportunities in life that we did not have. True there are lots of families larger than ours and families that have less than we do but their standard of living is not as high as it should be. We intend to give our children an education which will enable them to maintain as high a standard as we have set for ourselves and if possible even higher.

We feel that if we have any more children that we will not be able to do this and unfortunately we do not know by what means to prevent having a larger family excepting by unaturally denying ourselves. We also know that some people do know how to manage this. I do not think our doctors will assist us in this matter. They figure that the larger the number of babies the more money they make out of it. They are not so much concerned with the problems of the parents.

Five

I believe it would be one of the greatest blessings on earth for the working man if your plans could be carried out. Incidentally I am a working man myself, being in the employ of a local automobile plant. My wife and I are very devoted to each other. We have one baby girl about four months old. We have been separated for six months, first for financial reasons, secondly for reasons pertaining to the birth of the child which I have never seen. Think of it, a man with a babe four months old and never having seen it! I am a cripple too and can never tell how soon my working days may end. I expect to have my wife and baby with me in thirty days. Then I suppose a repetition of the same thing again. I simply cannot afford to have any more children or I should say support—though I am willing to do the best possible by the one we now have.

Six

I am thirty-two years old and have been married twelve years, my wife giving birth to four children. I doubt whether it is necessary for me to tell you of the hard struggle I have had to make a living for the family, while working in a tailor shop. I take it you are well aware of the fact. I took sick with tuberculosis four years ago, and have been "on the cure" ever since. I am pronounced fit to go home to take up the struggle again, and am expecting to leave the sanitorium about the middle of the month. The first problem that is facing me is how to prevent adding any more to a family that I cannot take care of properly.

Of course "abstinence" would be the answer to my problem, but both my wife and I are of an affectionate nature, and we could hardly apply abstinence with any kind of success. I know from past experience.

I have applied for advice and help to some of the doctors I know, but they have neither no advice to give me, or won't give it, which is hardly just, especially in my case.

Seven

I am only a man but my hat is off to you and I think you are doing the best work that ever was done. When I was married I was just as well as any man could be, but in two years I commenced to fail in health first with lung trouble and then rheumatism and was laid up for three years, but we had no children at the time and I had money enough to tide over until I got where I could work a little, but I am still crippled so I cannot do hard work for what money I can get and that is just enough to exist. Now we have one little girl nine months old and no one only a mother and father knows how we love her and my wife and I both would like if we could take care of them as they should be. Now here is the condition we are in. My wife not well, I am crippled up with rheumatism, with one little girl no money coming in, only what I make and I don't know how long I can hang on over night. When I hobble home I wonder if I will be able to work the next day and worrying what my wife would do. Now our doctor helped my wife get rid of one child two months ago and God knows I do not want her to go through that again but the doctor said he couldn't see what we would do with any more. I asked him if there was any way to keep her from getting that way and he said not anything that I know of. If I did I would gladly tell you. He has six children. Now I am afraid she is that way again and my God, what we are going to do is more than I know.

Eight

I realize you are a friend of humanity. If people would see with your light, the world would be healthful. I am a father and husband of my wife—father of six children in five years, two of them living and two sets of twins born prematurely. The first was six months and the second seven months, all dead. These two living children, they are sick in the first year, and my wife, she is very poorly, and had to nurse the last baby on the bottle. She do not have milk for it.

I am a foreigner and poor coal miner, and my earnings is not very good for all this expenses what come on us. I feel so bad about everything what comes on us, and write to ask you to send me information for us. Please do not tell me I am foreigner, not worthy help from you, but help me for God's sake to prevent having any more trouble, as we have already.

Nine

We were married thirteen years ago and had five children one of which died about three years ago. After the one died I talked my wife into not having any more children, using for an argument her own family of which there was twelve, that we are getting older, I being thirty-nine and don't know what may happen and so forth. I have tried all kinds of stunts and safety devices with no

results. Two and a half years ago my wife had a miscarriage having taken some pills, two years ago she went
to a doctor, one year ago a miscarriage, two months ago
her period stopped. She went to our family doctor and
the only thing he wanted to do was to make an appoint-
ment with some other doctor to get operated on. My wife
is afraid to go on the table and took some more pills. But
now for my main object in writing: Is there any way to
keep from getting pregnant? I am only working for a
living and God knows we don't want any more.

Ten

I am a married man with two children, but I am not
with my wife now. She left eleven months ago for the
simple reason that I teased her about there being seven
more children. And so far I have not been able to get
her to come back to me. I don't want any more children
any more than she does, but I don't know how to keep
from it. I think that if I could get that information I
could get her to come back to me.

Eleven

My wife cannot carry pregnancy through to birth. She
has had to be aborted twice "according to law" in order
to save her life. This has ruined her health, and more, has
almost destroyed our home. The doctors and hospitals are
very willing to make big charges for these operations, but
will not give any information regarding the prevention of
pregnancy, although they say it must not happen again.

Her condition of course makes conception doubly easy. I'm trying to protect her by practicing continence. But this is not desirable nor good for either of us. I am a poor man working on a salary. My wife is very timid and backward about seeking information, so I am presuming to write to you myself, as I want to protect her and save our home.

Twelve

Add me to your list of maladjusted, who for eight years of married life has struggled along, with a semi-invalid wife (caused largely because of ignorance of the sex function) looking for assistance we should have had at marriage. Today my wife is in a sanitorium, and I am trying to get adequate information that we may try again to take up life together, this time we trust more intelligently. Let me add that I am seeking to inform myself in every way possible to bring about a better understanding of the sex life, and believe heartily in Birth Control. With more "light" I hope to be a more effective propagandist.

Thirteen

I was raised up with eight. The ninth carried my darling mother to her grave and went with her. I have been living in prayer that someone would volunteer and do something for a poor woman who has to suffer the pain of having too many children. If my darling mother had only known of a woman of your kind I know she would have had mercy. I have a first cousin that has miscarried three times in four years and she wants to know of your remedy of preventing the birth of children. She has never had any she carries them from five to six months then loses them so I have asked her why not stop it. She said she couldn't help it. The doctor won't help her. She has ruined her health already and the doctors will say, I think I can gain your health back without an operation, that is all that she can get out of them, so I told her about your work. She has asked me to write you for the help. She is just getting up from the last time and she wants to know and is crying for mercy. Will you please send it to me? I also have a sister that is crying for the mercy of Birth Control.

I'm a man of twenty-five, not married but will be in June, if it's God's will and the girl I'm going to marry is only nineteen years of age. She practically has no parents, she can't live with them in peace and she don't want any children under twenty-five years at least. Says she don't want any and God knows as I see the sufferings of so many women and children I don't want her to have any and I have three sisters to take care of and send to school and I need a wife to help care for them.

I don't need any children. My youngest sister is twelve years old. I have them in school and I need a wife so I can put more on them and if there ever was a man that felt and had mercy on a woman it is myself. I see and know so many that ought to have your advice. I thank God for a great woman and I ask mercy for these three especially.

Fourteen

I have had a lot of trouble in raising a family and want to ask your advice in the matter. In 1915 I was married the first time. My wife was twenty-six years old and I was twenty-five. In 1918 the first child was born. She gave her life for the child not being able to give natural birth. The baby lived and is a strong healthy girl now. In 1920 I married again to a fine young girl the same age as myself. We were married in July and didn't have any children until a year from the next December and then a nice eight pound boy was born. She had a very hard time but gave natural birth to the baby and got over it all right.

After about a year she wanted another and the doctor said that probably the next time everything would be O.K. and it would be easier for her. It did not prove to be. She had to be taken to the hospital and the baby was taken from through the side and blood poison set in. She only lived about a week.

The children all lived and are rugged as bears. Now I am coming to the part I need your advice on. I am going to be married again in the Spring and it is the earnest wish of us both that we do not have any children. My family is large enough and besides I don't want to take the chances again. Can you help me?

Fifteen

Am twenty-two years old, married one year, father to one child now eight months old. My grandmother had seventeen children, my dear mother had twelve, seven of which died at birth or shortly after.

Me being the second oldest living, only one married out of our family. My parents are poor living always in a rented house in the city. Now to tell the dreadful tale of which I have prayed many and many a time that my family will not have to face or suffer like we children had to. My father works on the railroad and must I say he is a drunkard ever since I know anything? Many a time threatening our lives when drunk that we would go to a neighbor's house over night.

Must I say I was an unwelcome child, it looks so to me. When six years old was sent out on the farm for my board for two summers. Winters went home and to school. As eight years was sent on the farm again and never returned to my dear mother which I loved so dearly, the same with a brother younger than myself. Was raised in a Mennonite family. Started out in life at eighteen without any knowledge of life as all these things were barred from me, learning all these things from vulgars or low-lifed people. Here I am ready to go over the brink inexperienced along this line. Now please if you can tell me how to control birth of unwelcome children please tell me the truth as this will be a blessing to me.

Sixteen

I am a young man twenty-five years of age and married to a young girl eighteen years of age. I realize there is a difference in age and also my wife is young, but feel that the difference is not too great. We married sooner than we intended because of the fact my wife had a very unpleasant home life and I wished to free her from it. She is young and never had the chance to enjoy life as most young ladies do of her age, due to the conditions and oppressions she lived in.

Now I want her to have the same chance of happiness others of her age do and that she could not have while she was at home. I want her to enjoy her youth. I wish to say she is a fine sensible little wife, not a bit frivolous, and is making a very happy home for me.

Now this is the situation I am facing. Either forcing motherhood upon her before she is really best fitted to undertake its responsibilities both physically and mentally, robbing her of youth and adding burdens upon her before they should be, or I am causing a misunderstanding which is becoming very serious on account of my neglect to her. This condition is causing me a great deal of worry and unhappiness as well. I realize things cannot continue this way and my love is too great to cause her unhappiness. Will you help us out with your kind advice?

Her happiness is my chief desire and I know that when the time comes that we are fortunate enough to have children they shall be given the best start and protection in life we can possibly give to them. We want them to have a better opportunity than we have been given.

Seventeen

I have three healthy children and do realize and know that is all I can afford to bring up and educate properly.

My wife, I am sure, should not have any more for it would be just as you say in your book, an unwanted child. It is not that I do not love children, but I believe a man should not be the cause of any more children than he can well afford to support and most of all his wife can have or afford on account of her physical condition.

My wife is in the United States and I am about seven thousand miles away, my reason for this is that I am afraid of having any more children due to the fore-mentioned reasons. I do not want my wife to have any more children. It works a hardship on my wife as well as myself for we have had a happy life together. I would like to ask you kindly if it is possible to get your valuable advice as to a harmless preventive.

Eighteen

A few months ago certain hinted possibilities of Birth Control came to my knowledge quite by hearsay. By that I mean a friend of mine was told by a pal of his who knew of a friend, etc. To my mind the information was not convincing but nevertheless I wrote for my friend to this friend of his and asked him politely and discreetly just what he knew; result, no answer; why? couldn't say. Now yesterday your February number of the *Birth Control Review* came into my hands in a very roundabout way, having to my knowledge been read by at least three married men and their wives. They frankly admitted they had gained but little knowledge of the subject. I was handed the volume and from a general thirst for knowledge I read it from cover to cover twice and must openly admit I am at a loss to explain my thoughts which I have on the subject of its contents. I therefore have made myself the correspondent for the above mentioned three family men.

My case is roughly this. Oh, it's all summed up in your columns on married love. Why go over the same grounds as those correspondents of yours have so aptly done in letters so full of pathos which you have seen fit to publish?

I will but mention that I am in a like position though I have only been separated from my dear wife and son but twelve months. Separated in the pretense of building for them a home on the Western prairies of Canada. I have built them that home now and shortly will come the time when my loved ones are to join me. What is to happen? Shall I have to face my old bogey? God knows I love my wife. I love little children but I wish more to see my wife a smiling companion, my pal. I want to see her happy and in perfect health and a keep her life free from inopportune worries. Can you blot out our bogey? Material information would be greatly appreciated. Though I am familiar with the home life and general cases of my three married men friends I will refrain from writing of them herein, but will assure you they join with me in the sincerity of this communication and would discreetly handle any information you are willing to impart.

Nineteen

For five years my wife has refused to live with me. She has borne four children, two dead, and physicians have told us she would die if she had another. I had spent hundreds of dollars before the last child's birth in the effort to save my wife from the danger, but doctors either could not or would not tell me the true preventive. Her health now is very poor and the children's also. I would do anything to have her back for she is the only love I ever knew. She would be glad to come if I could safeguard her. The children need me, too. Will you not tell me what I can do to make my home happy again? It seems I must dispair and become utterly broken if I can't have my wife, children and a home. I've simply been heartbroken and almost dispairing for five years and dread the future more and more. I will be so grateful and happy and so will my little family if you will grant our plea.

XII

Marital Relations

UNDER the conditions depicted in the majority of these records, it is obviously impossible that normal, happy marital relations can be enjoyed. When a permanent fear of pregnancy has been established in the mind of the wife and the dire consequences of physical intimacies overwhelming in her thoughts, happiness in marriage inevitably becomes a thing of the past.

We present here a group of letters from wives who, despite all the vicissitudes of their married lives, are still in love with their husbands, and who have no complaint to offer concerning the behavior of the latter. Their husbands are still lovers and comrades, and all too willing to shoulder the full burden of their responsibilities as head of a growing family.

Yet the very strength and depth of this mutual love stand as obstacles to the realization of happiness. For the full physical expression of love brings with it too heavy a penalty. Acute dread of that penalty, in the form of another mouth to feed, another baby to clothe, poisons at its source the sexual communion. In its normal expression, this communion knits into an inviolable union the love of husband and wife. With fear uppermost in both minds, normal fulfillment eventually becomes an impossibility. Marital happiness vanishes forever.

More prevalent, however, in the confessions I have received, is the case of the so-called "selfish" husband—the man who, like those natives of certain primitve tribes described by anthropologists, have not yet learned to correlate, under the law of cause and effect, the sexual act and the birth of a child nine months later. Husbands of this type are imperative in their sexual demands upon the wife, and completely oblivious of the price that is exacted of her for their heedless moments of brute pleasure. To such men the marital relation is nothing more than the selfish gratification of their own physical instincts. If the wife must be condemned to the "solitary confinement" of incessant pregnancy, with all its hazards in the way of miscarriage, abortion, and still-birth, it is an easy matter to place the blame of such consequences on her!

Wives of such men may truly be described as "white slaves," with the exception that the lot of the prostitute in most countries is a far happier one than that of these legitimate wives and mothers.

It would be unjust, however, to blame all husbands for the suffering of the wives and families. With the denial of normal and satisfactory intercourse—and indulgence under compulsion may be legitimately condemned as essentially abnormal—the very foundations of marital happiness are undermined. The wife's dread of the approach of her husband—justifiable as this dread may be in the light of past experience—brings with it a greater and greater strain upon enduring marital relations, and eventually their rupture. The villain in the drama is neither the one nor the other, but the relentless, inhuman driving power of natural but uncontrolled impulses.

Downright brutality on the part of the husband is fortunately the exception rather than the rule—there are, however, examples in the present group of unspeakable selfishness. Cases of extreme nervousness on the part of the husband would undoubtedly, upon analysis, prove to be an unconscious reflex of the attitude of the wife.

After the perusal of these pathetic accounts of the gradual destruction of happiness in marriage one thing is evident: Contraception hygienically practiced renders feasible the fullest, freest and most satisfactory expression of mutual love through physical communion. This precaution makes possible the development and the fruition of true love and enduring marriage. Such marriages form the strongest and safest foundations of happy families—through the birth of children by choice, and the proper spacing between their births. Upon these foundations, the severest economic burdens would be lightened, and a possible way out of hardship and poverty indicated.

We reserve for future chapters other aspects of married life upon which our records throw significant light.

One

I wish you Godspeed in your noble work for us poor slave women. I am a mother of four living children. We are very poor farmers. My oldest child is seven years and my youngest is six months old. Neither my husband nor I know how we can possibly have any more children and care for them. We do not own the roof over our heads.

Oh, could you write me and tell me how my husband can come to me and know that there would be no more of this terrible, awful suffering as I have had to endure in the past?

I have seen my husband cry when he found out there was to be another siege of that terrible awful pain and suffering I always have to come through. Cannot you tell me through some safe way I will not have no more children? I am only twenty-five years old myself, not very strong, my average weight is ninety-eight pounds.

Two

I have six children and every time I have to give birth to a child I kiss myself good-bye. I have a most terrible time with every one of them especially my last baby. I have a strong healthy husband and he seems to have a strong nature because he tries himself to take care of me but he can't help himself. He is not the kind of a husband to make a slave of me. He is a very good man to me and a good father. He works very hard to support his family. Although he works hard to keep us going and I work very hard in the house, to take care of a family with six children is not an easy task.

I can't afford to hire any help. I have to be the housekeeper, the washwoman, the cook, the seamstress and many other things that a house requires. My children are none of them big enough to help me. My oldest girl is thirteen years old and the rest of them are all younger than her. I am thirty-two years old. I can have about a dozen more children, if I will not find some certain preventive. I could be the happiest woman if I could have my mind relieved for one minute to know that I am a little free. It is not only the most terrible time of giving birth that I fear, it is the great responsibility of taking care of a family, I cannot give these children the proper care. If you know of anything that is certain please, I beg you, to please give it to me.

How am I to help myself? Only one that has knowledge of a sure way to prevent having children can lead a happy life. It is through you that I seek that happiness. Please send me my key to happiness and I will bless you and I know God will bless you for it too.

Three

I am going to try to express as near as I can what I want you to know and want you to help me if you can. I am married to one of the best men in every way I most ever heard of though we are poor and not able to raise a large family. We have two sweet boys; one is three years old the other one is sixteen months old, they are fat and healthy never been sick any, I mean bad sick. Their father and myself are in good health so far as I know. I was twenty-seven years old when I was married, didn't suffer so very hard when they were born but we don't want any more because we are not able to do a good part for any more. We are so happy with our boys. I know there never was a couple any happier than we. My husband don't want me to have any more; he is ignorant like myself and don't know what to do, he is willing to try anything that won't injure my health, almost willing for no sexual union at all, that is the only way I know to express it. You understand what I mean of course. I would do anything on earth for my husband, he is so good. I feel like it would be an injustice to us both to bring several children into the world and not able to support them nor educate them, though I will avoid miscarriage if possible.

My husband works all the time we live on a small farm. I have lots of work to do myself, I can vegetables of all kinds to live on through the winter, makes it hard on me but I am happy. I can tell the world that happiness is something can't be bought with money.

Four

I am just twenty-three, mother of a darling baby who looks strong but really is terribly nervous and has spasmodic attacks which nearly kills me to see. For that reason I can never think of bringing any more children in the world which will more than likely have to suffer. Also I am just a nervous wreck from the suffering I went through before and at childbirth. I doctored with a few different doctors and they all said they never saw anything like it. I was sick from the start of pregnancy and have never recovered. Also I have been warned to keep out of such circumstances from then on or it would probably cost my life next time. That was some over two years ago. I menstruated regular through nursing the baby on.

My husband has been a regular man, I must say, to keep me from so becoming. But the suspense is terrible. I worry day for day until the month is up and I know for sure and I am just killing myself body and soul until I can hardly do my own work at all, as well as ruining his own health.

With this awful unsolvable problem between us life is not as sweet as we had supposed, but is a burden to us. We are poor, terribly poor, but would be happy if we only knew how to live and enjoy life.

Five

Eight years ago, a lady said to me: "Have you ever heard of Mrs. Sanger? She is a personal friend of mine. I will bring you one of her booklets on Birth Control," and she did. Now my older sister was with me and in all innocence I told her how I got it and she asked to see it and when she got home she put it in the stove before I had a chance to read it. I can only realize now the tragedy that was. I have now five children and I am now a physical wreck, no definite disease, just worn out, a nervous wreck. Miscarriages I could not count them. Three within the last seven months. Can you imagine? I begged the doctor to tell me but he said he knew nothing. My! I'm going crazy myself worrying from month to month. My husband does everything possible to try and avoid my becoming pregnant. He adores his children and we really love one another just as much as we did fifteen years ago. Picture a young woman and he is young too, thirty-one and thirty-three. I've got easily fifteen more years of childbearing. The suffering I endure carrying and the hard confinements I have make me weep. All this I would bravely endure but I cannot take care of more. It means taking the bread out of one mouth and try and feed the other. I am desperate. What else is there to do for me if self-control fails. I help myself when I can. What else is there but abortion? The pity of it. Another reason: my husband is not a well man. He has had three operations for ulcers of the stomach and has been under treatment in the hospital from six to eight weeks in each and he has been in nine times. Every one of my children has been born either right before he came home from a hospital or right before he went. I tell you we are both nervous from the fear of my becoming pregnant, fear of his becoming sick and leave us in want. If you knew more of my story you would have pity.

Six

My husband and I firmly believe in Birth Control. We have a baby boy and in due time hope to have more babies as our circumstances permit. It seems so much better to have fewer and to take good care of them than to have more and be obliged to neglect them. It took me over two years to recover from the serious time I had when this baby (two and one-half years) was born and because of this and expenses connected with it all we are more anxious than ever to feel sure of ourselves.

The constant strain of not feeling certain of just where we are is very nerve-wearing on me and does not make home any cheerier and better for my family. If you can tell us what to do it will be appreciated more than words can tell. I would like to say that my husband is a fine clean man and a splendid father to our baby and will be to any others that we may have. This too makes it seem important not to have them faster than he can provide for them.

Seven

I am married near five years and I have two small babies. My husband I were parted through quarreling and the fear of having more babies. At the present time he has not spoken to me for three days. My heart is breaking. I keep away from him as much as I can and that makes him very angry. I do nothing but cry and cry. He is so big and strong and I so small. Oh, please tell me or help me, what shall I do not to have too many babies for I feel as if I will have to raise them myself. My friends tell me as well as my doctor not to have no more children and to be careful, but I do not know what they mean. I fear my husband so. If you will come to my rescue I will never forget you. I can hardly see what I am writing from the tears in my eyes. I could write a book of my heartaches and unhappiness in my short married life. Oh, please help me, my heart is breaking.

Eight

I am a poor woman and already have three children and I have to work like a slave more than anything else, and my husband is not good to me, and I have a terrible life to live. I would be O! so glad if you would give me some advice.

It would have to be something that I can do without my husband knowing for he thinks breeding machines are

what all women are. Please, please, please do tell me
something; anything that is harmless that I can do;
Somehow I feel that my husband would treat me better,
be kinder to me if I did not keep away from him so much.
Oh, but I cannot have no more children.

Nine

I am a married woman with three babies. My oldest
child is a girl, she will be six years old. The next one is a
boy who will be four years old and the baby girl will be
two years old. I have my housework to do, my washing
and ironing and care for my three babies and am now a
month and a little over a week on the way for another.
I have tried everything that I knew to do and everything
any one else told me but it did no good. I am so nervous
I can hardly stand for my babies to come around to talk
to me or touch me. It makes my home life miserable.

My husband says he wants no more babies but I have
come to believe he cares more for his passion than he
does for me for he won't do anything to keep me from
getting pregnant. My husband is a man who could give
me a good comfortable home and make good money, but
he won't hold to his jobs when he gets one. That keeps
me worrying myself to death all the time for I am a
woman of ambition and want to be doing something all
the time. I have always claimed good friends and many
of them and been out in company all the time but since
I have been a married woman I have to stay at home
with my babies, for my husband says there is no pleasure
in going out and taking babies. I was twenty-one when I

was married, and am now twenty-eight years old. I married for love and a home for I wanted a home and babies for I love them and a nice home, but I did not marry for passion or to be bred to death. I would rather kill myself than to have any more.

Ten

If you will only for my sake and my dear children's sake help me please do tell me something so I can keep from having any more children because if I can't I will die first. I have seven children and I am a wreck. My life has been spoiled by having so many children. We are so poor I have to help keep the family by washing and I know I can't stand this very long. My children are none of them big enough to work yet. I want so bad to give them an education because this world is so hard when anyone has not been educated for it. One of my children needs to go to a sanitarium. His legs are crooked and I haven't the money to do it. We don't even own a home of any kind for my dear children. My husband is not strong and can't work all the time. Oh God, did I know when I was a girl that I would bring seven little mouths to feed and suffer in this world? If I had known I never would have looked at a man.

My husband is always quarrelling at me for having so many children and every time I have a child I can hardly live with him. Do help me for my own sake and my children's. I want to live and raise them. If you don't help me I will try something more cruel because I won't bring another little soul in this cruel world to suffer and live in want as my children are living.

Eleven

I am married and have three children but they are all very close together. The oldest boy is three and a half years, the second boy is two years and my little girl is six months. I am a small weak woman. I only weigh a little over a hundred pounds so you can imagine for yourself. My two oldest children are strong and healthy, but could be better, I think. My little girl is not so well. The doctor told me I was too weak to have children. He doesn't want me to have any for a while, but what shall I do? He won't tell me how not to have any. So I thought I would ask you if you know of any way. If I could only have one whole year so I could get my health back a little bit. It isn't that I don't want any children at all any more, for I dearly love little babies, and have always had a wish for about five or six anyway, but I want them to be strong boys and girls, but if I can't take care of them as they ought to be then I don't want to bring any more weaklings into this world.

My husband is a big strong man but he will not be careful. He always says he is going to be careful but that's as far as it goes. The doctor even tells him that he should be very careful. He says go and take something to drive it away, but I don't want to kill. Please try and help me if you can. I would be ever so thankful and I am asking only for the sake of these little ones that I have now so I can bring them up half-way decent.

Twelve

I am coming to you for advice like so many other women have done. I have been married seventeen years, had a child every year, got five living now, oldest fifteen, youngest eleven months old. My husband threatens to leave me every time I get that way. I, like so many others, don't know what to do and my husband don't know either, but just thinks I don't have to get that way. Is there anything I can take or do from being that way? No one will know. Help me please. We are very poor. Cannot afford any more children.

Thirteen

I have been married sixteen and a half years. My oldest is a girl and will be sixteen. I was only married about ten months till she was born and I have had eight and they came about every other year. I have five boys and two girls living and one little girl dead. She was next to the youngest. She only lived to be a little over thirteen months old and she never was strong and I always layed it to dope I took when I found out I was that way. Everybody saw her said I never would raise her but I thought I would. My youngest will be nineteen months old this month. I have thought of everything I would like to do, even to shoot myself, but I know I wouldn't be here to look after the others. I wouldn't care so much but our means are very little. He works every day but seems though we cannot get along with so much expense. Have to pay rent too and it seems to me since I think I am that way again it has made him so different. He wants me to get rid of it and I went to our doctor and he will not do such things at all. So Sunday he went away. In the afternoon after coming from work to fix his car he drives to town, and was brought home late in the evening so drunk he was unable to help himself. I felt so bad to think he did it for I could not think what the cause could have been for there had not been a word in any way. We all were laughing and having a big time and he hasn't talked to me since, so you know our home is not too pleasant these days. It is something he never had done in all the years of our married life. Of course, we have our little scraps but I consider this a real trouble. When we layed our little girl away it didn't go as hard with me as this for I felt as though she was better off out of this wicked world. He took it worse than I did and to think he will bring such a disgrace on the rest as this. I am only hoping it never happen again.

Fourteen

I am just about to have my fifth baby,—besides one miscarriage. The babies are a year apart and the situation in our home has become a tragedy. We are not able to take proper care of the babies in many ways.

My husband is a truck driver. The children become ill for want of things and mother's care which we knew they should have, but which I am not able most of the year to give them. But it seems sadder than all to find this year that my husband has lost patience and nerve and is failing to stand by me during this awful pain. I am nearly paralyzed and in great pain most of the time.

He scorns me now, and instead of helping me is positively cruel. Threatening to leave us without a mere existence.

I am not afraid of starving, but it is bitter, bitter to think of what our home has become.

Fifteen

I was always poor and when I married it was the same. My husband was hardworking and tried his best and did make a nice living. Eleven months after I married a baby girl was born. By then my husband made a pretty fair salary. He is naturally very, very close with his money, even for necessities. I could not begin to tell you how I suffered when I was handicapped with my child.

Knowing that I was tied down thus, my husband started to go out alone not wishing to be bothered with a baby. I suffered agony. For fully three years I suffered and I am beginning to open my eyes. My baby is four years old and a little lady and so my husband does not neglect me as he used to, but we have nothing. Oh, my poor child! I cannot give her so many things that she ought to have and I also am deprived of a lot of things. Five months ago my husband invested his savings ($2000) in a business. The rest he owes and some he borrowed. I am his main help. He is still very very close and I was not complaining but to my utmost misery I have become pregnant. I am now in the fourth month. If I had not been poor and ignorant I could have helped myself but it is too late.

Realizing my condition he is disgusted and says what will we do, who will help out in the store and the baby will drive customers away with its wailing? We live in the rear of the store. He says if he gets someone in the store he will leave on a trip. Can you imagine how I feel? Did you ever have a million pound weight on your heart? I hope not. Please advise me. I must die or the child. I can never stand three years or even months of the former agony.

Sixteen

I was married at seventeen to a man six years my senior. He is part German and all I have ever known seem to think that women are to rise early and work late and satisfy their brutal passions. The first winter I was married I had a three months' miscarriage. The doctor said I lifted something heavy. In one year I had a baby girl. When she was seven months I had an attack of appendicitis. When she was thirteen months old I was three months pregnant again. I had an operation for appendicitis. When my next baby boy came I had to get up and do the cooking and housework and take care of those two babies, when he was only twelve days old. In two years I had another boy, besides those three babies I had my invalid father-in-law to care for, besides my house work and a cow. In two and a half years a beautiful baby girl came to our home.

I decided that for poor people that if it was in my

power to stop the baby business I had better get busy. When the baby was three years old I had the same over again, but I had the flu real bad and miscarried at three months. In six months the same old story. I was six months and was hardly able to creep around and I was taken quite ill and the water broke and I had to go to the hospital and the baby taken. I was sick and had temperature every day for about five months after that, and sometimes would go all day with only a few drinks of water. When before I was strong the same old story over again, and in desperation I went to an old nurse and she caused an abortion. I had blood poison also and it took three doctors to save my life. That was last October and now it is the same old story again. I am a nervous wreck and I feel that now at thirty-one years of age I have had more than my share of babies. I didn't know what it was to be sick until I started this baby career.

It wouldn't be so hard if my husband was kind and sympathetic, but he thinks it all foolishness to be nervous and cross and will say the hardest things to me. If the house isn't spick and span and meals on the table when he gets home he says I am lazy. No matter how bad I feel before confinement or how soon after that his passion is aroused I have to submit to him. I am so sick from the first six weeks and sometimes until almost time for the baby to come. I never have any help and when the baby is three weeks old I have to do the work. I hope and trust that God will not judge me wrong, but I feel like I would rather die if it were not for my four babies.

Seventeen

I have six children, am forty-one years old, have very poor health, have reason to believe my husband has a venereal disease. He forces me to have intercourse whenever he wishes and will use no contraceptive measures, and I must have help. When I menstruate I remain in that condition for two weeks at a time, then I have relief for one week and then start all over again. You can readily see what danger I am constantly in of becoming pregnant again. I am in no shape physically to take care of the children I already have, not to mention any more.

To all of my pleadings my husband turns a deaf ear. He beats me, curses me and deserts us for weeks at a time when I refuse intercourse. I have begged him to provide himself with such protective measures as are available for men but he will not listen. He does not support us in a half-decent fashion and I do not feel that bringing more children into the world to suffer such poverty is right at all. The place we call home is only a hovel—not nearly as comfortable as most barns—bare floors, no furniture, cold and cheerless. Won't you advise me what to do and do so quickly? My husband has left me again, all for the stand I have taken, and we are destitute. I must live with him to get his support until my youngest children are older (youngest is eighteen months, oldest fifteen years), but to live with him I must indulge him sexually and whatever protection I get I must provide myself.

Eighteen

My husband drinks heavily and does not provide for himself and two little boys which are two and four years old and are very puny children. I lost my baby which was very delicate, but if she could have had proper attention and nourishment she might have lived. I hoped at first the good Lord had taken her to make her father see what a life he was living and causing his family to live, but he didn't change. So I try not to grieve after her for I know .how she would have suffered for necessities had she lived. I live in constant dread of getting pregnant again for my husband is unspeakably cruel when I am pregnant. I have so many heartbreaking trials to go through during the nine months that my babies are nervous weaklings when they arrive. So I am begging you for advice to keep me from bringing any more babies into poverty.

Nineteen

I am a woman thirty years old and have five children, have had six but one dead, oldest one twelve years old. My husband is a drinking man, gets drunk every week, and when he is that way he drives me outdoors. When he finds me in a delicate state he stays away from home two or three days at a time leaving us with no fire, no money and even food each time. When he stops I think he is going to do better but only gets worse. I am thinking of leaving him but what will become of my three little girls? When he comes home after being away he threatens

my life with a revolver, shoots through the house. Three
of my children are ruptured. He don't seem to care. He
only gets better when he knows my troubles are over. I
have just had a miscarriage which I caused myself and
I've been very sick but getting along nice now. I had to
do this as I owe doctor bills from all my children, only
pay some and leave some. So while I am all right now, is
there anything in this world I can do to keep from having any more?

Twenty

I have two children: one seven and the other, a boy,
will be a year next month. The first one is a girl. I have
had two miscarriages and I have been ailing for four
months but the physicians say I'm not pregnant. It was
either from cold and exposure just before my time for
menstruation and I was nursing the baby and gave that up
right away and started to fill myself with "poison drugs,"
not to please myself, but to please my husband, as he
says he'll not have any more children in the family. He
has all he can support. Well I've done something. I
menstruate all right but not natural and I do not feel
good and just feel like doing something desperate at
times. When my first child was born I asked the physician
what to do and he did not want to talk about it. Everyone else I asked just said what helps one won't help
another, try something and if it is O.K. use that. My
mother is insane, has been for twenty-three years and I
know that ignorance of sex problems was the cause. I was
seven years old when she was taken away.

My father was a "crab," plainly speaking, just like my man and there was no living with him, not even we two sisters could live with him. We had to leave him alone and go and board. I expect you have heard so many tales of woe you are tired of hearing them but I wanted to make it plain to you. My life, as young as I am, is not all peaches and cream.

Twenty-one

I married young and had children very fast till I had five and had to take in washings and any kind of work I could do at home to get along, putting my children to bed hungry at times. My husband was taken up for murder once, but got out. After that he stole an automobile and some brass, and then for murder again, and went to prison for life, leaving me with five children and not five cents in money.

I had to put my children out and work and try to help keep them. Then I met a man whom I loved and he begged me to marry and bring my children home.

In about a year I was to become a mother for this man, but at two-and-a-half months I miscarried and almost died. It was not long till I was in the same shape again and I miscarried, taking me to the hospital, where both nurses and doctor said they didn't think I would live.

I am in bed right now with a miscarriage. I bought one of your books some time ago and I and my husband both have been reading it and he begs me to write and see what you can do for us. We just rent, and me being sick so much is sure bad, so if there is anything you can do, for God's sake try and let me know what it is. I would sooner die than to go through this kind of life.

Twenty-two

Yours is a wonderful work. I have thought for several years that a woman has almost ceased to be a woman but a brood sow or something of the kind, with the difference that the animals are given more care and consideration than we get.

My husband has told me often that the sooner I am worn out, the sooner he will get to *break in another*. I have been married six years, and am the mother of four children.

At twenty-three I was a big fat healthy jolly girl. At thirty I am an irritable, nervous, rundown, diseased skeleton. Have never known a well day since my first confinement. Then I was torn nearly to pieces both inside and out. The after-birth was grown to the womb, and it in turn was fast to my side. When the birth was accomplished the womb was turned inside out and pulled almost entirely out of me. Since, I have always had to wear a tight muslin bandage around my abdomen, and during preganacy, use it as a sort of sling in which to carry the child. I never get through confinement with less than seven days of hard labor (once eight), and then it is a case of instruments. Pregnancy for me spells nine months of sickness and suffering untold. And on top of that I have to endure the abuse of a selfish cruel husband, so you maybe can imagine what an enviable shape I am in. When I ask to be spared any more children, my husband tells me if he can't be gratified at home he will go else-where. And he would. Even if my body stood another confinement I don't think any mind or reason would for I go nearly crazy with suffering at times. Anyway it has come to this, that I will not under the present existing conditions.

As a last resort there is suicide and that is no worse than bringing puny, delicate children like these of mine into these surroundings. I can not afford to have proper medical attention myself. And no one can expect me to have healthy children in the condition I am in. So much sex indulgence is not only distasteful but painful and I often sit sewing half the night to escape it. But that is terribly hard on me, for I am so weak. I hadn't ought to be doing my housework, but I have to.

Twenty-three

I have had two children, and two miscarriages within the last three months so will you please advise me so I do not get that way again as my husband is very mean to me and thinks if I am pregnant I will not leave him. But I cannot live with him much longer, so to keep myself out of trouble is the only way of getting away from him as I cannot stand to bear any more for him.

Twenty-four

I am the mother of four babies, two dead and two living twins. Lost my two first ones. My babies are only seven months old. Please tell me something that will help me to free myself. I'll say any mother that has had such a time as I did with my last babies, they would cry and beg for help.

For three months I almost walked the floor continually crying. I would catch the top of the door and pull to try to give more room to get a little relief. I was carrying my baby standing up, I would wake myself up crying and my husband of choice would quarrel and tell me to shut my mouth and go to sleep. He would say nobody on the place could sleep for me. Nobody knows except me just what I went through with nobody not even to give me a kind word and say face it. I'd rather be dead than face it again. Some girls will say I would quit him but how could I when I have two little babies and no home. Who would want me? Nobody. Please help me.

Twenty-five

I am twenty-eight years old and the mother-to-be very soon of a sixth child. I am a farmer's wife. My husband is a drunkard and so very abusive. He tries to kill me and beats at my door. I have to hide the butcher- and paring knives and the guns. He calls me the vilest things a woman can be called before my children and threatens my aged parents and I don't dare tell the neighbors. They respect him. He don't say anything before them.

I have so much work to do. I raise garden enough for seven or eight people to eat all summer. I canned six hundred quarts of fruits last summer. Always do. I have to raise enough chickens to eat, some to sell and enough to supply our family in eggs and help keep up the table. I do all our washing for our family and I have been injured when my first baby was born until I can hardly stand on my feet and no one knows what I suffer. We owe 114 acres of well improved corn-belt land. I have it thrown in my face how dishonest I am, and what a liar I am. He never trusts me an inch and will ask the neighbors and children questions—to see if I am lying.

He calls me a liar and thief and other names fifty times a day. He says I am no wife if I don't like the way he does, how can I help myself, and a thousand other things. I can't please him no way, shape or manner. My baby will be born the last of April. I don't want it.

Twenty-six

I was only a girl of eighteen years when I married. I have three children and married only four years. I am awfully worried about my periods, because my husband cannot support them. He works, but spends it all in drink and cards, and when I tell him I must have some money he beats me and tells me to get out of the house. I would go only I wouldn't leave my children behind or if the baby was only old enough and could walk I would go but before I can raise them to come to that point I find myself in that condition again. Really I would rather die than have any more children because I have a hard time to have them and then my husband is a drunkard and a brute.

Twenty-seven

I have two babies and suffered terribly in each pregnancy. After the last baby came my husband and I were never happy, as I was afraid to kiss him or go near him for I knew what it meant. That made things worse. He said I was cold like an icebox. He might as well not have a wife, and we almost parted. Finally there was a lady who told me of a douche that helped me a little, but that wouldn't work always. If I didn't come around I'd nearly go wild, so I take pills till they almost kill me, and I know in time it will kill me, for they upset my stomach. So please help me and tell me what I could do so that I can fulfil my husband's wishes and as soon as I get stronger and able to take care of a child, I will have it as I like them, but not when I'm not able to take care of them. If they cry, husband would say take that kid in the next room, how do you expect me to sleep. So you see how happy we were. It seems I could almost write a book of myself, you will get tired reading. But you are the first person that I could tell my troubles to and this is not half. How many times I thought, "Why is it the woman must go through so much and have a child against her wishes?"

Twenty-eight

My dear friend could you please help me out some way that I would not have no more children. If you won't help me then I *will take poison or kill myself* before I would have another child. I was married when I was fifteen years old. I had to get married for my father was a great drunkard and he hated me and would chase me away from home when he got drunk. So that is why I got married so young, but my husband is ten times worse. I have two children in four years. The boy is nineteen months old and the baby girl is two months old. When my husband gets drunk he beats me and the little boy, so why should we have any more children when these two children have a mean father. But if we would have more children he would be still worser, mean and still I am always sick. But my husband always tells me that I am lazy to work but not sick.

Twenty-nine

I was married when I was twenty and the picture of health. We were married eleven months when I had had a horrible time. They called a miscarriage. And the doctor told me to be careful for I could never give birth to a living child. About six months after I was caught again and had a little boy who was healthy looking but was so weak that when sitting on the floor at the age of two years could not get up unless someone would help him and he only lived to be two and a half years old and then I had another child, a girl who now is ten years old but was sick all of her life with epilepsy and I have another boy that is seven, only these two are living and I am in constant fear of bringing more unhealthy children into this world. I have to plead with my husband every time to please be careful but he said if he had known that that was all married life would mean he would have never married. To think he had to *support a wife and kids and not even have it as he liked.* I have bad health and my leg is a torture to me. Now after I've been married thirteen years had only three living children and three miscarriages.

290

Can't take care of the two as they should be because we spend all the money for doctor bills on confinement cases and for the afflicted girl.

Thirty

I am only twenty-two years old and the mother of five children and I have brought one child into this world each year since I have been married. You can't imagine how I feel. I am never rested and each day my health seems to fail me more. My youngest baby is now four months and I have decided to write you and see if you can give me some good advice so I may rest for a few years anyhow as I think it is cruel to bring so many innocent children into this world to suffer and especially when we are poor folks working hard for a living. My husband isn't any too good to me. He seems to love me but yet he treats me mean and I cannot understand him as I try to do my best. My husband is eighteen years older than myself.

Thirty-one

I am twenty-three years old and have had five children already. One boy died and I have three boys and one girl living. The oldest boy is seven years old and the youngest is six months. I want you to give me advice to prevent from having many children. I have a very hard time with my babies. When the last boy was almost born I was with pains for a month before he was born. When the child came out I was very tired and can hardly stand up. My children came too close together and they are very naugnty and I cannot do my job. I always worry and cry. They always want to be on my lap when I sleep in the night, the next morning I can hardly stand for my body with pains. My husband is working in the mill and do not win enough money to support the family and it cost high for living here. He is always drinking and drunk most the time and I am always worrying. Sometimes he slaps me when I tried to advise him. He is a bad tempered man and always had cough. Many things I want but cannot afford to buy them for we don't have money and the things are of high price.

Thirty-two

I am thirty-eight years old and have brought nine children into the world, one of which died in infancy. The babies were all close together. Also have had two miscarriages. I have tried sleeping apart from my husband but he insists upon his sexual satisfaction so does not help a great deal. We are poor and my husband takes most of the money for his comforts and needs and I and the family have to go without.

XIII

Methods that Fail

THE present revelations throw light on the chaotic conditions in which the intricate problem of conception and contraception lies buried. The whole subject is a battle-ground of mutually conflicting ideas and practices. This phase of life, of the utmost importance to the well-being of the race no less than to that of the individual, has, according to the testimony here presented, been left to chance and the clumsy devices of unguided experience

The inherited prejudice of centuries transmits from one generation to the next a vague idea that contraception is a sin. The harsh realities of life relentlessly challenge this inherited idea. Upon the consciousness of the individual they press the imperative necessity of conscious control in any successful struggle for existence or for happiness.

This primary conflict is fought out not merely in the lives so graphically depicted in the present material, but among scientists, legislators, and moralists. If the leaders of civilization have failed to reach any ground of common agreement, need we be surprised that this disagreement is reflected in the unrecorded tragedies of thousands of lives?

While theologians, moralists, legislators and jurists have been splitting theoretical hairs, and medical science has remained content to stand aloof from the problem of contraception, necessity has compelled men and women —and in the vast majority of cases women without the aid of men—to seek such fragmentary knowledge of Birth Control as may be available to them.

The present testimony indicates first of all a naïve recourse to the advice of neighbors. This whispered— or often withheld—neighborhood gossip might well be dismissed along with "old wives' tales." In efficacy it is on a par with all accumulated masses of folk-lore and "household remedies." Time after time the appellant records the failure of neighbors' advice, to forestall an undesired pregnancy. Usually it consists of vague counsel concerning the so-called "safe period," or the lengthy and indefinitely prolonged nursing of the already existing infant at the breast—during which time, legend says, pregnancy cannot take place. No causal connection between such preventives and the act of conception has ever been scientifically established. Suppression of the orgasm on the woman's part is another widely prevalent idea. But this too is usually found to lack efficacy.

When advice is obtained from the local physician, it is likewise of so rudimentary a character that it proves to be scarcely more effectual—if at all—than the methods obtained from neighbors or friends. Nor can we avoid the lamentable fact that there are numbers of quacks and charlatans who profit by the credulity and ignorance of thousands of harassed mothers.

When mechanical contrivances are resorted to, they are

used with no apparent recognition of the necessity of individual adjustment or the physiological peculiarities of the special case.

The methods used by the male are often uncertain and usually unsatisfactory. In the majority of cases, they are to be condemned because they prevent the satisfactory fulfillment of the act of physical communion, and produce a nervous reaction fatal to the well-being of both participants.

One conclusion from an examination of these cases concening methods that fail seem inevitable. That is, the necessity for the development and standardization of a sound scientific body of knowledge that may be taught to all parents and parents-to-be. Toward this development and standardization certain steps are necessary:

1. Removal of the obstacles of prejudice and ignorance on the part of the public, the press, and the churches.

2. Repeal of obsolete and unjust statutes which are responsible for the present chaos and conflict in public opinion, and hinder the distribution and dissemination of education in sexual hygiene.

3. Establishment of clinics for the free education of adults in the technique of parenthood—in conception as well as contraception, so that wilful ignorance can no longer be offered as an excuse for destitution or race-deterioration.

One

It seems I can find nothing to help me from falling pregnant. I am married ten years on the tenth of this month and I have five children, the oldest nine and the youngest fourteen months. It seems it doesn't do me any good to do as I have heard from my neighbors. I try to do as they do, but without avail, it seems. My husband is just a laborer but he makes good when he is working. But it seems it takes all he makes to keep us and when he happens to get out of work it is very hard on us. I have to do all my own work and have to sew a great deal. Many a time I have to take in sewing to help along. I am not able to do it, as I am always in such poor health for so long after I have been confined. I have had a false conception with my first baby and had to have it taken away without giving me anything to put me to sleep. With my fourth I lay between life and death for four weeks as I had uremic poisoning. At the end of that four weeks I had to get out of bed and crawl downstairs on my hands and knees and make the oldest child, not six years old, slide down with the baby, as we could not afford a woman any longer. So you can see I have suffered my share. Please for my sake and my children's, help me find something to keep me from falling that way again.

Two

I am thirty-three years old and have had six children, four of which are living. I was married before I was sixteen and it just seems I have had nothing but children, sickness and death ever since, but I feel that maybe the future may be brighter. I am not very well myself now. I have been taking treatment for over eight months now for inflammation of womb and see a slight improvement. I am just worried sick every month for fear of getting pregnant again.

I have asked doctor to tell me something but he always tells me there is nothing entirely reliable, and that is all the answer I receive.

My husband is so good and kind to me and would do most anything to keep me from becoming pregnant but he is human and so good to me I like to do the best I can for him. We are buying a home now in a neighborhood where the children are pretty well grown up. My baby who is four years old is the youngest. When I asked one woman what she did she replied she had a good recipé but *didn't intend to tell* anyone else except her daughter.

Three

I must come to you with my troubles. I have just been married six years. Will soon have had four children as I expect the last in June. None of my little girls are two years apart. With my fourth one which I now carry, it just seems like I haven't any strength left and am a sick woman all the time and I just cry and wonder each day will I live through it this time. Each time one has been born I've just prayed it would be the last one but just as soon as each one of them is not a year old I am pregnant again. I bought something from a lady but that done me no good. I got that way just the same. So another lady told me about a thing for men. But that failed and I got that way again which I could hardly believe how I did, no matter how careful we try to be, I get pregnant anyway.

Three ladies live right by me, two of them has each one boy, one eight and one seven, and the other one has no children at all. Still they must know something. But they won't tell me. Just sit at home and laugh each time I get that way. Now the two won't even speak to me when they see I am pregnant again.

It hurts me so I just cry and wish I wasn't here at times, but it is just for my little girls I look back to and know not what they would do without their mamma, or I believe I could take something so I could die and leave all the suffering I've went through.

I know when I get through this and get well again it will be the same old story. Then I will choose death before ever I go through it again.

Four

I had thought from my reading in magazines, etc., that after marriage the direct information necessary to prevent too large a family would become mine "on demand." But to my amazement others older and supposedly wiser seem as ignorant as I. I was nearly twenty-five when we married and had I realized this condition I should have remained single a while longer. I was never very strong, and now as the mother of three children I feel my little strength slowly going and know that the demands of motherhood is the cause.

Already our doctor has warned me to take care of my

health. Heart weak, liable to lung trouble. Since we lost our second child I would not object to one other but I would like better to be able to choose when.

After marriage I lived in the country on a farm and since I was from town *many neighbors thought I knew and appealed* to me. It was almost with tears I had to refuse to aid the poor creatures who seemed to think I knew because I was from town. Oh, you indeed know their despair! I too have seen it. A woman, the mother of nine children, appealed to me, but I was powerless to aid her.

Five

I am a woman forty-four years of age and have five daughters, the oldest twenty-three and the youngest two years. I was just getting to the place where I could go out and be a companion to my girls, the youngest being eleven years when this babe arrived. The only thing I ever did to prevent children was to *watch my time*. I feel if I have another it will be a tragedy and am seeking a safe and sane way to prevent it.

Six

I am the mother of five children, one dead, four living, of whom the oldest is nine and the youngest eighteen months. Am expecting another within two months. When my last child was born I said I'd rather die than go through another childbirth, and yet I can't do it, as my children would suffer more without a mother.

My heart just aches to think I must give life to an unwelcome child. How I kept away from my husband to avoid having any more! He even said my own brother was my sweetheart and said he would support his children, but he did not have to support me; all this I had to endure because I did not want him near me. I took the advice of a nurse not to have anything to do ten days before and three days after menstruation and yet why, oh why! must I be this way? I tried something that the midwife gave me which was no good. To go through an abortion I would not do, as a friend of mine tried and she almost went insane, six weeks she could not sleep, and after that she was pale and sickly looking.

Seven

Seven years ago I married, and in ignorance have brought into the world four children. I am thankful they are all strong and well, but I am not, and my recovery from this last childbirth is very slow. If I can regain and keep my health, we shall be a very happy family. My husband and I both desire to have this knowledge, that we may live in happiness and without fear. He is a strong vigorous man of thirty-three and continence is impracticable in his case. He has been very considerate, but I am one of those women who have *no safe period* and the simple contraptions I have used have all failed.

We planned for this family of four, and have been given two boys and two girls, but being so near of an age they are a great care, and as our means are limited, we shall have to put forth every effort to care for the family we have now.

Eight

I am thirty-one years of age, mother of five, and I am not sure, maybe the story will be six later. I have the best husband in the world and I truly love my precious boys but we are trying hard to care for them properly and buy our home too. It is indeed a struggle. I have to work very hard, do all my own work, sewing too, even to the coats, knickers, overcoats, etc. It seems my heart will break with the burden if I have to have another—much as I love them—because they are a part of "him" and I have no fault to find with him as he is so kind and considerate always.

I have tried many things. Doctor says wait eight days —imagine that helping!—I was mad. Why is it so terrible to tell of a contraceptive when most doctors will perform criminal operations or give something to bring the period? Can it be the penalty for giving the Birth Control knowledge is greater than for murder of an unborn babe? I don't know but I'll never commit murder. Can you and will you help me?

Nine

We have been married nearly two years and already have two children. We didn't want them. We had intended to have children later on when we could better afford to have them. After our first girl was born she weighed only three pounds. I was doing most of my work again when she was eight days old and I nursed her till she was five months old though she wasn't gaining and it didn't agree with her at all, only hoping that by nursing her I wouldn't have another, but when she was five months old I found that I was again to become a mother. Now we have another that weighed six pounds and is now seven weeks old and ever since it's birth I have lived in fear and terror that I would again become pregnant.

Ten

I am of the same opinion as you. I say women are so ignorant of things they should know, but as they are unable to obtain the right information from the right place and the law so one-sided, we can but live in hopes you will be able with our united help to let the suffering world know what they should. This is what I would like to know, as a mother of five children, and a laboring man for a husband, age fifty years this coming birthday. Isn't this a large enough family for any working man? Is it possible there are any real sure-enough things women can do to keep from having children when they have enough, that is, without injury to themselves? I have tried dozens of preventives my neighbors advised only to find myself pregnant again. I live in perfect dread from month to month. I will say *I have a perfect control of myself,* but is that enough? I learned that of an old nurse after she had twelve of her own and a none too particular husband.

Eleven

I was married when I was seventeen and became the mother of a ten pound boy when I was eighteen. I was constantly ill during pregnancy and when my boy was born I was very sick for a long period and was badly torn.

After his birth my husband insisted upon resuming sexual relations immediately. I succeeded in keeping him from me for a little over three weeks. The first month after childbirth I was again pregnant although I was so weak I was hardly able to be around and had all my housework to do also the washing as we lived in the country where there were no conveniences. I then resorted to abortion which left me weaker still.

After that I refrained from all sexual feeling and succeeded in keeping from becoming pregnant except once when I carried it for a couple of months and lost it, being so weak. A year ago my husband left home and left me with a great many bills to pay. No one knows where he is and although they have taken all the stock and things I had worked so hard to help earn, I still have nearly $200.00 to pay on bills.

I was granted a legal separation some time ago and have met a man whom I care very much for and whom I am to marry very soon. I have been working for him for about six months and he is ready to assume my responsibilities. But I would like to be assured that my sexual feeling for this man would not be killed as it was before by fear of too frequent pregnancy when not in proper health.

Twelve

I am a minister's wife with two babies, one ten months and the other twenty-three months and have just gotten out of the hospital where I underwent an appendicitis operation. What I want to know is what I am to do to keep from having another child for at least two or three more years. My whole physical condition has been at a low ebb for six months or more. I have had gall-bladder trouble too, but my nerves were so bad the doctor would not make the major operation now. We are poor and not able to keep help either, only have part of my washing done.

My husband is trying to rise and I know I am a hindrance to him. I am cold to him because I fear another child if I warm up to him and even love him. He loves me now I know but he says it is hard to be loving to an icebox and I know we are growing apart and it makes my heart bleed. I fear for our home. My husband goes a great deal and wants me to go too, therefore I don't see how I could halfway care for another baby even if I were physically fit to bring one into this world.

Thirteen

Can't you help me for I am near out of my mind. Here I am at the age of forty the mother of ten children all living, oldest is twenty-one years, baby ten months old and just had a miscarriage. My health is all gone. My baby is a very sick baby, have to walk the floor at night.

I wouldn't mind it if I had strength or health but neither. So I go to my doctor for baby and self and I asked him to please tell me what to do so I won't have any more children. He says "Take care, you won't have any more." Thank God I had a miscarriage now. Having so large a family and no health is awful hard for me.

Fourteen

I have devoured "Woman and the New Race" greedily, and the thought that comes to me is "is she like all the rest, if she gives any information at all, will it be so veiled in medical terms or high-flown language that only a medical student or college-bred person would understand and in the end it would mean 'use a warm water douche and be careful' and send a bill for $10.00?"

Forgive me if I am skeptical. I gave a doctor $150.00 for a package of dope and in less than six months I was pregnant. Do you wonder that I am skeptical and discouraged?

I am twenty-seven years old and my husband twenty-nine. We have been married seven years. My boy was born eleven months after we were married,—another boy eighteen months after that, but only lived five hours; between that and the little girl (now almost two years old) were four miscarriages, one at five months and if I mistake not, there will be another!

My husband is a prince among men; he does things very hard for him to try to save me all this, but it is no use. I am not strong, never was. It seems sometimes I shall certainly lose my reason. If it continues it would be easier for me to leave this world except for the thought that I am sorely needed. I would rather die than bring another little one into the world to be half taken care of, for I know that I will not live another seven years if the past seven are an example of my life for the future.

Fifteen

I have told you things that I have never breathed to any human before, and if you do not tell me what to do, it is really a crime to withhold this knowledge from a woman, and if ever a woman begged for knowledge it is certainly I.

My mother had only two children, myself and a sister younger. Whether there would have been more I do not know, for she didn't believe in telling these things and don't to this day, so we were brought in absolute ignorance of such matters, and that it was an unpardonable sin to be caught talking or even thinking about such things, and now I and my sister, who is less fortunate than I, are paying the price.

Sixteen

I have three children, the last one four and half months. It was nearly a case of losing mother or child. I had an abscess on my breast and had it operated on, money for doctors and a nurse for ten weeks has left us hundreds of dollars in the hole. I feel at times I'd rather die than have any more, but what would the babies I now have do without a mother. I am twenty-seven, five feet three inches tall, and only weigh ninety-seven pounds, and am always in very poor health.

My husband and I fear so that I might have more that he seldom touches me, and then he uses his own method and that I know from his poor health lately is running him down, and it is not natural for either of us. It is making us very unhappy, we generally quarrel often and I cry constantly always wondering how I can satisfy my husband's passion and yet not have any more little ones. We love our babies dearly and want to do for them, but with my poor health, we do not feel we should have any more. Is there any way you could help me?—by this I of course would not want you and I to get into trouble or go against the laws of the United States at least write to me some words of encouragement.

Seventeen

I have five children and have had three miscarriages. I am thirty-four years old. I have tried every thing any one has told me but to no avail. My husband drank for ten years of our married life, but is not drinking now. Since the birth of my last baby, which is twenty-one months old I have not worried quite so much for I had coaxed him into using certain precautions but now he has given me to understand if he cannot get complete satisfaction at home he will not bother me but will go somewhere else.

The tragedy of this would be if he did this it would break my heart completely for through all the suffering I have had to endure I still love him. Again common sense tells one it would cost money and he does not earn enough now to properly provide for the family needs. I am fearful every moment for fear the inevitable happens and I again find myself either deserted or in the family way. I am not asking you as a woman would ask a physician but as a woman asking a woman who knows how to help. I know God will bless you greatly for your love for women in helping them through the vision He has given you. You will pardon me I know for speaking so frankly but it seems I have known you a lifetime and I am in a terrible place and need a friend.

Eighteen

I am writing in the interest of my two daughters. I would like to save them the sorrow I have experienced of a broken home and I think one cause was we tried to keep from having so many children by practicing what was not very pleasant or satisfactory for either and then had five children, and I think he has gone to other women always for full satisfaction. Three years ago at the age of forty-four he got in with one thirty years old, good looking and slick and she has stayed after him until she caused him to waste not only what we had accumulated but most of my inheritance as well.

Both of my daughters are married and I think the oldest one and her husband are trying the same thing we did though with no more success, since their fourth baby was born before the first one was old enough to go to school. The other girl has two and will have the third in May and the oldest three and a half years old. Her husband is a mechanic and can't make enough to keep them going now, so I wish for their sakes you would write and tell me what to do.

Nineteen

I am twenty-five and my husband twenty-three. We have been married not three years yet. The first year I had a miscarriage which lasted for about a month and which made me an invalid for about six months. Again last year I had another from the effects of which I have not yet recovered. The strain endured at these two times brought on a case of leaky valves of the heart in a serious way. Up to that time it had not been serious. Even now to go upstairs or a sudden fright affects me seriously. However, the doctor informed me that with good care I might lessen the danger. So you can imagine how I should hate to become pregnant again.

My husband says that if I do not want intercourse with him however, he will go where he can get it and I should break my heart if he did that. He doesn't realize my feelings in the case altho he is so good to me otherwise. . . . I had often wondered if there was any certain safe way and am so glad to hear there is. Please will you let me know what they are? You would relieve my mind of so much worry for worrying can't be helped every month. If I could only be sure of not being pregnant while I am in this state. I know that were I stronger I should want to have it so but I worry all month for fear I am pregnant and am also making my husband dislike me for the same reason. Please let me know what the contraceptives are and I will do all I can to help you. I could help so many of my friends also.

Twenty

I have been married fifteen years and I am thirty-six years old. I was married at twenty-one and at twenty-five I had three children, seven years after I had another which is now five years old. We have managed Birth Control from the third to fourth child and from the fourth until now because my husband uses . . . but as we already have more than we can support and educate properly I would like to know something that would help us with a surer Birth Control. My husband is the only one working to support the four children and myself and like all other people we try to give our four girls all that is possible for their education, as they are getting older it takes more money every year and I have had to work in the mill to help. Now that I have one fourteen years old I would like to stay home with my children. As I am only thirty-six years old chances are that I could have more children.

Twenty-one

I am coming to you as a friend and am going to tell you some facts I would not trust to tell my best friends. I am a married woman. Will be twenty-five years old in February. I was married when I was nineteen. I was married just thirteen months when my little girl was born. I was very proud and glad because of pregnancy. I did not want to have any more right away so heard about the man's protection which we tried. When my little girl was twenty-two months old I gave birth to a boy, so you see that did not help. I think I have just the right size family for me to take care of now.

We live on a small ranch, own some cattle and horses. If I can only keep from having any more children for about five or six years we could be out of debt and easily afford more babies which I would not hesitate to have. A friend of mine told me of a doctor that would give me a dangerous gold internal appliance which was a sure preventive, and it cost me $10.00. After I had used it about 3 months I had a hemorrhage caused from it. Well, I feel it my duty to tell you the truth to obtain help. After trying this three months I missed one month, became pregnant. I consulted this same doctor. He brought on a hemorrhage. I had another doctor. They took me to the hospital and scraped my womb. Well, since that time I had a three months' miscarriage. My family doctor told me not to become pregnant again until at least one year. I asked him what to do. He advised separate beds. Now I certainly do not approve of that, because denying men their sexual desires is what causes them to run after other women. Isn't that right? Then other doctors have told me I couldn't do anything to prevent childbirth as the neck of my womb was torn a little at the birth of my first child.

Twenty-two

I have had six children, only five living. My oldest child would be twelve years old if she was living. She died at the age of twenty-one months now I have two girls and three boys, all two years apart, not so bad as some poor women that have one every year. Yet I am not strong and with my last baby the doctor wanted me to go through an operation so I would not get any more children. I was ready to go when I was in bed with my baby but after I got up and around I saw I just couldn't make up my mind to go for I just love babies and the thought of not having any more, I just couldn't go. Yet I knew in my heart how I have to suffer to have a baby but oh, if I could just have a couple more years of rest! If you could only tell me what to do. I avoid my husband whenever I can, but any married woman understands a man. My sister is thirty-nine years old and single. Often tells me let well enough alone. I am thirty-two years old and married thirteen years now.

Twenty-three

I am thirty-six years of age, am the mother of seven babies. One came at seven months, the other three had to be delivered, the fifth I carried six months dead, had to undergo an operation, then one came to time, lived. And in March of this year I had to be conveyed to a sanitarium, lay on operation table three hours and forty-five minutes and had seventh one delivered dead. It weighed sixteen pounds, measured twenty-three inches. Now the doctors will say you can't live over another one and I feel that way as I am suffering from Bright's disease and have tumor. I just live in constant dread of becoming pregnant again and sometimes I think I will go crazy. I menstruate every two weeks and sometimes as long as five or six months at time. I don't feel like I will ever be well again as I haven't been able to do any work since last November. I am on diet. I have stated just part of my case to you and if there is any means of getting information to me please do send it and explain things. Doctors say for me to have an incision made and cords tied to stop breeding but I can't stand that.

Twenty-four

I am twenty-three years old. I have been married five years. I am the mother of three living children, the oldest four years old, and have had two miscarriages since the birth of my last child. The two miscarriages have been harder on my health than the first of two children would have been. I haven't, as yet, recovered from the last one. My doctor is one of the best surgeons here and has attended me in all of my illness since childhood, says I must submit to an operation as a means of preventing pregnancy or else lose my life in a few short years.

I am affected with anemia, my father having died with pernicious anemia, and I also have weak lungs. In fact there is no organ in my body that isn't weakened. I have asked my physician repeatedly for information concerning a means of preventing pregnancy but he absolutely refuses to help except to operate.

I would so love to live and raise the three babies I have. In my present state of health I doubt very much if I would survive an operation besides at my age, only twenty-three, I do so hate to submit to one. Surely there is help for me. Could you, will you send me information concerning a means of Birth Control. Is there anything you could tell me, or send me, or that you could tell me to get?

Twenty-five

I am coming to you because I have nobody else in the world to go to. I have been married nine years and have four children, all very healthy and whom I worship, and two abortions which I never quite got over and I fear I am pregnant again. I have tried all of my married life to find a sure preventive but could never get nowhere. It seemed as though I couldn't take a long breath without becoming pregnant which was ruining my health as well as my home because my husband never wanted a family and could never understand why I could not keep from having them, not realizing I was as ignorant of sex and my body when I married as my little eight year old daughter is now. I thought at times I would lose my mind as I worshipped my husband and children both and it was maddening to have such a discontent in my home when all the time I was eating my heart out for happiness also.

I thought I knew a safe method of Birth Control but four months ago for some cruel reason I found myself pregnant again with my fifth child. When I tell you my home is ruined I put it mildly. My husband puts the blame entirely upon me and has given up all interest in life caring for nothing, taking no interest in the children, almost ignoring me and staying away from home a great deal. It is driving me crazy because I so wanted a happy home and to raise my children up right but how can I with such prevailing conditions. I do not tell you this to degrade my husband because he is a very good man and wants the children that he has to be well provided for, but I do it just to show you what a problem I have. What am I to do after this one? I feel as though now there is nothing that would be sure for me.

I have thought very seriously lately and I am willing to be operated on so that I can't have any more because I refuse to submit to abortion any more and I know if I keep on having them it would be better that I should die. I don't want my ovaries taken but if that is the last resort I will. Couldn't I be sterilized and what is the process of the operation? Will you please give me your honest opinion as I must do something for the safety of the family I have and as I said before I have no one else in this world to go to. I haven't told you that my husband and I are both just twenty-seven years old so you see we are so young yet. May I add that we are $10,000 in debt and only renters and struggling so hard to get out and give our family a decent standing so you understand we have a real problem and to succeed we must have content and happiness.

Twenty-six

Being that you understand these things I wish to ask your advice. I'm a woman of twenty-five years of age. Have been married for six months. On account of a broken leg I couldn't go thru my first motherhood so I consulted a doctor. He took down all my ailments which consists of the after-effects of scarlet fever. I have a still knee which was caused from operations and the disfiguring of the kneecap. Then I have a spell which causes me to sleep more than normal, that is I have to. All this is caused from the scarlet fever, thirteen years ago.

When I got through telling the doctor all this he sentenced me to be sterilized. Being a poor girl and as I don't quite understand this sterilizing business, I went to another doctor who helped me out of the pregnancy. I also asked her what she thought of it and she had different ideas altogether.

Twenty-seven

I have read all your books which are very interesting so I am coming to you with a very important question hoping you will be able to answer me as I am pinning all my faith in your answer. This is my question: I have two children, one six years and one two and a half years, both girls. My husband or I do not care for more children as two is all we can take care of as they should be. Also if it is too late and it is born will it harm me if I go through an operation at the time of birth or after so as to become sterilized. I am only twenty-two years old. My husband is thirty-five years old and he does not want me to suffer and ruin my health by having children as I am sickly and nervous. My physician is willing to perform the operation but he advises me to think it over he says I am too young and that after the operation I will have no sexual desire and that I will be lazy also that I will become stupid and wouldn't care for anything. I think if I was sterilized I would be very happy and would have no cause for worry. My husband is also willing, but I want to know the truth about it first. I will close and wait your answer as soon as possible as all my happiness depends on your answer.

Twenty-eight

I am a married woman twenty-three years of age. Three years ago I was married and I now have a boy of fifteen months. I am not very strong and only weigh one hundred pounds. I am in constant fear of conception, not only because I am not strong but because I am still living with my parents and find it hard to save a little money to buy a home, so I can scarcely afford to raise any more children. My husband, who is very good to me, and I are very fond of children and wouldn't like to part with our little boy but we both realize we have our hands full at present to try to buy a home and give our baby the necessities of life on $27.00 a week.

I am the oldest of six children. My mother is a broken woman and a nervous wreck trying to keep a large family and doing all her duties. Twice she had miscarriages because she was too weak to carry her children.

She is a great advocate of Birth Control, but my father is not. I am sorry he couldn't be a woman. The worst part of my story I am about to tell you. I believe as you do. Why don't doctors give you a preventive for conception when they say to have a child would be a calamity, it would mean death? I have a sister who last month reached her nineteenth birthday. Since she was nine years old she has suffered from a bad heart contracted through diphtheria. Four months ago she married against our wishes. We have had specialists for her and they all say she has a leaking heart and it cannot be cured. Since she married her heart has become worse and the doctors told her not to become pregnant or it would surely kill her. None have told her how to prevent this though. Now we find that she is pregnant two months and is getting worse every day. Her doctor, a specialist in obstetrics, is at a loss what to do. He don't know whether to commit abortion or let her carry it as long as she can. He said he should catherize her and her heart can't stand it, but he thinks she will have to go to bed and stay until the baby is born, or until he will have to take it from her on account of her heart, as he thinks she can only go six or seven months at the most. Should she come all right he would remove those organs so she could not become pregnant any more.

Twenty-nine

I was told to write you for information for which I applied elsewhere. I have been married two years and have two children and am constantly in dread of there being another one as the methods of birth control I have been able to get have proven wholly inadequate. An uncle of mine died of epilepsy, as did also my sister. For this reason more than any other we don't want more children. Here is the information I want or rather the questions I want answered: Will a reputable surgeon perform a vasectomy operation? Or would he think one demented to volunteer for it? Or is it a fairly common operation?

I understand it is not a very serious operation, is it? What is the approximate cost? I know this letter reads as though I were ignorant of everything. Of puritanic parents, reared in a sparsely settled country, among reticent people, is it any wonder I don't know these things?

Thirty

Although I am the mother of nine children and a sufferer from epilepsy my doctors would not or could not give me a remedy for preventing pregnancy. I began these spells when I was pregnant with my first child and most always have from one to five of them every time I am pregnant and if it is in your power to give me a remedy I can depend on won't you please give it to me. My doctors had me use douche which I used until I saw it only helped me to get in the same condition again and at once as you will see when I tell you my oldest child is thirteen years old and youngest three months. I have tried every remedy I could possibly get but nothing has helped me one bit in my trouble. Now I am told there is no remedy that is safe only an operation for my husband which he is willing to undergo for my sake but I am now trying to find a safe remedy outside. Won't you please write me and tell me the safe preventive and where to get and how to use it for I am desperate. I live in constant dread all the time that some or all of my children will inherit my most dreadful disease and if it had been in my power to prevent I would never had but one. I am a farmer's wife and live in the country. Will be thirty-six years old and so I have a good many more years in which to bear children as my health is good, only for the fits I have which I have mostly when I am pregnant or just after child is born.

Thirty-one

I am a young mother, twenty-four in August, and by that time will be a mother of four children, my oldest only six. I have one of the best husbands in the world, he has always been so kind and thoughtful, and has done all he could to make me happy. We dearly love our children, but are poor working people and only get $50.00 a month. We want to limit our family because we cannot support very many, and it endangers my health. I only weigh one hundred and eight pounds, and have always suffered with female trouble. I went down into the Valley of Death at each birth, besides suffering untold agony for a month before and after birth. I have hemorrhages and am very weak. The doctor told us to be very careful for it would be only a matter of time for me. He didn't give us any advice other than there was a "safe" period. My husband was afraid of the advice, and did not touch me for a year, and you know too well that we were not happy and content as before, so at last we risked it. My monthly periods do not stop when my babies come, and I have to put them on a bottle in about six weeks. My periods come about every two weeks and am weak and sick for several days and have to go to bed. I have fainting spells at times. I have done everything anyone has told me to keep from being pregnant but everything has failed. I wouldn't want to live without children, but must not have any more and do justice to the babies I already have.

I believe you can give me some information to help me, and if you will I will fight for you to the end. You can't know how happy I would be to live and raise my four little bright faces, if I could only protect myself from becoming a "slave mother." I don't know anyone else to write to except you, and I hope I won't cause you any trouble.

XIV

Self-imposed Continence and Separation

IT has been a difficult task to limit the letters included in the present chapter. Almost innumerable apparently, are mothers and fathers who have deliberately chosen the path of self-denial rather than to bring unwelcome children into the world. Each of these letters, many written by men and women of the middle class, of superior education, contains a pathetic drama of married life. A hidden tragedy uncovered because life has been sacrificed and love denied.

Continence, unless I am misinformed, is the only form of Birth Control countenanced by the Church. In proffering this wholesale, though evasive, solution to human beings to whom the Christian faith promises "life more abundant," Catholicism joins hands with Puritanism. Both, apparently, close their eyes to the inevitable consequences of this precept. These consequences, as the following records indicate, are for the most part kept secret. They may be read easily enough, however, by any competent student of human nature. In the strained, dissatisfied expressions of the women who have been thus forced to curb their deepest impulses the secret is often exposed. One mother describes this inhumane régime as the "strenuous, heart-breaking, nerve-racking prohibition of love-life that we have been through. . . ." A young and loving husband of thirty-three attests to the disastrous mental and physical effects of his "intense desire always balked." Love cannot survive continuous denial. If it is to blossome into beauty and happiness, it must be nourished like all other living organisms.

Here we have records of the disastrous effects of self-imposed continence: the petty quarrels, the dissensions, gradually increasing and becoming more dangerous, establishing a breach which widens into estrangement. In certain cases, it is the wife who has imposed the armour of continence upon the husband. In others, it is the husband who, keenly cognizant of the impending dangers of possible pregnancy, makes the decision. In still other cases, husband and wife mutually agree to this abnormal mode of life.

Two consequences, both equally disastrous to happiness in marriage, are evident. Either there is a gradually drifting apart, and the separation becomes a permanent one; or an eventual surrender to impulse, and the forced recognition that after all, the prohibition of the love-life had created unhappiness, and has moreover failed to produce any tangible benefits.

The evidence here at hand supports our conviction that continence as a remedy for the problems of marriage is invariably productive of greater evils than those it seeks to cure.

Pregnancy, as I believe the testimony offered in this volume sufficiently demonstrates, usually interrupts the normal development of the growing love between husband and wife. Psychic adjustment and the establishment of an enduring harmony between the two personalities is seldom based on a sound foundation. Romantic love is one thing; procreation is another. As long as the two are entangled together in an inextricable and inexplicable mess, it is not likely that any great success can be made of either.

In the following group of confessions, we may study the unhappy accounts of those futile efforts to escape from the tangled mesh of life by the wholesale denial of love, and of the penalties they have inevitably suffered.

One

I have been married ten years and have two children. I am not quite thirty, but my husband is past forty. He is very good and true to me, and not at all a passionate man. There is four years' difference between my children, but the fact of that is severe, for this reason, and why I am writing you. We do not have the love-life because he is afraid. He doesn't want any children because we are farmers and we have a great load, financially, and he says we cannot have children. He believes that a child should greatly be desired and there should be some money in sight for that child. For three years about after our little girl was born we had no love-life. We either slept apart or he refrained from his desires. That did for awhile. Then when I was sure I wouldn't be caught again I implored him to live naturally, and he did then, for one month, and then the second child, the little boy, came. That was or will be five years ago this coming March. I must be very susceptible for I am not passionate, but try to treat the sexual embrace the way I should, be natural and play the part, for you know, it's so different a life from what all girls expect.

I was only nineteen when I married and just out of the convent school. I do not regret my marriage, or would not undo any part of it. I would gladly go through all the agony of childbirth again if I could help my husband. I must tell you all this so you can know, so you can advise and help me, for I'm sure you will. I nearly died in the first stages of pregnancy—frightfully ill, couldn't stop nausea day or night—that alone my husband can't forget. He brought me tea, crackers, did what he could for me, but nothing could help. He did things here in the house and then worked sixteen hours on the farm. He can't forget it. Do you blame him?

I would go through it again if he would live naturally, but his will power is so great he won't. Here is my trouble now.

He needs me terribly. His health is not good, he is nervous and I am worried sick because he has these night sweats some times. I'm a Catholic which is one reason my husband has not taken his love-life, fearing that if it came to the life of mother or babe, baby would have to be spared. I would rather not think of that, but even if I am a Catholic, I am broad-minded in really every way and if I was caught I really would go through with childbirth which, after a month's time, has already taken root and is considered wrong by the church.

But I am worried now over my husband and want to help him. He really suffers and, as he says, we can't keep this up forever. This is the fifth year now and not once has he taken the chance. He seems to be under a terrible strain now, is troubled with pains in the back. In your book you speak something of the harm of practising absolute denial.

Oh, please help me to let my husband come back to me and tell me what I can do. He loves me but not like he would if he could have me. I am not ashamed to write that because the time this afternoon has been ripe for me to write. I feel he will love me more because it's dreary enough back here on the farm and there are other men who live happily and do not have a lot of children, but the fear of having any more simply obstructs the love-life with us. It really can't go on, and he is not well and happy, so I want you to help me. I don't want to lose all my good looks or health, but I want to live for my man. I would die for him, of course, but that's why I'm writing you. I don't want to go on like this either, it's really impossible and so unnatural.

Two

Unless something is done of the order you indicate we will always have divorces and miserable marriages, as I feel most of it comes from the causes you say. Take my own case for instance. A few weeks before my marriage I fell from a horse and injured my spine. The doctor told me if I went on with marriage I took a grave risk, but my fiancé thought there would be no children. In eleven months there was a boy, after months of torture; at birth we both all but died after hours of agony. For three years I was an invalid. Then I went to the hospital for an operation.

In four years and a half, after using the only method of prevention I know, I found myself that way again, with days unbearable with suffering. The doctor said absolutely no more, but when I asked what to do he would not tell me anything. I used a method I heard of, but it failed and once again the torture of days and nights of continual suffering, getting up in the morning and praying for death to end my suffering before night. But I lived and gave birth to a baby girl again. Seemingly everything fails. My health is entirely shattered, my nerves are weak and the suffering has unbalanced my mind.

Do you wonder I avoid my husband and live in deadly fear of the companionship that should be a joy, with the result that our home life is spoiled because he don't understand why I avoid him?

Three

I was just one of ten children and after the last child was born my father disappeared, leaving my mother to raise the brood. She worked at anything she could do, but my three older sisters became prostitutes, no matter what or how much she did to save them. I being the fifth child, married at seventeen because I believed it was my only salvation. Now at twenty-three I have four children, one boy and three girls. The girls are only one year apart.

I have a wonderful husband but a laboring man and it is as much as we can do to make ends meet. Sometimes

I try to keep away from him, but he tells me I am hardened and I am afraid I shall lose him. I cannot bring myself to the abortion idea because I fear for the other children if anything should happen to me. I have repeatedly asked for advice and have been told of one method, which I know now is no good. I was as faithful in using it as I could be, and still I got pregnant.

Four

My husband and I have been lovers from babyhood, but were married just before we were thirty. We have five children, beautiful gifted children—two sons, twenty-four years and twenty-two years, three daughters, twenty years, fifteen years and thirteen years old. We lived a normal sex life up to the birth of our fifth child as we had waited so long living chaste lives up to our marriage and I did so appreciate his coming to me pure after twelve years of separation (he travelling with an invalid mother) I felt nothing was too much to do for him.

When the babies came one after another and we were so very poor it did not seem right for intelligent people to live thus. The last birth nearly caused my death and my doctor said that "this must not happen again." Meantime I had contracted T. B. and nearly died with hemorrhages and heart trouble but begged to live to raise and educate my children. Finally when the baby was two weeks old and the nurse left, my husband and I agreed to try to forget our sex relation until my "change of life" was complete, for the children's sake. It was easy to adjust at first, as we were both very miserable and tired, poor and had to work so hard. Baby was frail after five months nursing poisonous milk from a T.B. mother.

So time went on (we occupying bedrooms in different parts of the house and trying to avoid anything that would stimulate passion). Meantime we have both gotten well. We have sent the two boys through school and both are university graduates, the oldest girl is attending university and the other two are in high school, so you see our self-denial has reacted beneficially for the children.

But the last two years and especially the last six months, my husband has been begging me to live in the sweet old way and I want to but I'm afraid. The relations between myself and my husband became so strained a year ago I consulted our family physician but he said I would be more susceptible than ever now after this long separation. He said at this time in my life with my weak heart, another birth would certainly finish the story. I have had to tell the three older children what the trouble was, as they have noticed their father's apathy for me (for it has almost reached that) and I am afraid my own heart will turn if relief does not come soon, as I can hardly endure the indifferent ways he shows after all our loving lift together from my earliest remembrance.

It is unthinkable that our lives should drift apart after all these years. My two fine sons have always confided in me and I hope may help in the next ten years to get some legislation that will sanction Birth Control without parents having to go on indefinitely bearing children whom they cannot educate or else living the strenuous, heart-breaking, nerve-racking prohibition of love-life that we have been through.

It was the only way we knew, and we have borne it through thirteen years but the end is not yet. There has absolutely been no sex relief in all those years for either of us. Can you please help us before our hearts drift too far apart?

Five

I have five living children averaging eighteen months apart. I am now expecting my seventh baby in about ten weeks, coming just before our tenth anniversary. Hemorrhages were severe the last two births. The doctor said those muscles have become too weak to do their duty.

Not knowing that sterilization is against the law even though another childbirth may mean the mother's life I asked a physician if I might have such an operation if I live through the coming confinement. It seemed to me he purposely took my intentions to be criminal and gave me a long moral lecture. I told him that my periods are irregular and asked him if it is possible to doctor and get those organs in health so that I might have Birth Control. He would have it that I was wanting to bring on the flow and get rid of the baby. How could such an operation give health to those organs?

If my husband were not willing to practice absolute continence much of the time our children would be much closer. I doubt if the best of men would be willing to practice absolute continence ten or fifteen years.

I am thirty-three years old and I believe look fairly healthy but never feel really well. I seem to be somewhat subject to pulmonary trouble. Our children are not rugged and the doctor bills for them are too much for us. My husband's salary is less than a hundred a month. We moved on an acreage thinking the children would become stronger and that it would be less worry for me to take care of them. We have to borrow the rent money and are now paying $50 a month on the loan out of my husband's salary.

Six

I am the mother of two small boys, aged two and four. Last June I had a major operation, all organs put back in place and much repair work done. The surgeon told me I ought not to have more children. However they do not say how not to have them.

After the first baby came I felt we could not afford more and for nearly a year my husband and I refrained from any intercourse. His nerves broke and for some time he was mentally unbalanced. The doctors thought his doing without the sex relation had something to do with it. After he was somewhat better I had another child.

Since then we have not been without satisfying ourselves that way tho I doubt if the means of prevention we use are very good for us. He seems perfectly well, but I feel terribly nervous and irritable. In fact I never seem to be fully satisfied after intercourse as I would were we natural in our relations. What I want to know is what precautions can be used that will not injure one's health?

I feel I should not have more children not only because of my own physical disability and because I fear lest the mental disorder once shown in my husband might appear in the children. I am thirty-eight years old, so unless I take precautions I am still likely to become pregnant. Can you help me? I love children and would like to have more if it were wise. But it is not.

Seven

We have been married fifteen years and have five children. Of course we would have twice that many but we really don't live like man and wife because we couldn't take care of a bigger family than we have. We have to work early and late now to get food and clothes and that's all we do get. I sure hope you can help me out so we can live the normal married life.

Eight

It may be you will never read this letter but I must write it at least for my own benefit even though I will be forty-nine years old in September. At my age I should have the big problems of life well settled and I thought I had but developments of the last six or seven years have almost driven me to desperation, and I need help.

I graduated from a denominational school when twenty-seven, getting an A.B. degree. That spring I married a girl one year older than myself. She graduated from the same school two years previous. The fall of that year we both entered a university for graduate work. My wife is a fine woman of high and noble ideals. She is an unusual leader in whatever activity she engages. Now all this is by way of a background for what follows.

For ten or more years it seemed to both of us that ours was almost a perfect love. Our joy and satisfaction in each other's companionship were of the highest order. But things have changed. Our first boy was born a little more than two years after our marriage. This was an instrumental case and nearly caused the death of both mother and child, but both are strong now. Our second son was born three years after the first. During the interval between these two births we had but few sexual unions. The first childbirth had made us afraid. But the mother had no great difficulty this time. Five years after the second son was born our little girl arrived without difficulty but not at our planning.

Before she came we had not had but three or four sexual unions since the second son was born, for my wife was not strong and feared another child. For nearly two years after each child was born we were continent as a protection to the mother. Since the last child was born we have remained almost completely continent and for five years we have been together but twice, the last time nearly a year ago at which time conception resulted. We could not face the prospects so we had a doctor help us out.

But the tragedy is what follows. In this forced continence to which we both agreed as a preventive measure, with, I will admit, less firmness on my part than on my wife's, there grew up little differences and discussions and dissensions, quarrelsomeness and bitterness, until now my wife is completely disgusted with me and says I can never touch her again. She would be perfectly willing to have me get a divorce but I cannot bear such a thought.

333

My wife is a highly intellectual woman and would be perfectly happy with me if I could respond in intellectual intercourse alone, but she wants no physical associations. My own conviction is that this attitude is an outgrowth of her constant fear of motherhood and she would rather die than give birth to another. She will soon be fifty years old and tells me she is past the days of youth and all sex interest and believes me to be mentally and morally and physically diseased because I have sex desires.

The last six or seven years of continence have preyed upon me both mentally and physically so that as I write I feel that I am almost a wreck. My wife says I should be strong enough mentally and says I should become so absorbed in my work that I would be entirely free from any sex desire, and I apply myself with renewed vigor to my work in such a hope but it is all a nightmare to me.

I feel so surcharged physically and I feel my life is so empty without the love and companionship and physical union with my wife that my life is miserable and empty and without hope. She has told me repeatedly that she no longer loves me, that I am beastly and unworthy of any attentions from a pure cleanminded wife. I have tried to think she is right and many times have thought I would break with the past and start my life anew in some foreign country. I have done more thinking on this one subject than anything else during the last few years and have come to the conclusion that our unhappiness is all the result of our fear of more children. I believe if we had known of safe harmless methods of prevention we could have lived normal lives and would now be happy. My love for my wife has never waned one bit. I will do anything I can for her.

My purpose in writing to you is to learn whether there is any hope for our future. If I could rid myself of all sex desire and give my life wholly and completely to intellectual pursuits and intellectual association with my wife, we could get along fine, but somehow I have been unable to do this. My wife has grudgingly admitted that Birth Control is right but tells me that my knowledge is coming twenty years too late to be of any value to me in our family relationship. I know these are sacred and personal problems. Will you be impatient and disgusted if I ask you to tell me out of your wide experience in contacts with men and women thruout the country whether I am abnormal when I experience the sex urge at fortynine?

During the earlier years of marriage my wife displayed no antipathy for our unions and it was not until the fear of additional children began to prey upon her mind that she developed a dislike for me. At present her state of physical and mental make-up is such that almost barely the mention of sex upsets her and she has developed a distinct loathing for anything of that kind. We have occupied separate bedrooms for five years and I crave her kisses and affection which under the conditions cannot be satisfied. I see only two alternatives: Either some mental and physical change must take place so that we can again find the proper companionship physically and mentally or perhaps advancing years will put me beyond the sex urge or I must seek separation.

Nine

I was a school teacher when I married a poor farmer boy. We have worked very hard and I have broken my health down so badly. I suffer all the time from over-lifting and heavy work. I have borne four children and since the last baby, now two years old, it seems my abdomen has fallen right down on to the pelvic region and supports will not get me back to normal shape; and the pain is almost unbearable after hard work. Am sick four or five months before my babies are born and a year or more after their birth and just begin to feel like myself again and I get that way again.

It seems just like I cannot go through with it again and I have been almost living apart from my mate till he has threatened to leave me and the babies and go to town where I know he could find relief anyway.

Now, we have both consulted doctors as to obtain some way of prevention but both were told they could not tell us—against the law! Now I have no desire to break up our family nor am I shirking my duty to do all I can for the good of our little home and babies, but I am getting pretty desperate when I think of bearing another child, as I can only feel it is so great a peril to go through again and between the two conditions—separation during life or suffering and pain through many years; or maybe death and leave them all. I appeal to you. Can you send me a way to prevent conception or direct me to where I can find it out?

Ten

In the first place, my husband and I started all wrong. We got married before we had enough money to keep house. We went to live with his folks where we still are and thought we could soon save enough to go by ourselves. Thirteen months after we were married our first baby was born, and in fifteen and a half months after our second baby came.

We love our baby girls dearly, but are so afraid of having more that we have had no intercourse since before the birth of the second child, three and one-half years ago tomorrow.

Although my husband says he is still faithful to me (and I have seen no indication that he isn't) naturally we are not very happy; we have a good many quarrels and he has told me a good many times that he could divorce me because of my refusing him. It is not that the sexual union is revolting to me, for it is not and has not been in a single instance, but I dread the expense of rearing more children and I am not very strong and everything worries me so. I cannot sleep nights through worrying about losing my husband and it makes me so cross and irritable and naturally I feel tired all the time. Can't you possibly help me?

Eleven

I am the mother of two very sweet children, a boy of seven and a little girl of five, but ever since the little girl was born I have been a nervous wreck almost, run down and unable to do my work at times. I am thirty pounds underweight and the children's playing and even talking worry me most of the time. I've went to three or four doctors and taken their medicine but still am nervous, worried and run down.

I keep house for my husband but we each have our own room as I cannot endure the thoughts of going through another ordeal like I did when my two children were born, especially the last time. My husband is not happy with this way of living and neither am I for I think the world of him and the children but I'd rather die as to have another in the condition I'm in.

I believe if I could find a certain sure preventive that I could depend on, so we could live together again and be happy without worrying about my becoming pregnant, I could maybe feel lots better and lose some of my nervousness and stop worrying. Perhaps put on a little weight too. My husband is just an ordinary working man so I cannot afford anything extravagant in price but I have come to the point where I have either got to do something or quit altogether.

Twelve

My husband is a day laborer, log scaler and woods camp foreman, by profession, and has been successful in making us a fairly comfortable living in the ten years that we have been married, since there is only him and I and the two living children to provide for. Although I try to do all my housework, including milking and working in the

338

garden through the summer season, I am not at all healthy and we were married only four years when I had given birth to three children. The third one died only a short time after I had given birth to it. Then in the three years following I had three miscarriages, brought on, I suppose, by my prevailing ill health and having so much hard work to do. The last time this happened I was in a serious condition for several days narrowly escaping death.

The physician informed us that if this was repeated again it would result in my death and advised continence as the only safe means of prevention. This is very unpleasant and hard to endure but my husband who seems to just adore me said he had the same regard for my health as his own, so we have practiced this strictly in the past three years and when the matter is referred to between us he only says jokingly that he doesn't mind it much, and only revealed to me recently that he had been suffering seriously from his self-control for nearly a year. He is looking bad and I know this is injuring his health. I have great sympathy for him. We are both very young yet and as he is healthy, and has strong sex desire, I can hardly stand to treat him thus.

Thirteen

I have my family of three sweet children, all of whom we welcomed and wanted. Three is all that we can possibly care for financially. Give them the education and advantages we want them to have. My husband has been kind and my wishes have come first, and in order to prevent further conception, has practiced complete continence. It is his kindness and sacrifice that moves me to write you this letter. To be informed means so much to our happiness and that of our children. Thank you so much for your interest and for all that you are doing for mankind.

Fourteen

Would you please send me some information about scientific contraceptives and how I could keep from having any more children? I would hate to admit it to anyone else but I frankly admit it to you (as you are my friend). I practice absolute continence with my husband, as I am forty-three years old and menstruate very regularly yet, and I am so afraid I might have another child at this age and I know I would worry myself into my grave if I should ever become pregnant again and some of my reasons is this. I have two girls now and one dead.

On my husband's side his own father is in an asylum for the insane for a time and my own father was in one for quite a while, and I do not think it is right to bring children into the world under those conditions, the insanity in our families developed after my two little girls were born.

I do not wish to bring unhappiness to my husband by practicing absolute continence for I feel more so than ever since I read your book that it is not fair to him for he is a real, good kind and indulgent husband, but he knows as well as I do that if I became pregnant again that I also might go insane from worrying about it. As you say in your book "Woman and the New Race," we

are much healthier and happier if we have intercourse
with our husbands. Now if you please tell me something
I could do to not become pregnant? We, I know, would
be so much happier because I as a wife, want to do the
right thing by my husband and make him happy, if it is
in my power to do so. I do not want by practicing continence to drive my husband to prostitutes or anything
disastrous like that.

Fifteen

I have a problem which to me and to those with whom
I am concerned is very serious and in the full meaning of
the word, vital. I shall try to be candid and brief in stat-
ing it knowing that with your great work you cannot afford to spend much time on any individual. I am thirty-
three years of age. Have been married for ten years. We
have an adopted child.

My wife has always been delicate and was some years
ago severely injured in an accident and a doctor told me
she could never bear children. Knowing that it probably
meant her death if conception took place I have refrained
from sexual intercourse, for my wife's welfare is more
to me than anything else.

Now I am not under- or over-sexed but am a healthy
strong normal man. Yet the strain is very very hard not
to live and have intercourse naturally. The intense desire always balked has ill mental and physical effects and
I fear may lead to estrangement. But I need not dwell
on this as you will understand it. I love my wife dearly
and if she could only obey nature without the shadow of

death as a penalty it would enable us to live normally and happily and do our work with mental faculties clear.

Sixteen

I am thirty-four years old and am the mother of six children now and expect to become a mother again shortly. I dread the months to come very much as we haven't the means to hire help. I expect to do all my housework, take care of the children, do all the cooking and milk six cows, as I have done before, up to the day my baby is born. Being a mother, you know this is too much to expect of any woman. We live on a farm, but my husband is working at public work at the present time and don't have much time to work at home. I would not mind my work so much but about five years ago I had a very bad case of typhoid fever. I was bedfast for eight weeks. Had to have two trained nurses all that time. I was unconscious and had many hemorrhages the first few weeks of my sickness.

The worst thing of all is this: I love my husband as much as any woman could and it nearly breaks my heart when he is not affectionate to me or the children or when he says anything harsh. We get along good only for one thing. He says our family is already larger than it should be to take care of them right. I think too, that seven will be as many as I can care for properly.

He would rather stay away from me and not have intercourse at all rather than make the family larger. This don't please me for I know every time he doesn't come to me for a week or two he gets so contrary with me and children that there is no pleasure living in the house with him. I have never refused him his privilege once. He is very moderate in his passions. He has always been true to me and I to him and owing to my afflictions and desire to live happy with my husband.

I think Birth Control would be all right in our case. I love babies but I think we have had our share after we get the one we expect in a few months.

I am a Catholic and would not think of destroying a child after conception. Can you tell me of any sure way by which my husband and I can enjoy the privilege of married life without conception. It seems some people know how, but we don't. I know my life will be a torture if I cannot find a way of satisfying him without conceiving more children. He says this is our last and I know he means it and that he will keep away from me rather than conceive more.

Seventeen

I have poor health and have not the strength nor the time to give our six little children the attention that we want them to have and its hard to support them well.

I am thirty-four and my husband two years older. We have lived in continence for more than two years. I thought I would like that but have finally come to think that I don't want to continue that way the rest of my life. It has indirectly been the cause of conditions that are far from ideal. My husband and I are about as far apart spiritually as any two could be living under the same roof and rearing a family together. His once passionate affection seems to be dead. He tries to do what is right but he seems not to enjoy my company, although I can see he does enjoy the company of certain others of my sex. I have no way to appeal to him now it seems.

I believe that if I had a sure knowledge of Birth Control it might in time be the means of bringing happiness to us.

Eighteen

I am the mother of four boys, the oldest fifteen years and the youngest four. I had the first three in two years and seven months, then shortly afterwards I found myself pregnant again, with the result I submitted to an operation. I had also taken pills through this one and that one's advice which is the ruination of young married women. Then my health was poor and I had the doctor myself for a few years, also my husband's health was affected and he went to one of those quack doctors and made his case worse, then after nine years my last little boy was born. I was very far through then, had kidney trouble and was six weeks before I could get around.

Now I am a woman forty-three years old and since the last birth my husband tries to live apart and takes all precautions, but oh, I know it's injuring his health awful for he doesn't even seem to have a pleasant word and he looks bad in health, doesn't eat and is not himself at all. I would rather a hundred times be as happy as I was having my family. Life doesn't seem the same. My home life seems wrecked. All love seems to have gone and I do want to keep the home together on account of the boys. What is life to be separated? My husband is very indifferent and has very little to say. I can't get him to talk on any subject. Do you think this living apart life is doing it? I am sure it is, yet he won't hear of me trying anything myself. He was so scared with my health being so poor, so dear friend any little advice from you will be appreciated very much.

Nineteen

I was married four years ago and have two children, but the doctor says the next one will kill me. My husband is a fireman. We lost everything we had in a tornado. I work in the underwear factory and I am running a sewing machine and have been working at it for years. Is this why I come pregnant very easy. The doctors say not to believe anything about being sure of antiseptic and will never give me one only that makes me come pregnant again.

I often think what's the use of living. We have not had intercourse in a year and a half. I long for my good husband's love but we can't have it the right way because he said he would go crazy if I died. I have heart trouble and often faint three times a week, and am nervous. Every week my husband comes home I can see it is telling on him, but he tells me to wait as he knows what the doctor told him and he does not want me to die. Please give me a good contraceptive. Then I could give my husband my true love for him. Please let me know if there is any way at all.

Twenty

I am twenty years old and married two years and have two children. My girl is two years old and my boy six months old and I'm afraid of getting in a family way again. I had them too hard. I had to have chloroform and am so afraid to even think of having more. Am weak and thin and bad appetite. Please help me. My husband is not working for two years now. He is a coal miner.

I keep away from my man as much as I can, and it causes quarrels and almost separation. He thinks I want another man and he curses me. Please answer as soon as possible so I can help myself before it's too late. I've been to doctors after the girl was born and they all turned me down saying there is no such a thing as preventing from getting pregnant. Please help me before I get caught again.

Twenty-one

I have three children, the youngest eighteen years old. My husband was absent from home nine years and when he returned I had during his absence developed cancer, making eight years of this affliction. I am the picture of health and have reached the change period and he is a healthy man. We have not lived as man and wife for eighteen years. I had a horror of giving birth to any more children and I was unable to nurse them. First boy sick for two years. The girl came when he was two years old and I can't bear to review the misery of mind I went through when I found there was to be another child. She is not robust and when the third son was born I could not nurse him, either and fed him on condensed milk. Result a healthy boy but with poor teeth. An expert dentist is caring for his teeth and we are paying a $300.00 dental bill and he has the knowledge that he will loose them before he is in his mature age. The other two have the same experience.

There is no need for me to go farther. We used all sorts of foods, life was a burden and I fully realized the bitterness of a mother giving birth to children that she was unable to nourish.

So we choose the safe way, but it is a humiliating way to me. A wife in name only and my husband a man with a companion and no more. Fortunately he realizes the position we are in and lives a moral life and never complains. Physicians tell him at my age there is no danger of conception. I menstruate every three or four weeks, sometimes two. They are very careful not to offer any assistance to make the fact sure though. My daughter soon will be facing the same conditions and all the advice I can give her is "don't get married" is the only safe way I know.

Strange our laws will not protect us in this way but are keen to tear our boys from our arms and send them to war.

Twenty-two

I am twenty years old and have a little baby girl who will be two in December. My husband and I have just separated because he drank so much and would go out and stay for one and two nights at a time, and I would have to sit at home alone with the baby and worry. We have just sold our furniture and put the baby in a home, and he seems to be very sorry for his mistakes. As he is ten years older than myself I should think he would have known better. But I think he is going to try to do better and perhaps we will go back together. But I am afraid he will never do better. But nevertheless I will go back to him for the baby's sake. For she just loves him and cries to go home. She has a very bad cold and fever. She is so restless at night and cross in the day. She was never like this at home when I took care of her. I am about worried frantic. I think if the baby will be happier and healthier with us we had better try and make it go.

The main reason I left him was the fear of having more children under our financial and domestic conditions. Can you picture anything more heartrending than a large and very poor family of innocent little children, suffering because of a drunken daddy? It isn't so bad for just one child. In fact it is better than having no home and being sick all of the time but as more children come there would be more poverty and he would get drunk oftener.

So please, please tell me of some way to keep from having any more children. People who donate to these homes should help you in your cause for these homes do not soothe the aching hearts of mothers and children who have to be separated. Your work is not trying to mend a broken heart but to prevent hearts from breaking.

Twenty-three

Through the death of my mother when I was eight years old I was taken out of school young and kept house, also worked in the factory, and always got the hard jobs because I was strong. I worked too hard and am not so strong now. The doctors told me I should have an operation at the age of nineteen, but I escaped that. I suffered from ignorance along other lines not having a mother's protection. After I married I gained a better sense of health. But I made so many mistakes in my life, seems I must always learn by experience.

I married a Catholic, a Roman Catholic, and I am supposed to be in the family way all the time. They don't care for a woman, they only care to have children. I did not turn Catholic and I never will. Our home is broken up now such as it was. We have been separated for about six months. He drinks a little and is spiteful because I don't want to have a lot of children, but he says he would not care if we didn't have more if I could keep myself from having them. But he does not want to do one least thing to protect me. My children were born eighteen months apart but I could be caught every ten months. I made him use —— sometimes but that's what broke up our home. He won't use them. In my case there may not be anything at all to help me but that's what I want to know. If there is a way a woman can protect herself the doctors won't tell it. One doctor told me the safest thing he knew was what I asked my husband to do, but he won't do it. If I'd never have to have another child I would try to live with him again. I am living at my father's house now but the children are always asking for their daddy. The best thing that I know to do is ask you if you know a sure way. I'd rather be dead than live with a stubborn man like him and have a large family. He did not support the family he had properly and the children must be Catholic. I won't have children for any priest—not any more. It's the priest that makes them do that. I believe so, anyway. He is getting more stubborn all the time. If it means another baby I'll never go back. I was made for some good in this world besides that.

Twenty-four

I married when only seventeen and will soon be nineteen and during the time I lived with my husband we had a mighty sweet little boy. But after he came my husband and I couldn't get along. He was a bottle baby and of course I didn't want any more children and then and there we had our spats. After the baby came I have never had good health and that is one reason my people don't want me to go back to him. They don't want me to have more children. But I truly love my husband and would suffer anything in the world for him and I think he would for me too. He doesn't want me to have any more children. He is afraid I will die next time instead of the baby. But of course we don't know anything that will keep me from getting in the family way and I haven't lived with him since the baby was three months old. We are both young. My husband will be twenty-one this month and we didn't have much to start on and you can't imagine how proud I would be if you would only answer this and tell me please what to do. I want to live with my husband but I am afraid I might get into worse trouble. My husband's salary is very small and times are so hard I think it a great sin to bring little innocent children into this world in poverty. And please think of it this way: if it were your daughter or for instance you, and some one knew how to prevent it, wouldn't you think God would bless them to tell them how to keep from having so many? I believe it a sin to destroy one after you are already caught up but beforehand I don't think it is.

Twenty-five

My first baby will be two years old when my next one is born. I am continually under ill health for I have attacks of asthma which can only be relieved with hypodermics of adrenelin. Life, since I have been married, is not worth while and if you cannot or will not help me to prevent any more births, we have mutually agreed, my husband and I, to separate.

At least I will regain my health and will not have any more babies to board somewhere, for we have no home of our own and my first baby now lives with my mother. We can never get a home for the babies, if I have to stop working every two or three months to be confined every year. It is not worth it anyway and is not necessary. Will you please tell me where and how I can get in touch with some good Birth Control method?

Twenty-six

I have three children, seven, six and three years old. Between the one six and three I had three losses and since the last one three years old I have had three losses. I was taken to the hospital twice and operated on because infection set in. I was there twice within three months. I am all right so far but I am worried sick because my husband said he cannot keep me out of trouble much longer as it is ruining his health and if he gets sick what will my three children do? I am living in three rooms now so I can try to pay some of my bills as I still owe the doctors and part of the hospital bills. If I can't get help from you I guess we will have to separate as we can't afford to bring more children and nothing to support them with. This is my last hope. I do pray you will help me. I am only twenty-five years old, my hair is turning white and I look like forty. No one will believe me when I say I am twenty-five. They say, "you mean thirty-five or forty."

Twenty-seven

Your book appeals to me because of the fact that my wife and I are living apart today and have been for almost seven years, only seeing one another once or twice a year. We have two sweet children, a boy ten and girl seven, and we both think that is as many as we can care for properly, so through fear of becoming a mother again and rather than to do it we live apart, not because we do not love each other, but because the ones who know these things will not tell me what to do or what to use to prevent conception. If I had this knowledge I could be living with ·my family and be happy. I guess this is a foolish request for I suppose you get thousands of them, but when a father is separated from his children and for no other cause than not knowing what to do and the doctors tell me there is no way without injury to the health of the woman, what is a fellow to do?

Twenty-eight

I have two children, a boy born November, 1921, and a girl born November, 1922, now in a few weeks I will have another. Both of my children have been sick all their lives. My little girl has kidney trouble, inherited from her father. My little boy has indigestion which keeps him very poor. I weaned him at six months old on account of being pregnant again and not only that birthing my last child for forty-eight hours I was lying right at the door of death without strength to bring it in the world. The doctor said if I got that way again in the next eleven months I would hardly rally.

My husband and I stayed apart for six months as that was the only way we knew to prevent it.

My mother died when I was a small girl. She had consumption and birthing her fourth child she died. My little sister and brother also died of the same disease. I have been sickly all my life.

Some people said if I married it would improve my health. Well, I married but I am weaker now than before. I can feel my strength leaving me. I feel that two babies will carry me to the grave yard where my mother lies. If my body survives the next birth I want you to please tell me something that I may not bring any more sick children in the world to suffer and die or be left motherless as I was. My husband and I both are willing to try anything to prevent the fourth birth. Please excuse my writing you such a long letter but I feel so bad over my condition some nights I can't shut my eyes to sleep. Please answer me as soon as possible as I would feel so much better to think this was my last one.

Twenty-nine

I am coming to you for help. I have been married three years and have given birth to two children in less than two years. I live in dread now for fear I will find I am pregnant again. My baby is six months old. I would not mind having more children if only they would not come so close together. I did not have time to regain my strength after my first baby came until my second one came. Now I am nervous and so weak I can hardly do my work. Before my first baby came I was as stout as anyone would care to be. Won't you please tell me about a contraceptive? No one will ever know and so it will never harm you and will be a wonderful blessing to me. My husband and I have talked of giving up all sexual intercourse but you know how miserable that would make us. I could not do it. I would rather be dead.

Thirty

I am in deep trouble over having too many children and only hope you could tell me something that would help me out. I have been married seven years and have six children, three of which are living the others dying before one year of age. My eldest now is only four years and the youngest is six months. We love our children and want to bring them up in the right way but I know that if this keeps up our home will be ruined for now we are heavily in debt to the doctor for so much sickness.

I have been trying to be so careful not to get that way and keeping away from my husband. That is making him so he cannot care for his family in the way he should. There has been no pleasure in married life for us, because of the children coming so fast. We love our little children and my husband is a good father; he brings all the pay he gets. Even now it is not enough to keep us on top. The thoughts of having more children to care for and me not accepting him in the way I should is driving my husband to do wrong, for he has told me so. We have a very happy home only for that one thing and I know that it will ruin our home and maybe his mind.

So what can I do? I only pray that there is a safe way and you can help me for the sake of my three children that they might have a home with both a father and mother to care for them. I am in constant worry of becoming pregnant again now when I know we cannot care for our children in the way they should be. Don't stop your good work for I know it must be appreciated in many homes like my own where one trouble of having too many children so close together is ruining them. Hoping and praying that I can hear from you and you can help me or tell me some way I can care for myself so I can have Birth Control in my home.

Thirty-one

I have just read your wonderful book "Woman and the New Race." It is just as I always supposed that it was, that the rich had a preventive while us poor people who had the hardest row to hoe had to have the children. I am a woman twenty-four and have had four children in six years, although we tried to be careful. I live in the most awful suspense from one month to the next, for fear I am in the family way again. My mother never told me anything about those things for she had nine children herself.

I married a poor man because I loved him but it is hard to hold a man's love and try to avoid close relationship. I fear that it will break up our home if I do not find something to guard against conception. I had my babies so close together that I am almost a nervous wreck. I am that poor that it was three months after I saw the ad in the paper before I could get money enough to send for book.

Thirty-two

I am a married woman. My husband is working at one place for his board and I am working at another. It is impossible to draw wages so we are kept away from each other. We are afraid of raising children if we live together and I decided to ask you how to prevent it. We haven't the means to keep ourselves so how can we possibly keep children? We have a chance to work for a bachelor the first of April at $40 a month for the two of us. It will be hard to do on that small wages. I want you to tell me how to keep from having children until we have a home and money to keep them with. I feel as if I'd rather die than bring children into the world with nothing to take care of them with. I hope you will answer my letter as soon as possible. I will be anxiously waiting for your reply. Please help me and I'll do my best to help you in return if I can.

Thirty-three

Will you please give me a sure remedy on Birth Control as I am very nervous and sickly since the birth of my child five years ago. I don't know what a well day is hardly. I have mighty bad spells with my sides. The doctors said I would have to be operated on before I would get well. I have to have chloroform and after all my child has to be taken and poor little thing don't know what a well day is hardly. He been sick all his life. It is mighty hard to think about bringing these little bodies and souls into the world to suffer and be sick all their little lives and we do not own a roof over our head and are in debt $2000.

If you can give me a sure remedy on Birth Control please do for the sake of my husband. He is gradually drifting from me to another woman, for God knows how I love him. I love him better than any man in the world, but to keep from bringing the little bodies into the world, I keep away from my husband. All I can say, it causes us to have hard quarrels, almost separation, and I am so afraid I will get pregnant again and I haven't got strength enough to care for any more children and I just drag around feeling so bad. I can hardly live at times and at times I wouldn't care if I was dead. I get so discouraged. Been down in bad health and for the sake of my husband and dear child I have to pull myself together and do my housework and washing. We are not able to hire it done.

XV

The Doctor Warns—but Does not Tell

WHATEVER criticism of the medical profession we
find implied in the documents presented in the following
group of letters does not justify the conclusion that all
physicians are as limited and as merciless as the majority
of these described. In other words, we should restrain
ourselves from rushing to any wholesale condemnation.
On the other hand, we cannot escape the recorded uni-
formity in the attitude of the family physician in rural
districts and in the small towns of widely distant states.
It is perhaps not mere chance that two of these letters
record an almost identical retort on the part of the doctor revealing complacent and jocular indifference in the
face of human misery.

What defence have the doctors of the passive indifference here reported? Why do physicians remain silent
in the face of a great human need which asserts itself, we
may assume, daily or almost daily in their ordinary practice?

I do not believe that the doctors are indifferent to human suffering. I do not believe they are as heartless as a
class as these documents would have us believe. It is impossible to believe they would willingly be responsible
for the wholesale slaughter of mothers, or by heartless

indifference willingly sentence mothers to lingering death.

"Do you wonder that I, a physician, should ask for such information?" asks one of the doctors who have, like the thousands of laymen, written for help. "I will tell you that in all my four years in school this information was withheld from the students, and whatever I have learned I have picked up in a practical way since I have been in general practice." This confession throws light upon thousands and thousands of physicians practising in the country.

They do not know! Medical education has suffered by the general prejudice of church and society at large. The individual medical student, like the doctor, has been afraid to challenge the laws against contraception. In addition, he has feared to destroy the faith placed in him by his patients—in brief he has been afraid to admit his ignorance, which he tends to conceal by a jocular, good-natured evasion. The Hippocratic oath has been interpreted as placing contraception in the same class with criminal abortion. All the while this misunderstanding has been perpetuated, illness, misery, and human suffering has been permitted through uncounted generations to multiply.

On the other hand, we may witness on all sides the living benefits derived from the proper advice. The more intelligent physicians, conscious of their function in human society, have realized that contraception is an important phase of medical science, and have indicated to their patients the way toward the creation of happy and healthy families.

Among the poor, as these letters suggest and as thousands of mothers have affirmed, the doctor warns against further pregnancy, but refrains from giving any technical advice concerning contraception.

We are forced to conclude that less intelligent medical gratuates naturally drift to the lower strata of society, and the less profitable practices. They tend to become more mercenary in their attitude.

When one views the whole history of the medical profession, when one has come in close contact with its practices, one cannot escape the inconsistency of the ordinary doctor's attitude of self-sacrifice. Long hours, lack of sleep, curtailing of leisure and interruption of domestic habits are all borne uncomplainingly in the interest of his professional duty. The average doctor works courageously to save the lives of mothers and babies in childbirth. But to her appeal to prevent the conception of an unwelcome child he turns a deaf ear.

There are not words enough in my heart to express my gratitude for the nobility and self-sacrifice of the individual doctor, with whom I have worked in season and out. But one cannot work among women, or do social work, without eventually coming to a realization that the profession as a whole has been woefully blind to its responsibility to society and to the race in failing to respond to the almost universal demand for hygienic methods of contraception.

What has been left undone—or ignored—in the past has brought about a racial condition which the physician can no longer afford to ignore. Progress, civilisation, humanity at large are all calling upon the profession to prevent the recurrence of dysgenic conditions of human breeding, and thus to aid in the solution of lamentable social conditions.

Until the doctor is awakened to a full responsibility toward the safeguarding and creation of racial health, he cannot truly fulfill his legitimate function in human society. More and more medical science and therapeutics are concerned with prevention of disease instead of the amelioration of individual maladies. In the important program of contraception, the average physician has stood aloof, all the while jealously guarding his lien over matters of individual health. The time has come when he should recognize his power and his duty in these larger issues.

One

I was born and raised on a farm. My mother had nine children. I was the fifth and since my birth mother has been practically an invalid though she bore four more children. I married at the age of sixteen. In just six months I became pregnant and my health gave down. I spent almost the entire nine months in a hospital and a month afterward. My baby seemed normal at birth but never was very strong and when he was six months old I took to bed with lung trouble (T.B. in the early stages). We spent everything we had and could borrow for doctor and hospital bills until I got better—I thought I was well—then when the baby was three years old I became pregnant again.

My husband took me back to the hospital and I remained there hanging between life and death for three months, then when they were sure I was dying the doctors consented to operate and remove the cause. They found nothing but decayed clotted blood. No formation at all after three months of the most painful waiting. In just one year the same thing happened again and the operation was the same. Now my baby is five years old and my health is some better but I live in a constant dread of another pregnancy. I love children and would be more than happy to give birth to three or four more strong healthy youngsters, but I am not willing to bring weaklings into the world to suffer as I have suffered. Besides I do not believe I could possibly live through another pregnancy. So there is my story and here is my appeal to you. I love my husband dearly and he is very good to me but I am almost afraid of him to come near me and I can see that my fear of him is resulting in his paying less attention to me, and I don't blame him in the least because I can't be a real wife to him. I love him and my heart aches to be a real companion to him. He tries to make me think that it makes no difference to him but I know it does.

After the second abortion I asked my doctor to tell me if there was any way to live happily with my husband without the constant fear of pregnancy and its dreadful results and he said there was none, that I must either get a divorce or risk becoming pregnant again and if I did he would not operate again but just let me die.

But I notice that he has been married longer than I have and his wife is strong and healthy but they have only one child.

I consulted another physician and he said it was against the law to tell me. He has only one child too yet I must

363

not know that which means happiness, maybe life itself. Is there no way for me to get this vital information? Must I just live—nay exist—in dread because an unjust law says I must?

Two

I am a woman twenty-six years old, the wife of a laborer, and the mother of three babies, and am not hardly able to get around. When my last baby was born I had a terrible time and it was almost the end of me and since he was born I have had three miscarriages through no fault of mine, and there just seems to be something wrong with me all the time.

Now my doctor has told me that I cannot carry another child over two months. But he will not tell me how to keep from getting pregnant. Says it would be a sin for him to do so. I cannot understand why a doctor can be so hardened that they can let a person suffer when just a little advice would stop it all. All I have to look forward to is just one miscarriage after another and every penny we can save goes for doctor and hospital bills.

The worst of all is that I cannot even give my three babies half the care they should have for I am never able. They tell me that if I can keep from getting in the family way that I have a good chance of getting much stronger and oh, what a blessing that would be in our home! Will you please tell me some way to keep from getting in that condition without denying my husband altogether as that seems almost impossible for me to do, and sometimes I have almost given up and wished that God had taken me when my last baby came.

Three

What I want to do is to tell you something about my past life. First my age is thirty-eight years. I married at the age of fifteen and I have been the mother of fifteen children, eight girls and seven boys. Last May I brought birth to triplets, two girls and one boy, but I have lost all three babies. The last one I lost was just nine months old and I was so weak before my babies were born I could not stand on my feet but a very short while at a time. I had some kind of smothering spells and my limbs swollen and was so heavy that I could not walk hardly at all. But now I am getting some stronger but before I lost my babies they were sick all the time and I had to be up at night and lost so much sleep I could not gain much strength. But I am thankful to be gaining grounds and I hope I will get in the prime of health again. I am in need of knowledge and proper means as to keep off conception in a harmless and healthy way.

I have been instructed wrong by my home doctors. I have been putting all confidence in what they would tell me and later find that conception had taken place again. I would go to them again and they would say go ahead now you are stout and strong and you will make it all right. But I have judgment enough to know that I am breaking down as fast as time can move. I know my feeling better than the doctor, and I must seek for knowledge somewhere.

Four

I have had two children. I am married five years. I was married two years and four months when my first one came. In twenty months my second one came. Both were born dead. The first could not be washed or dressed. We had a midwife. She couldn't tell me anything, only insisted on having more children. The second one died while being born. I had to take chloroform.

Had two doctors—then almost lost my life. The doctors didn't know the trouble. One insisted on more children, the other thinks I might never get through again, but never made an effort to give me a preventive. My last baby would be eighteen months old now. I am a nervous wreck. I am constantly worrying that I get pregnant again. I am afraid because of my nerves, that it might be an injury to the child.

Five

I have asked my doctor oh! so many times to tell me something to do to prevent conception, but he won't tell. It is easy enough for him to say "Now you take your life in your hands if you have any more children." It's easy for him to say that, but he won't tell how to prevent it, and I am determined to find out.

I am twenty-three, or will be soon. Was married when I was nineteen, a woman in years but a child otherwise. All my life it seems I have been ill, first one thing and then another. I was raised by one of these mothers who believe girls should be kept in and know nothing until they are married. I love my mother but she believes, "let nature takes it course, what God sends take and keep quiet." Is it any wonder I am asking, yes even praying for help? I am so weak I can hardly stand up and I have my home to take care of and my babies besides, as we cannot afford help, it's just a case of get up and do it. I have had two operations this last year, one for the appendix and the last one for removal of the gall bladder. Is it any wonder I am weak and my baby is dead? God only knows what I have suffered and am still, but I have to live for these two boys of mine or else all would be different.

I am a Catholic and the Church believes it is wrong to prevent it but am I sinning, as the Church believes and teaches, when I don't want to bring little ones into this world to suffer and die or else live and grow up without the care they should have and no telling what they will be or become? I know deep down in my heart I am not sinning in trying to prevent but would be if I became that way and waited until I were three or four months along and then got out of it. That is why I want to find out what to do. My husband is only a boy twenty-five and works day and night. He is losing his health and worry. It seems as if it's all we can do. He is a laborer, a helper on the railroad on forty-seven cents an hour. That is no money now-a-days to try and live on. He works all day and takes the night shift whenever he can get it to help out and earn a little more.

It was enough when we were first married but babies and hospital and doctor bills make it too much and we cannot go like this having a baby every year.

Six

I have given birth to three children. They all died. I have also had several miscarriages. I asked the doctor why this was so, also if he could give me something to prevent childbirth. He would not answer either question.

My husband is sick and is not able to go to work half the time, so naturally the burden falls on me. At times it is very hard for me, so I am writing to you to ask for advice.

I would rather have the children, if they would live, but I can't seem to go full time, or to have them alive, and yet I get pregnant again and again. Surely it is not intended that a woman should go on like this. Some one told me that my babies die because my husband has a disease, but I do not know about that. The doctor will tell me nothing.

Seven

I have been married twelve years and in that time I have been pregnant nine times, bearing five living children and two born dead and two miscarriages at about two or three months, and my third child was too weak to stand this world and left us at seven months. The rest are well and strong, but I am not. I am just now recovering from a miscarriage and am very weak.

I have been home from the hospital only a week and the two doctors that took care of me told my husband: "One more child and I won't answer for her life." I asked them what we should do to prevent conception and they said "you must be careful," that is all they would say. My husband is very much worried. We are very dear to one another. He is very good to me but we both realize that we have our life and our four remaining children to care for and we can not go on like this with the suffering and worry and expense and nothing to show for it when we are done. We are both very fond of children, too much so to see them brought to this world to suffer and die or die before they ever enter this world.

I am certainly in favor of Birth Control. Think it is a fine thing where one's health is at stake or the income not sufficient to maintain all expenses. My husband is not a rich man. We have enough, if not too much sickness and doctor's bills, and hospitals come in to eat it up. We can live and care for what we have but if we have too many more or too many sick spells between, we will have to begin to think.

Eight

I am a young woman but feel twice my age, after what I've gone through. My baby will be a year old this month but I am almost wasting away. Before I was married I was healthy and always felt well, but after my baby was born I suffered something terrible. I am built very small and the doctor had to cut me into a form of a triangle and when I was brought home from the hospital I was worse than ever. I couldn't walk for four and a half months and I used to cry myself to sleep.

The doctor said I should consider myself a lucky woman that I am here today, as he thought I'd never pull through my confinement. He said I was terribly small and did not have the strength and doubted whether I could go through it again. When baby was five months I became pregnant again and had my womb opened. No one knows the agony and torture I went through. My organs weren't healed and I had to go through the same thing a few months later.

I haven't got much strength left in me and when I do washing or wash the floors or stand for any length of time I get the most awful pains in my back to the top of my head that I get so weak and dizzy I fall to the floor and lay there till I have strength enough to get up.

I don't know what to do.

The doctor sends you away, saying, "Now don't do it again" or "be more careful" or "you had better get wise," but that is all. It seems as if I get caught so easily and don't know what to do. My husband is healthy and looks fine and when I look at myself, oh, I don't know what to say.

Why do the women have to suffer and go through so much and it seems as if the men are happy-go-lucky all the time and they don't go through anything? I have no one to tell these things to and I've got to get it out of my heart as it seems as if someone put a knife into it and cut me into a million pieces.

Nine

I am the mother of five children. Six years ago I was in the hospital for seven months. The doctors said I had T.B. and I couldn't live more than three months. At the same time I was pregnant. I wouldn't give up and my baby was born, but was sick about five months after.

The doctor said she would not live. Thirteen months later I had another baby and twenty months later my last baby was born. After he was born I couldn't pull up. The doctors said I must go away at once. I had to wait to get into the sanitarium, but eventually when my baby was ten months old I went. I was in bed nearly eight months.

The doctors wanted me to stay another year but I said I would do the best I could and be with my children. My children had to go to a Children's Home as I haven't a relation in America, having come here nine years ago. My baby (the only boy I have) had pneumonia twice while I was in the sanitarium. They despaired of his life each time as both lungs were involved. The sanitarium doctors said he must have T.B. I cannot get him in any insurance and still he is a fine big boy for his age.

The doctors all tell me I must not have any more children. But I have never met one yet, and I have come in contact with quite a few, who would give me any information to prevent my getting pregnant again. I am young enough to have several more children, my age being thirty-six. I am trying my hardest to regain my health

371

on account of my children as I cannot bear the thought of having to leave them until they can take care of themselves.

Ten

I have been married thirteen years and have three children, ages eleven, nine and two. Last year it was discovered that I had syphillis in the tertiary stage. How long I had had it no one knows or where I got it, but it ate a hole through the roof of my mouth into my nostril. My husband's brother, his wife and four children have the disease so I imagine I got it from there, but I can't prove it. I discovered this in August and in September I was pregnant. Thanks to the disease I had a miscarriage in March. Since then I have kept away from my husband as much as possible. Now I could not bear to have a child until this is out of my system. Please help me.

My doctor says I must be careful and not get pregnant but when I asked him for information he said there is no information and won't be until Mrs. Sanger gets her bills through and then the medical profession will do research work. I hope you continue your campaign. If the woman had the controlling vote in this state legislature it would be an easy matter. I would like to help but I don't know how.

Eleven

I was married seven months ago to a man, most loving and kind. I have just recovered from an operation (abortion). Even now I regret having given up the little life I carried for less than three months. We wanted it, my husband and I, but I suffered an attack of tuberculosis six years ago and am just recovered therefore my physician who has fought with me for years against the "white plague" said my health would again desert me if I bore my baby, naturally it frightened us, so I submitted to this operation. Everything went better than the surgeon expected and am recovered and the condition of my chest is fine.

But I am puzzled at both the surgeon and the lung specialist, the latter our family physician, for neither one or the other told us what to do before they discharged me from the hospital. Yet they tell us to wait a few years before we have our baby. Now could anything be more discouraging? We have quite made up our minds that I will not go through the dangers of an abortion again, for after all the pain I came back from the shadows with empty arms. Yet we know it is best not to have a child until I am certain of enough strength to come through the ordeal, strong and well, so as to be able to take care of it properly.

Twelve

While a girl scarcely in my teens, I was operated on for an abdominal abscess. Adhesions resulted that crowded my maternal organs to such an extent, that my uterus was crowded out of place and the continual pressure caused me considerable annoyance, so much in fact that I submitted first to a minor operation, then a major operation to relieve me of the pressure without any results.

Physicians advised me to have a baby; I had been taking no precautions and of course continued married life as before. About one year after my third operation, I became pregnant. I gave birth to a baby boy at the hospital. Scarcely a week passed by when septic poison set in. For a month I was just hanging on, then I had to submit to another operation, an abscess had developed; and I had three incisions as a result again. Finally on April 30th, I came home, after being there almost four months. (January 5th to April 30th). Doctor told me I should have no more children and I live in constant fear. Yet when he might have attended to me he never did. Could you, would you, Mrs. Sanger, impart your information to one so crippled bodily as I am? I would rather lose husband, baby and home, than submit to such an experience again.

Thirteen

I just came from the hospital and am too weak to write so I am asking my husband to write for me. I have three living children now and in 1918 I had a serious operation. Since that, I lost one child at birth and had two abortions, the last I was five and one-half months.

I have to pay the ambulance doctor, hospital, and undertaker all at once. Ever since the operation, I am getting weaker and losing weight and color, but with all my pleas with doctors, they won't do anything for me. I went to several and they think that what I ask for is an insult to them. So since I read your book, I didn't ask any of the doctors for help as I know I won't get it.

Fourteen

My wife is the mother of a normal boy now four years of age. During the three or four months just previous to his birth she was in a generally bad condition. Labor was extremely difficult, lasting forty hours and relieved then only by surgical assistance. For two months after delivery she was unable to stand on her feet.

The doctor feared for more than a year that her kidneys were permanently diseased. However by the end of the second year she was fairly well recovered.

After four years rest she is again pregnant and for the first three and one half months showed no signs of sending down albumin. However between the end of the fourteenth week and the beginning of the sixteenth she began to send down albumin and now at the end of four and one half months she is sending down so much that the doctor is very much alarmed.

The doctor tells me that she is in a dangerous condition if this continues to increase and says that it is worse in this case than in the first; that it meant a hard fight ahead and that a third pregnancy would be fatal. However he admits that he has not had the training that will allow him to tell her how to prevent a third pregnancy if she survives this one.

After a long hard siege my wife's pregnancy came to an end near the first of the year, with no greatly aggravated results to her kidneys, and with a healthy baby girl.

However, a serious ventral hernia resulted with other damage which will necessitate an operation as soon as she is strong enough to permit it. The doctor was of the opinion that this was the result of her first pregnancy but of course cannot be sure. However, he made it plain to her that if she became pregnant before this operation was performed she "would not come through it" and then turned around and refused to either give her information that will prevent it or to cooperate with me to get this information. He is iron-clad in his stand and about the only reason he will give is that it is too dangerous a subject to take chances with, since it is open to so much misinterpretation.

Believe me, if I never was a Birth Control advocate before, and had any feelings that the present law was adequate and the medical profession capable of handling all legal cases, I have certainly changed my opinion, and I certainly won't hesitate to tell a few of our legislators what I think about it. When laws are so drastic that they either blind the medical profession to its plain duty or else intimidate it so that it is afraid to do its duty it is plainly time they were changed.

Fifteen

I have suffered from heart trouble ever since my two boys were born. I have three living out of five.

I have so many times asked many doctors for help, only to be kicked out of their offices. When I went with my last baby my whole body swelled up so I was so fat I could hardly drag my legs with me. I dragged myself to my doctor's office and asked, and with tears begged him to help me, that if I pulled through with this one now couldn't he help me so it would be my last one. He got so angry at me, his eyes looked so terrible fierce, I got so scared, I don't know to this day how in the world I got home, but I cried for two days over the many shameful names he called me. He said he would give me a good licking till I was black and blue if I ever dared myself to ask him such questions again. I thought I would go mad. I just cried. I could not stop myself and I got awful sick. I got my boy—a eight months miscarriage. Good thing it was dead for so he don't suffer any more, but I still cry like a fool for a little thing but I can't control myself. It is very hard for me to hold a job because they seem to think I am not right in my mind. I feel terrible bad but what can I do? I managed to keep away from my man but he quarrels often. Now isn't there some way to control the birth so I could at last cast aside this suffering and fear and win my way back to myself again or must I go on like this always and my children after me?

Sixteen

My husband was brought up in a strict Catholic family, but he is one of the broadest minded (as well as the most considerate), men in the world, I'm sure. We have been married three years and a half. We are devoted to each other,—but in that time I have had one baby and two miscarriages, and no one will tell us how to prevent having any more children, until I am able and willing to do so. My husband is young and it is cruel to deny him any sexual pleasure. Still I don't know what else to do.

Our doctor seems not to want us to have any definite information. He says "The only way to keep from having children is to live in different parts of the town."

Whereupon he laughs heartily at his own joke. Isn't there some way that I can get some real, reliable information? That sickening uncertainty every month is a real nerve strain.

Seventeen

Now I'm stuck. I don't know how to say what I want to say. I haven't a very good education and I certainly am no writer but I'll just write what I think. Of course, I want to know how to not have any more children. I am twenty-two years old and have two children—a boy four years old and a girl almost two—and I am glad I have them. They are both normal and healthy kiddies but I am not so strong as I used to be. Not sickly but just thin and get tired out pretty easily. Backache on washday and other small troubles. I'm not bad off like some women but I want to keep my health and take good care of the babies I have. I am always scared to death every month when my menstruation comes a day or two late. I try to be careful but I am never sure. I have had two miscarriages besides my two children and have been married barely five years.

I went to my doctor and talked to him half an hour but he just beat around the bush and wouldn't tell me anything. I look healthy so I suppose he thought it wouldn't hurt me to have more children. Anyhow the more children women have the more money he makes.

378

I know he knows because he has been married a long time and has only one or two children. He declared there was no certain preventives but you say there is. A women I know says there is too. She was a nurse several years before her marriage and says there are certain methods but she won't tell because she is afraid of getting in trouble. It makes me sick. I'd like to start a Birth Control clinic myself if I had the knowledge but I haven't and it is "against the law"—what a jumble of crazy uncivilized words. I think nations that make Birth Control unlawful are uncivilized.

My husband is a coal miner but we are buying a small tract of land—twenty-six acres—and have built a house on it—a three room wooden house that he built and I helped. It cost us about $125.00. He has to keep on working for wages for quite a while yet, but we're going to try to make a chicken farm out of this. I expect to help a good deal and I can't do much if I am forever washing diapers. I hope you will tell me how to keep my family down to two children so I can give those two a good home and a better education than either of their parents have.

Eighteen

We have two small children, one continually ill, brought on by my poor health. I worked till two days before his arrival and was back again in three weeks to the factory. Owing to so much illness and him being out of work three months seems to be such a drawback, one cannot get on their feet and give justice to the wee mites.

I went to my doctor and he said the only thing to do is

for my husband and I to live apart or an operation if we could afford it. Now I do not want to do either as both court danger, not only that, but we love children and if in time, when we get on our feet and wanted more, we could suit ourselves.

We are both young, twenty-three, with years ahead and we want to see them grow sturdy and happy, not underfed and have to have the care of some one else. We live with my mother and she cares for them, but is getting feeble and if we could get on our feet in six months or a year we could manage. There must be some way honorably. The rich have it: why not the poor?

My doctor said at birth, "Well, this is just a good start," but when I paid him half of his bill, wanted to know when I'd pay balance, he said at the time, "Oh, you'll get along." I said "What about education?" He says, "Oh, they don't need that now." Well maybe not, but they need a certain amount to get anywhere and no one likes to see their children not given a half a chance and to be in the home to give care and know what they are doing and that they aren't on the street.

Nineteen

I will recite you my own case. I will have been married seven years this coming September. I have four children, two boys and two girls. The first two children were welcome. I suffered quite a lot with them, but I was proud to have them. At that time my husband was earning $25.00 per week, and we were able to manage fairly comfortably, but six months after my second baby was born my husband met with rather a serious accident from which the doctors say he will never fully recover the use of his arm. What few dollars we had managed to save for a rainy day were all eaten up by the accident, and he will never again be able to follow his old occupation, and has to take another position at a much smaller salary.

Since then you will see we have had two more children. I love them dearly but felt it a crime to bring them into the world under existing conditions. I am not able to give them the care and attention they should have. Neither am I able to give them the proper nourishing food they require. With having so many mouths to feed on such a small salary I had to forego the nourishment I should have had while being pregnant with my last baby. The consequence is after my last baby I cannot seem to regain my strength. I am almost a nervous and physical wreck, with continual worry and what is still worse, I am pregnant again (about three weeks).

I am distracted, what to do I do not know. I cry myself to sleep. When I told my husband the tears came into his eyes. He has tried hard to avoid it. Were I strong and able and had sufficient coming in to support them I would not mind. I would be glad to have them for I am passionately fond of children, but what are we to do when we cannot feed those we have already? And I do not feel I shall be able to go through it again. I am entirely discouraged. I dread the future, the results of our ignorance. I feel worn out.

I asked my doctor after my third baby was born, how I could avoid having any more. He laughingly said "Tell your husband to sleep in the woodshed." You see he gave me no satisfaction and I am suffering today untold agonies.

Twenty

With a sad heart this evening I am going to write you that which I have confided to no one before. First I will tell you a little of myself that you may understand. I am thirty years old, been married twelve years last October. Have four boys, and in a few short weeks will try to give birth to the fifth. I am in dreadful health, and am dreading confinement as never before. I have such unusual hard times only one of my children have come into the world without instruments after hours of untold suffering. I am now almost paralyzed in my hips and back, can't walk a hundred yards without help, hardly and will be down in March. Just think what I must yet suffer to say nothing of the last hours if I live. I can't live through much more such trials. I have tried all things I could hear of and the only result is I have no health, a bad diseased stomach and soon be mother of five children.

I just pleaded with my doctor once after my third baby and I was down three months and had seven knife operations to save me from such suffering. He said if he were to save the ladies such illness doctors would have nothing to do.

We are just poor people, my husband is a railroad man and a devoted true man any woman need not be ashamed to call husband. He don't want any more children. He never wanted any, but I did until I found out I could not give natural birth, then I didn't want any. He has tried to save me from these months of suffering but in a short time a baby would be on the way. I am not a highly passionate woman and have been told that was why I conceived so easily, but I thought it was because I had no health much. So please write me a long letter and give me some advice. Please tell me how to avoid any more children and how to be a better wife for my husband. I can't deny him when I love him dearly and I know he loves me true.

Twenty-one

I am thirty-two years old and have been married ten years and have three children, a boy eight, a girl five and a half and a boy over two years. I have a bad kidney and liver trouble and it is best I have no more—both for myself and for a child. I always have a partial paralysis while carrying and while in bed. I narrowly escaped when the last was born and you realize what kidney trouble means at childbirth. It is a constant worry for fear I get that way again and another horror of using any advertized appliances for fear of injury to one or the other of us.

I never could see how young married teachers in school could keep from having children, some have one others none and go on teaching without having more.

I have talked with a few friends and our experiences are: One doctor will tell you "Don't play with fire and you will not get burned." Yes, he wants that $30 or $50 or more he gets for maternity cases (no difference under what circumstances). What are we to do? Married—yet shall we send our husbands elsewhere?

Another will tell you there is no sure preventive (of course different things for different people I suppose). He also wants the "long green," and yet he and his wife only have one or two.

Another will give you a wink and say "abortion." I don't want anything like that.

Twenty-two

I am a woman of twenty-three years of age. I have three children living and I have had six miscarriages in seven years. Time and my health is failing me very fast. I positively do not want any more children until I see if my health regains. I have lost fifteen pounds in two months time. It is not very pleasant to have children especially for a man who cares nothing for anybody but himself the whole time I am pregnant, and that is the cause of all my miscarriages. I have ruined my health trying to keep from having too many.

I am doctoring all the time and the doctors tell me I have all the symptoms of consumption, which they tell me came from losing so many children but I have asked almost every doctor here to give me anything for prevention. They would almost eat my head off and tell me that is what women are put on this earth for. I do not think it is right to bring delicate children into the world. If it were not for my children I would no longer be a married woman, for I am in constant fear from month to month and more so since doctors have told me I was going into a decline.

Twenty-three

I have been deceived by druggists and doctors who have pushed us off with false preventives only to quiet us. I have searched for four years to find some true, safe, reliable and harmless preventive, but sorry to say, in vain. I am a mother of six children and neither my husband nor I want any more. I have suffered of female trouble since my second baby was born. My normal weight is between ninety-three and ninety-eight pounds. I have one baby thirteen and a half months old and is no more than a six months baby. She cannot sit alone and doesn't try to creep. My smallest baby is only two weeks old. Two babies were born to me at the birth of this one, one being only half developed and died but still remained in the womb until the completion of the live baby girl, which seems to be healthy so far as I can tell. This was caused by my unhealthy condition. You can well imagine my condition these nine months. My oldest child is a girl of only nine years of age and very little help. She has to help her father most of the time when she is not at school. It makes my heart ache to see my husband wash the clothes and napkins for two babies besides doing all of the out door work and all the work on the farm by himself, only because I am not able to help any and we are not able to pay any one else to do it for us.

My husband always says that if he had as much money in the banks as he has notes and doctor bills to pay he would be a happy man. These heavy doctor bills will stop when I get relief from this most dreadful thing of having one baby after another.

Twenty-four

Have had four children, all dead at birth, and bear that I am pregnant again. I am the short stout type and am very susceptible to pregnancy. My doctor only laughs when I tell him I'm pregnant again but what good does it do to go through with the whole affair when at the end I realize nothing but intense suffering and add one more death to the family list? If I am pregnant now, which I think I am, I shall go on the table for an abortion.

Twenty-five

I am twenty-nine years old, have been married nearly eight years and have a son five and a half years old. When my son was born I went to the hospital I had also made the trip there the year before where after fifty-four hours of suffering I was anaesthetized and my baby girl born dead. When my little boy was two and a half years of age I had a miscarriage of six months conception and I had a local physician. By this time I had gained considerable confidence in this man who has always evinced an especial interest in us and our acquaintance with him. The muscles across my abdomen have all been broken so that I have no support and I had had severe internal and external lacerations which he himself had remedied by an operation, and he knew would be torn again in the event of further childbearing. But I obtained no satisfaction

386

and the case went on and on, all the time in his hands but nothing done, until finally after an examination he placed me in the local hospital and he and another physician operated on me, not however, until after he had ascertained that I was sure it was over eight months and he thought he was sure the child would live. Well, words are inadequate to describe what went on during the two hours that I was under ether. Suffice it to say that boy was dead and I came near passing to the Great Beyond. I have been in bed five weeks and am just beginning to be up. My physician admits now that he should have operated sooner, yet in spite of the fact that I should be thankful I am alive and not in the "happy hunting ground," both he and the doctor who assisted him decree that I shall never have another child or my life will pay the forfeit. I am of too slender build, the pelvic bone is too low and on all four occasions I have been anaesthetized and high forceps used.

Now in the face of all this, will my physician give me any light on the subject of how I may protect myself in the future? No, he will not.

My husband has tried several times to learn from him some expedients which would protect me but without success. His illogical reply to me, when I talked with him, is "Don't get that way!" But he will not tell me how not to get that way.

He even said to my husband that he had better go "down the line," that I oughtn't to have any objections as long as he let me alone. This, to a young man of thirty, who has always been exceptionally clean-minded and whom I have never had the slightest cause to doubt. He would not give us any medical knowledge that would help us, yet he would make such a suggestion as this! Now this doctor is a fine man, one of the most prominent and respected citizens. He is more than our family physician to us, he is a friend and has enjoyed the hospitality of our home time and again; yet he will permit medical ethics to disrupt my family.

Twenty-six

I am only twenty, been married two years, and have two children. Both my husband and myself are just scared. I don't know what to do,—I love children, dear God, yes! and because I do love them I want to rear them properly and give them the best advantages. But just because our mothers are ignorant, and my doctor, I have been to him and pleaded with him to tell me, won't tell me (maybe he don't know himself) and we are so young and suffering already for we are afraid of intercourse and are avoiding it and that doesn't help matters any for I love my husband dearly and want him so, and as for him, poor kid, he's as nervous as the devil! Oh I should be so happy if I weren't so ignorant, could develop and grow and help my husband to be big, make life a joy instead of a nightmare!

Twenty-seven

Help me for humanity's sake, also for the babies I have to neglect that I may not bear any more to be neglected, not that I shirk my duty but because I am a cripple and you may judge when you read my story as follows: I have five living children, one I lost at five months, the last three were born within four years. When the oldest of these three children was three months old I was stricken down with what some doctors called milk-leg, others called glandular rheumatism. I was unable to move any part of my limbs or body except my right hand and turn my head. A year I was in this condition, and will always be a cripple.

When the doctor was about to discharge the case he told me not to become pregnant as I may not be able to pull through. I begged him for some knowledge but all he would give was the so-called "safe period."

I asked the trained nurse and she would put me off saying she would tell me before she left but failed to do so, hence in a short while, after using every precaution I knew, found me pregnant. I prayed to God for strength to pass through those nine months which He did, giving me a baby boy.

My husband tried several doctors for this important information but they assured him there was nothing they could do or tell. When this baby was nine months old I found myself pregnant again. At last I passed through another nine months and gave birth to a little frail girl baby. She has always been sickly, is now eleven months old, cannot walk, and I live in terror as each month rolls around.

This spell of sickness cost us so much we had to borrow money, mortgaged our place and lost it. The babies coming so fast also cost a great deal. My husband works from morning till night trying to make a living and pay off these debts. I do not have a servant because we cannot afford it so do all my work and I tend my three babies. Sometimes I have to neglect the work and at times the babies suffer. With my crippled legs all the time and being on my feet so much makes them hurt worse, but there is no help for it. I must go on and on trying to get around and somehow get it done. But if you will help my ignorance and tell me what and where to get a contraceptive I will bless you till my dying day.

Twenty-eight

I have been married for a year to a man of twenty-four. I am eighteen. Four years ago he discovered that he was syphilitic and began an immediate course of treatment under a great venereal specialist of this city. At this time he has been pronounced "negative," but takes a course of treatment for three months of every year. By doing this he is taking precautionary measures, and in time will be entirely cured. But this being the case it is impossible for us to have any children for several years. I have already had an abortion the operation taking place in March. It was done by a competent physician and I am in good health, and I think none the worse for my experience. I asked my doctor if he could tell me of any reliable contraceptive and he said there were none, or rather, refused to tell me of any.

Twenty-nine

My wife is a permanent invalid through too close child-bearing. One may say my case was an exception. I say no, nine women out of ten in the rural districts where large families prevail are not in a physical condition for conception when it takes place.

Now let us get to the bottom of this thing and see why it was necessary for my wife to have this child while she was not fit physically. Don't say I am a radical! You cant get results from any case unless you get the facts first and no honest man should rebuke me when I speak the truth and can prove what I say. During my twenty years of married life (that estimation small) with a view of gaining information whereby I could avoid conception, and I am telling you right here that there wasn't one in the whole bunch that would as much as reveal the method commonly used by men.

Now I am not trying to ridicule the medical profession, for we could not get along without it, but I am speaking the facts and if the shoe fits it must be worn. Why wouldn't these doctors tell me what I pleaded for when my family was all that I could handle? I can tell you: because a great many of them would rather see a woman lay on a bed and suffer death and untold agony than miss that fee that comes from the transaction. O, you may say, the law prohibits them from avoiding conception! Yes, and the law permits them to cause abortion too where there are greater chances to save the woman's life by so doing. But it's seldom that you will be able to obtain this even in cases of necessity. Why? generally because there is a difference of about $50.00. Now hold on, don't say I am off about that. If you are a married man with a large family of many years experience you know that I am telling you facts.

Thirty

I wish I heard of you long years ago I would have been well and happy now instead of being a wreck. I am thirty years old, have been married fourteen years and have eleven children, the oldest thirteen and the youngest one year. I have kidney and heart disease and everyone of my children is defected and we are very poor. Can you please help me? I am so worried and I have cried myself sick and if I don't come around I know I will go like my poor sister. She went insane and died. My doctor said I will surely go insane if I keep this up but I can't help it and the doctor won't do anything for me. Oh! if I could tell you all the terrible things that I have been through with my babies and children you would know why I would rather die than have another one. Please help me just this once and I will be all right. Oh, please, I beg you please. No one will ever know and I will be so happy and I will do anything in this world for you and your good work. Please, please just this time. Doctors are men and have not had a baby so they have no pity for a poor sick mother. You are a mother and you know so please pity me and help me. Please, please!

Thirty-one

I am writing for this information that I may use it in my professional capacity for the benefit of my patients. I am doing a general medical and surgical practice, and I think it would be much preferable to advise the use of a proper contraceptive than be compelled to give a curett-ment to relieve them of the results of an ignorant attempt at a dangerous abortion.

Do you wonder that I, a physician, should ask for such information? I will tell you that in all my four years in school this information was withheld from the students, and whatever I have learned has been picked up in a prac-tical way since I have been in general practice. Any in-formation you may give me will be appreciated, and I assure you I will hold it in confidence.

XVI

Desperate Remedies

W E have seen how, in her efforts to escape compulsory maternity, the enslaved mother seeks information concerning contraception from any and every available source. The methods suggested by neighbors or women friends too often prove of no avail. Physicians, as the testimony presented in the preceding chapter indicates, withhold such knowledge as they may possess. If her past experience in bringing children into the world has been one of suffering and of a kind to strike terror to her heart, the mother is forced into a situation in which she is ready to attempt the only way out—abortion.

This desperate remedy is more universally resorted to than is commonly supposed. Condemned for ages by moralists and theologians, it has been denounced as a crime second only to murder. Despite the laws against it and the severe penalties inflicted upon the doctor or midwife who performs the illegal operation, it would be difficult if not impossible to produce evidence that there has been any decrease in the practice. This despite the advance of civilization and the manifold efforts that have been made to safeguard maternity.

To save the life of the mother, therapeutic abortion has indeed been countenanced not only today, but in the past. Now, however, it is more often the privilege of the well-to-do. In the present records we are confronted not with legal, scientific abortion, but the desperate—often self-imposed—remedy of utter hopelessness.

There is no more tragic or revolting aspect in the drama of enslaved motherhood than is exposed by this practice. The case of the mother who in desperation plucks from her own womb its unwelcome and immature fruit is uniquely tragic. This gesture, always taken at the risk of her own life and health, is a final protest against the overwhelming power of those blind, relentless forces of which she is the plaything. If she be the child of one of the great churches, she is made to believe that this act is the unpardonable sin. In committing abortion she is condemning her own soul to an eternity of torture. Yet in her desperation she challenges that edict. The revolting aspect of the practice is exposed in the vast number of midwives and abortionists who batten upon the never-ending misery of mothers in bondage, and who wax prosperous by the suffering and desperation of the mothers of the poor.

It would be the very height of folly and inconsistency, however, to condemn the evils of abortion while we close our eyes to the causes which make this practice inevitable. Not without significance is the demonstrated fact that in all countries in which the use of contraceptives has been prohibited, and the sale of preventives made punishable by law, the practice of abortion has increased immeasurably. Practiced illegally and secretly—often performed by the woman herself by crude mechanical or chemical means—reliable statistics concerning it are impossible to obtain.

One thing seems self-evident. Women who are ready and willing to take their own lives into their hands to avoid bringing into the world an unwelcome child—often out of pity for that flickering embryonic life,—prove themselves fully conscious of their own situation. Whatever their mental limitations, we cannot condemn them as irresponsible of their racial duties. Until the contrary has been demonstrated, we must assume them capable of self-education in the practice of hygienic contraception.

It is an easy task for priest, politician, legislator or magistrate to condemn the mother who submits to abortion. But do these worthy gentlemen with their urbane sophistication and untroubled lives ever stop to realize the long chain of antecedents, the physical tortures, the bleeding mutilations, the agonies that have driven the mothers of our race to this last and most desperate of remedies?

One

I am a young girl eighteen years old, and have a fine baby girl fourteen months old, but I live in a constant fear of becoming pregnant again. I have a blind mother to care for and I cannot have any more little ones. Please help me. I will do anything on God's earth to get a sure way of not having children.

I have been married since I was a little past fourteen. I was married in March, the next July I had a three-months' miscarriage. The following February I again became pregnant. On October this child was born, a fine healthy baby. The following April I was pregnant again.

I went to a doctor and had it taken away. I suffered death all summer and in August had to go to the hospital and have an operation performed. I had not stopped being unwell until I had the operation, but I swore I would go back no matter if it killed me.

I would rather die than bring another child into the world. Not that we don't love children but we haven't the money to care for them.

I was told it is a sin to have a baby taken away but I wonder which is the greater sin to have them and not be able to take care of them or get rid of them before one learns to love them?

I have asked my doctor to tell me how to keep from having children but he won't tell it. My husband tried to keep me out of it but sometimes there's a slip. Won't you please tell me something so I won't live in such a nightmare? This month I was two weeks late and those two weeks were a living nightmare and when I found out I was all right I got down on my knees and thanked God. When I am carrying my children I am as crazy as any lunatic ever was. My life is one constant dread. I have not only ruined my health by doping and having abortions but I have nearly lost my mind worrying if I am all right. For God's sake help me! I am still a child myself.

Two

I have a boy two years and a half old. He is a darling boy but I dread thinking of any more. I have had several miscarriages and have caused them myself, for my husband works hard to keep us three and now I am out working. I have a girl to come to the house to care for my baby while I am away, for I like to have respectable clothes and furniture for my house and can have more when I can work and help. My mother-in-law thinks it terrible because we haven't had a child every year, like she did. She thinks it's a sin to keep from having children but I just laugh and never say a word when she says those things. I know I am injuring my health for doing what I mentioned I did in this letter.

Three

I am a young woman of twenty-three years. Was married at the age of fifteen years. I was married just eighteen months when my baby girl was born. In seventeen months I had a baby boy, in sixteen months another boy, in twelve months a miscarriage of five and a half months, again. My health is gone. I weigh a hundred pounds and should weigh a hundred and twenty-nine pounds. We are very poor people. My husband is a good man and a hard worker but it is all he can do to feed and clothe these we have got. I have been practicing abortion though I know it will kill me in time. I would rather die than have any more children when we cannot take care of them.

Four

I was married when eighteen, my husband twenty, both of us ignorant in regard to sex matters. Our first child was born premature—six months, and didn't live. Two years later we had a boy, then a girl twenty-four months later, six months after that an abortion, because I couldn't stand the strain, as it was, from the two children besides taking care of the house, washing and ironing. I was a nervous wreck. Nine months after that another abortion, and I went through the horrors of twelve hours steady agonizing pain. One year later I had another abortion. Then I felt I could never go through it again and when I again became pregnant two years later I did not do anything and I now have another darling to take care of, but sometimes I wonder where clothes and everything necessary for a child's comfort are to come from. It is impossible to save for the rainy day, and I feel this must positively be the last one.

Five

Seven years this coming December 15, I married a railroad man of meagre circumstances and we lived comfortably till the children started coming. For the first three years after I married I did very well, not in keeping from getting pregnant but in getting rid of one every now and again. But then a baby girl was born. Fifteen months after that a baby boy was born, then I managed to get rid of several again and in December, 1924, another baby girl and when she was two months old I had to wean her and give her a bottle, as I was that way again, but I succeeded in getting rid of it.

My husband is very disagreeable when I am that way, he seems to think it is all my fault. All he seems to think about is the expense it will be to him, not the suffering I have to go through to bring it into the world and the care of it afterwards, for he certainly doesn't bother his head about their little wants, its always mother that has to do their things for them. And when they are right little I really believe he fairly hates them.

Six

I am just up out of bed from an abortion, the twelfth one, and four children, making a total of sixteen in seventeen years, and am only a little past thirty-six. I have sacrificed everything but my life,—my health is gone. I have four of the dearest children that I must try and live for, three girls and a boy. My dear little boy now seven, was born for some cause with his left hand missing. We came here from the east for my husband's health, tuberculosis. I have to work in a factory all the time to help provide for this dear little family. It seems some times that I cannot stand up under it all.

Seven

I do not understand the awful life the poor working class of people must live while the rich that could afford to have them, either have none or just one or two. Life sure is hard on poor people. . . . I read about you in the paper. I only wished I could scream things to do from housetops to poor women only. God! I would talk from sun-up to sun-down for Birth Control if it would do any good. I believe in it and hope and pray to see the day it rules supreme. For God's sake keep me from committing murder on myself as well as these innocent little lives, if you can tell me. Please tell me something to take, do or use and save at least my life and maybe prevent me from getting rid of any more. Am almost scared to go to bed.

Eight

At the early age of sixteen I met the man who is now my husband. My mother seemed to think the greatest event in life was an early marriage, so at the age of eighteen I married, ignorant as a schoolgirl of the laws of nature. One year later I gave birth to a five-pound boy. It was a frightful ordeal, the child as well as myself horribly torn by the instruments. Three months after his birth I was again pregnant. You being a woman can understand my predicament. My little son was a sick, puny child, bottle-fed, ruptured, (because of hard birth, the doctor said), and I a nineteen-year-old mother inexperienced, inefficient and in despair. I know you will not condemn me when I tell you I resorted to an abortion. Three months later I was again pregnant. I again resorted to an abortion. After living the life I did of poverty and too many children. I cannot bear to see my little boy have to live that same life. I love my husband and little son and my ambition is to rear a happy healthy home. We cannot afford a large family, we haven't the means to raise them properly.

Nine

I guess I am the most unlucky and the unhappiest woman in this world. I feel like there is not another woman in this world who has gone through what I have, if there is God have mercy on her. I have been married six years and I have two children, a boy five years old and a girl eighteen months old, and I have had *twelve* miscarriages. When my two babies were born I had to lay two days before they were born, that is the way I have to suffer when I give birth to a child. I would rather die than go through it again. The miscarriages were all brought on through abortions and I nearly died from blood poisoning three times. I am just now getting over one terrible spell of sickness. I am only twenty-nine and people think I am forty.

I guess my husband is a brute he doesn't care for no one but himself, but when you have two sweet babies you have to endure a lot to live for them.

Ten

I was married at nineteen—young husband who knows how to spend money too well; three abortions performed; in family way again and thought husband would change if baby came. Baby girl now fifteen months.

In May I performed abortion on myself and nearly died. I suffered so and the funny part of it is I have to suffer alone, no husband around, as he says I complain. I am now twenty-three years old and the good Lord only knows how many more abortions I have to go through for the sake of ignorance as I would not be guilty of bringing another child into the world as I have my little baby boarding out and I work in the laundry nine hours to provide nourishment for her. My husband is another "happy-go-lucky." It's the woman who is responsible, I ought to know by now. My mother-in-law knows but she won't tell me. Still she knows how I suffer every time. I want to have a son sometime but cannot afford a baby now as I have to save to go buy furniture. I now live with my father-in-law. Mother-in-law had six children and if she knew then what she does today she wouldn't have had so many. Even now I can see myself in her shoes, but no, I will see myself in hell before. I told my husband lots of times I don't want to be married and to stay away, but as soon as I am a little better he's Johnny-on-the-spot.

Eleven

At childbirth I suffer something terrible and after birth I feel very weak. I am married only two years and nine months, and to think just for the sake of others I am ruining my health. My husband does not want any more children, so why for the sake of others should I go along having more children when I cannot give them all the proper care that should be necessary.

What I would like to know is if you could help me in some way to have me miscarry this third baby of mine for I think there wouldn't be very much trouble to go through, and also to help to prevent from having more children, for I just dread the kind of life that I am leading. I never can have any recreation in this world because I have no one to leave the children to.

Twelve

I lacked one month of being seventeen when I was married. No one has a better husband than I. Five months after I was married I had a miss of about six weeks caused from a diseased ovary and going up and down steps. Four months later I became pregnant again, and had an eleven-pound baby which has always been healthy. But five months before conception and the nine months of carrying the baby I had the very best of medical attention. I nearly lost my life in giving birth to my baby. When the baby was sixteen months old I became pregnant again. It was an awful thing to do, but—I couldn't face the future with another child. I have never seen a well day since. If I had known what Birth Control was I could have saved myself suffering. For days I couldn't raise my head off the pillow. For seventeen days my foot never touched the floor. The doctors said they wouldn't give two cents for my life. The suffering was horrible, but I would rather suffer it again than bring another child in the world whom I am not able physically to take care of. And I know it would be rather hard on us financially. My one desire is to be well like I used to be. I am a little past twenty.

Thirteen

I am only twenty-one years old and my husband is twenty-eight. We have one little girl just past eighteen months. When she was born I nearly died. I laid from Tuesday night until Saturday evening at about six-thirty. I had two doctors, two of my neighbors and my sister with me. At six-thirty the doctors chloroformed me and took her. She only weighed four pounds. In taking her they tore me, and I didn't heal back right. Walking through hundred of miles of fire could not have been as bad as what I suffered for her.

I am afraid now to give birth to another and that fear is causing me to break my health with drugs. I am pale and weak and sickly. If only I knew what to do. Lincoln freed the negro slaves, but who is going to free women from the bonds of slavery that hold them?

What are contraceptives? To show you how ignorant most of we poor women are I can tell you I never heard of anything like that until I read your book. Oh! if you will only help me. I just can't bear to think of giving birth to another and I know I can't stand poisonous drugs much longer. Help me, please, and I will do anything to help your work along; it is the best thing in the world. You are the only one I have to pin my hopes on now. It means death if I dope many more times and I can't leave my husband. I love him. God knows how I love him. I'd rather die than leave him. The doctors around here say there isn't anything that won't kill you after you've used it for a while and I believed them until I read your book. It was a Godsend to me. I didn't mean to write so much, but you are the only one I have ever opened my heart to. I pray for your good work to continue until it reaches every woman in the country.

MOTHERHOOD IN BONDAGE

Fourteen

I was going to come over to see your doctor at the clinic but I discovered I was pregnant. I thought I was all right as I had been going every month for four months to a midwife. Last month I became pregnant and my husband would not let me go to her again. In the first place it was costing us too much money and as we did not want any more children it was difficult to know what to do. So my husband advised me to go and be examined by my own doctor as I had in mind I needed cleaning out. I was willing to take that chance and have it done as I done that before and I know what that is. It means some pain.

The doctor examined me and he told me somebody he didn't know what they had done for me but that they have been putting one over on me. He said I was pregnant about two and a half months going on three perhaps and he thought it best for me if I valued my life any to go through with it. But God only knows it will be awfully hard as my baby is now only eleven months old and she makes no effort to walk. I do not have strong robust children and my husband makes small wages and I do not know what on earth to do with this one. This will be my fourth living child without saying how many in between, and I have taken all kinds of chances, but now my husband says he does not want to lose me. That is not the thing.

Why is it that women have to suffer so much for a man sometimes that is not worthy of it? I have it on my man,

406

as I truly know he goes with others, and still God makes me suffer so much in these ten years I am married to this man.

Fifteen

Am the mother of three children, twenty-seven years old, married twelve years. Have had at least twelve miscarriages, some due to having had bad hemorrhages at time of birth, and not being able to carry the children.

With three I have been to a doctor who made a business of it, as it is more rumunerative for him undoubtedly than giving advice on contraceptives. A friend of mine just died last week, leaving four small children, a victim of abortion. Nor is she the only one that died through that death in our acquaintance. A midwife not living far from my home has between thirty and fifty callers a day. Have a friend who is married five years, has two children and has gone to this woman at least four times to my knowledge, and yet the doctor who attended her gave her no more satisfaction than the doctor I had. All my doctor said was, "Don't stay with your husband, then you won't have children." Now I have a sister in M —— who is just one wreck, two children are nearly cripples from infantile paralysis, and taking care of seven children, and two almost cripples, you can imagine her plight. Amongst our country-women—German-Hungarians—there are so many that are compelled to go to work to help along in these times, and most of them find themselves in the abortionist's clutches. If you would please give me advice I would spread it in German and Hungarian to hundreds of poor women.

Sixteen

My soul cries out to die rather than have more babies. One or two more we wouldn't mind, but would that be all? I'm only thirty years old, have one of the best men in the world, but I don't want to kill him nor myself with a big family. I am one of a family of sixteen children of which only seven ever lived longer than three years. My mother died at thirty-eight or I suppose she would have had more, for she too believed it a crime to prevent having children. I have had four of my own.

I was told by our pastor at church that if I didn't promise to quit prevention I would go to hell for it was going against God's will. I didn't promise, for, dear friend, I feel if I had any more babies I would go there anyway trying to get rid of them (especially if I induced my husband to quit the little prevention we do use). The only advice he would give me when I ask him what to do was that if my husband didn't want a large family to sleep in separate beds. But I told him I loved my husband and could not do it. So I guess I am considered out of the church and on the road to hell. But Lord I can't help it! We are paying for our little home and have had nothing but sickness since the first of the year and its all I can do to make ends meet. There are six of us. My husband makes $28.00 per week. I would so like to raise my three boys and my girl right. We have a nice home but I get so disgusted trying to make $1.00 go as far as two. I do all my own work washing, ironing, sewing and cleaning, and I'd be happy if I wasn't constantly under the shadow of more babies. I believe my married life will be one long honeymoon if I don't have too many babies.

Seventeen

I was always a frail, delicate girl, the last of seven. I guess my mother had no strength left to give. I was overjoyed when my first baby was coming as I had always loved babies so I planned such wonderful plans. I went to the library and read all the books on the care of babies. This baby was to be perfect. I had a frightful time and was in the hospital a long time but it was all worthwhile. I arrived home very weak and with all my own work to do, as we could not afford to have anyone. Before I fully recovered my strength I found myself pregnant again. All the joy went out of life, all the hopes and plans. I was too sick to enjoy the baby I had wanted so much. There is fifteen months between them. I never was well after her birth. Then in a short time I found a lump on my breast. They found it cancer and removed my entire right breast. They hardly expected me to live but I did to come home to try to do all my work with a weak right arm.

There is no use telling you of my suffering. You know. Soon I found myself pregnant again. The doctor admitted I was in no shape for it but would do nothing for me. We found a doctor that would but although I begged for something to prevent my becoming pregnant again all they would do was order tonics when all I need is knowledge so I can stop worrying and get strong. I cannot tell you how unhappy I am but I feel you know, you seem to understand. I want strength to take care of the two I have. I feel I could have it if I could free my mind of this awful worry. I wish my life away until I am too old to have any more.

Eighteen

I have worked in a factory eleven years and the majority of the women of my acquaintance procure abortion as their means of family limitation, regardless of the suffering and ill health which it produces.

XVII

Life, Liberty and the Pursuit of Happiness

OPPONENTS of Birth Control never tire of proclaiming that only women who immorally shirk the task of maternity are clamoring for contraceptives. Sane, healthy and loving mothers are opposed to it, according to these worldly wise gentlemen,—mostly priests and bachelors.

The present group of letters refutes this maliciously false claim. Whatever their limitations of education, these mothers reveal an intuitive understanding of life and its most fundamental problems. They are resigned to their fate; they are unselfish; all of them are ambitious for the education of their children. Their example justifies the popular American worship of the mother. In passing, would it not be a splendid thing to transfer that worship attitude which now satisfies itself in the singing of sentimental songs and the shedding of tears at saccharine movies, into some concrete and intelligent activity that would assure all American mothers "life, liberty and the pursuit of happiness"?

Our previous chapters have consisted of a sort of Dantesque pilgrimage through the Inferno of motherhood. The present records, it seems to me, throw the first rays of hope upon a heretofore depressing outlook.

Some of them have been written by young women standing at the threshold of marriage who aim to establish a sound foundation for family life before assuming the responsibility of bringing a baby into the world. Others, from young mothers, recognize that more children might bring with them economic ruin or a deplorable lowering of their present standard of living. Others from mothers of larger and healthy families express a determination to feed, clothe and educate each one of these sons and daughters in a manner befitting all who come into the world.

In this resolution that the children shall have a better and more abundant life than has been the lot of the parents there is nobility. Of such stuff is true progress made real.

In none of these records do we find, if we study them without prejudice and in a spirit of sympathetic fairness, selfishness prompting the request for contraceptive knowledge. In none do we find evidence of the mother's effort to shirk maternal duties or responsibilities. On the contrary, every one seems actuated by the noblest of motives —the welfare of the children, the protection of the family, the cementing of the bonds of enduring love between husband and wife.

Most gratifying is the testimony of these mothers who confess that they want more children, when they are physically strong enough to bear them. Our opponents have claimed that the knowledge of contraception would encourage and permit women to remain forever childless. The present records eloquently refute this fallacy. Voluntary motherhood is not looked upon as a punish-

ment, but as a fulfillment of desire, the natural and desired fruition of every normal woman's life.

That does not mean that the normal, sane woman
wishes to be immolated incessantly upon the altar of
maternity, in season and out. "To everything there is a
season, and a time to every purpose under the heaven,"
declared the sage of Ecclesiastes. So with motherhood.
Properly understood this function does not consist of
giving birth to an endless series of babies, left at an early
age to sink or swim, to survive or die. It consists not only
of conception, pregnancy, parturition and nursing, but always, more and more, of the more prolonged rearing and
education to full maturity of healthy children. Above all,
it means the assurance of security and self-realization in
life—in short the certainty of "life, liberty and the pursuit of happiness."

These rewards the present group of mothers claim, not
only for themselves, but for their children.

One

I am a young girl, nineteen years of age, and have
been married one year. I have had one baby nine months
after our marriage. She died at the age of two months.
I have good health and am fairly strong. My husband
will soon be twenty-one. What I want to know is this:
how can we prevent any more babies coming? We love
them and want some but not now. We want to enjoy
some of our young life together with just ourselves and
while I am in good health I would like to stay that way
and not become a wreck by having too many children.

Two

I am the mother of a five-months-old boy. He is very dear to us but I must confess he came to us a while before we had intended to begin "raising" our family. He was born one year after we were married and in some ways it has kept us from being quite the same to each other, as we could have been had we waited a year or so, because we had not become adjusted to one another before the baby came.

I'm not regretting this, but my problem and worry is that there may be another child within a year or so, and more after that. I fear for this to happen because it would injure my health and we are not financially able to have another child soon since my husband is only a day laborer. I do want another child but I would like to wait two or three years. I know I won't be able to do this if I can't learn of a contraceptive in some way.

Three

I have been married ten years and have had five children and two miscarriages in seven years. My first baby died at eight days. Have three girls, five and a half, three and one and a half years and one boy three months old. They are all fine, healthy children but all bottle babies. I have no milk after the first two weeks. The first abortion was caused by sudden shock when my nephew died five years ago. The second was last February and March and was a twin to the boy I now have. Both of these occurred during the first two months and have not injured me, but I have all I can do to take care of such young children. I have an excellent doctor and have had two weeks in a hospital at each of my last confinements. We manage to pay the hospital bill but we still owe the doctor twenty-five dollars on the last baby girl and seventy-five for the boy.

We expect to move on a farm early this spring and though it will be a fine place to raise the children we now have, I do not care to have any more. The care of the children and the farm work would be too much for me, so I probably could not give enough strength to another baby. I am small, five feet tall, and weigh one hundred and ten pounds. I have never done anything to prevent conception except to have separate beds for myself and husband. He is very considerate and never expects any intimacy during pregnancy and for some months after childbirth. In fact, there were only a few times between one birth and the next. We think we have enough children now, since we have our boy, at least until they are old enough to take personal care of themselves. My first confinement and baby's death was on a farm where I could not have proper care and there was no good doctor for several miles, so I certainly do not want children unless I could have hospital care and my doctor who has taken such good care of me these four times.

Four

We have been married five years and have two children only twenty-one months apart, the oldest two and a half years, and the baby nine months, so instead of having any more babies we both want to raise them with proper care. We feel that we have an "ideal" family. If you can give us any advice it will be very much appreciated,— and let your good work continue.

Five

I have borne three in four years and this is all I want to have, at least for some time to come. I have managed my home and family without outside help. But common sense will tell anyone that it is impossible to have children this close year after year without neglecting your present children and husband.

Six

We have four dear children. The oldest about six and a half years and the youngest one year. And goodness knows we wouldn't take the world for one of them after we get them. But, it's this: the mother can't stand any more for a while at least (that's me!). I can notice so much difference in my strength since the last one and then one can't care for them so well, and that worries any one so.

Seven

I am the mother of five children and feel that I do not want more. They are all strong healthy children, though one can see a difference in the first one and last one. I feel that I have raised my share. I do not want to bring children into this world that are not and will not be well. We can take care of what we have nicely but another or two would wreck us entirely. My husband works hard and long each day to keep us with little rest. I cannot help feeling that I would like to see him have more pleasure and perhaps if we have no more children it won't be long until he can. I myself am becoming a nervous wreck. Seems I could not stand it at times, so I am asking you to please help me and I am sure if you do I will help you in your work all I can.

Eight

I'm twenty-one and mother of two children and more coming. Please tell me which book is fit for a poor mother like me so I can read it and know something. It doesn't pay to be green in that case for it is a miserable life I would be laying up for me.

Nine

I am seventeen years old. We were married five months ago. When I was married two weeks I became pregnant. When I saw how easy it was for me to become pregnant I was worried because I was in fear of having a large family. I'm really happy now because I'm going to get a little baby. I know now that after you help me I can choose the time to get another. If it wasn't for you how unhappy I'd be. I'd be worrying about having the baby because after I'd have it I'd maybe find myself pregnant

again because I love my husband so much and I respond
to him easily. Oh, I'm so happy now and I wish you all
the good luck God could give.

Ten

My mother was pregnant thirteen times and out of the
thirteen she has five children living. There were five miscarriages and one born dead and one living only a few
hours while the other never reached its first birthday. I
was the fifth child, there being one older than myself
living. Since the three oldest were all dead before either
of us were born, there was just us two until I was ten
years old. I can look back on those happy childhood days
and think of the misery that too many children cause
and wonder why it is that this knowledge is withheld.
When there were just us two children we had a happy
home but when I was ten years old my mother brought
another baby into this world and in thirteen months another and in three years another with a miscarriage between; and as my mother was not able to take care of these
children that made the burden so hard on my older sister
and myself for we was not able to have any help.

Eleven

I am a widow with a boy twelve years old and am engaged to a very nice young man. I have repeatedly put
off marrying him until I can't get away with it any longer.
Next month I take the second step. My first marriage was
a failure. Was married at nineteen, knew nothing, my

husband turned out to be a gambler and drunkard and worse than that—other women. I was married one year and had a fine boy. When he was two years old I had to go back home to my people because my husband through drink, etc., contracted consumption.

My mother had a living family of ten and buried four, a total of fourteen births for her, so you can imagine how nice I felt when I had to go back home. I have been working ever since, which is seven years, and now I would like to be married again because I know that I am to have a nice home and I love the man dearly. My boy has been deprived of lots of things because I couldn't afford them and if after I marry again another and another baby comes perhaps all the attention from the father will go to his own which is natural. My aim would be to get my little boy so in the love of this man first and then when the others come we will be alike in love and attention, but what to do is what I am hoping you will tell me. My doctor told me to take something after conception has taken place but why not something before it comes to that I asked him. He says there is nothing to be depended on. I am thirty-three years old and I would like to sit back and be comfortable knowing that my little boy can have a few things he wished for.

Twelve

I am twenty-three years of age and was formerly a teacher, but gave up my profession to marry a man whom I dearly love, and our marriage was just recently, and we are now getting settled into a little home of our own.

While we have already spent some nights together, we have not had intercourse, although I feel intensely passionate toward my dear husband as he does to me. Our mutual understanding and sympathy is so complete that I can tell him things as I am going to tell you now.

I have female trouble that sometimes makes me ill and causes me intense pain, so that I fear if I ever should become pregnant, it might result fatally, so I want to avoid the condition if there is any possible way out.

Now I do not want to deny my darling husband, who is everything in this world to me, the fulfillment of the desire that his great love for me creates in him, nor do I want to deny this to myself, but I am ignorant of any means by which we can enjoy ourselves without danger to myself, and for this I am going to call on you. You see I am standing before a great problem that I know I have to meet in the very near future, like looking into the black darkness of the night.

Thirteen

I am twenty-five years old and was married eight months ago to my childhood playmate. We are very happy but always there hangs over us the fear of bringing children into the world, which we cannot financially afford and who physically may be unfit. I developed a tubercular bone in the right leg from the knee to the ankle at the age of eight years from then until sixteen my folks had me all over this part of the country to try to affect a cure without the knife, as the year before I had submitted to an operation for hernia. My health was such that all doctors agreed an operation at that time unwise.

At sixteen years I entered a sanitarium and began to fight for life and to save the leg. The doctor operated every few weeks for four years on that leg. It is now well and I am not lame, however it is not as strong as the other and I cannot stand on it long at a time. And to bear children now I feel would ruin my fast regaining health. My lungs have been affected with the tubercular germ, but examination now show all spots to be dead. Two years ago my husband underwent two serious operations and has not fully recovered and is under weight, weighing only a hundred and four pounds. So I feel we are both while loving each other dearly, unfit to bring offspring into the world until such time as our health assures us healthy offspring.

Fourteen

I have been married two years but my first year I was in training for a nurse and my husband was away at school so we have been together only a year. I wanted to finish training so badly but during my last year I took sick and after a couple of months in the hospital the doctors thought I had tuberculosis of the spine. They were not sure but the X-rays showed some kind of infection. I knew I would have to miss several months and my husband did not want me to go back in training for by proper care we thought that perhaps I would be all right. After we went to housekeeping I found that I was pregnant. During the time I took the very best care of myself for I did not want a weak and sickly baby. My baby boy is now three months old and the very picture of health. Lately my back has hurt some and I have such a tired feeling. During the last year I have felt so well and gained but now am losing. While I want another baby I feel like it is not right to have any until I know that I shall be strong. I have seen the effects of so many things used to prevent childbirth and the suffering it causes but surely there is some contraceptive used that is safe. I shall be very grateful for any information that you can give.

Fifteen

By denying myself, a poor tenant farmer's daughter, many pleasures and entertainments, by working and saving with the help of my parents, have gone through a normal school. After I spent four years in a small country school I had saved enough to pay for the expense of my education, but my health broke down and I was compelled to leave the schoolroom. Again I returned to the farm and my health was somewhat restored and as I have a natural love for children I decided to marry, at the age of twenty-four years. I started to be sickly as soon as I became pregnant with our first baby, spending most of the nine months in bed. I have never been strong since, and most of the time unable to do my housework or tend my child.

The doctor advised me not to have any more children as I was physically too weak and almost on the verge of consumption, only telling my husband to be careful, but that didn't avoid me from becoming pregnant. Thus when I was just beginning to feel my strength return, although our first baby was two years old, I am pregnant again and am in a worse shape than the first time. Although I am doctoring all the time I have very little strength and am almost nervous to distraction. I can see no relief if I continue to have many more children as life presents just one round of misery after another.

Sixteen

I was a school teacher and was in a run-down condition when I married three years ago. My husband had been married before, which fact immediately brought the responsibility of mothering a child to me. A month after marriage I became pregnant and because of hard work and worry I lost my first baby two months later. However three months after that I found myself in the family way again. This time I avoided such work as may bring on another miscarriage and instead taught school for a term of four months. When I discontinued teaching I still had the care of the home which was too much for me since I felt so weak and wretched. When confinement came I had to be chloroformed and the baby taken from me. Baby is now twenty months old but I have not gained a bit of strength since his birth. I think with horror of ever bearing another child when I am so weak.

Seventeen

I am a young married woman of twenty-eight and in my years past I was always working and gave all my money to my parents, as they were in need of it. When I met my husband we both loved one another. Of course, the best of luck was not with my husband so that he could save a few dollars. We married for love only and we are happy, but poor, realizing that we are not in the circumstances to bring any children into the world until we have a few dollars saved, so that when we do have children we can give them the proper care and education they should have. My husband is one of twelve children and had to help bring his other brothers and sisters up, as the father only earned $13–$15 a week. On that no parent can give their children the bringing up they should have, but they are all well and helping along. We both realize that it is not the proper thing to do for the children as well as for our country and therefore come to you for help.

Eighteen

I am a woman of thirty-five and mother of nine children, eight living. Having married when I was sixteen, ignorant of nearly everything pertaining to life, my husband told me we would have two children as he thought that would make an ideal family. He himself came from a small family; I was the only one left of four born to my mother in three years. She died when I, the oldest, was four years old, two dying ere she did and another a few years after. Having knowledge of the unhappiness and misery of my three aunts with their numerous unwanted and inadequately cared-for children, I certainly wasn't in favor of any more. But alas, I seemed to be particularly fecund and when my oldest daughter was twenty-two months old my second daughter was born. By precautions on the part of my husband and one two months' miscarriage my first son wasn't born till the second daughter was thirty months old, he living only five weeks and another son in eleven months after that every two years.

They have been healthy children, seeming to have the best of constitutions. But I haven't the means to care for them as I know they should be, and there is the trouble. I cannot see how I can take care of any more, for we cannot now live up to an American standard of living on my husband's income of $108.00 a month.

Through struggle and sacrifice of every member of the family and her own efforts at working at anything she could get to do, our oldest daughter got her high school diploma last spring, age eighteen. She is working now at a resort to buy her books and clothes to put her through County Normal. The second daughter is also working to keep on in high school. The six of them at school we cannot keep clothed as they should be or give them their proper food and home environment. I realize it so terribly at times it nearly drives me frantic.

As far as I am personally concerned I can refrain from sexual intercourse but it seems impossible for my husband to leave me alone, and I fear now again that I am pregnant. I have missed once. The terrible qualmish nervous feeling that I always suffer is coming on me and I am tempted to use abortive measures. Yet I know of no sure method and have always been too timid to go to a doctor and the last time by trying everything I knew and miscarrying at two months I felt so conscious stricken. Of course I was terribly nervous. It isn't that my children haven't been healthy but we cannot give them the proper training and care. My husband works twelve hours a day and seven days a week. He has such a little time to help and five of the children are boys and seem to me need looking after more than my girls.

Nineteen

My mother is of the old German type and she said everybody could and should have all the children they could even if it kills them. She is a good mother, but I don't think it is right to raise children like cattle and then throw them to the street or poorhouse to be brought up or die. If I could get one good contraceptive that would not fail but would be sure so I would not become pregnant till I can get strong again I would surely be glad. Then I could give my husband my true love and do my children justice.

Twenty

We have been married going on five years and have three children, a boy and two girls, and expect another addition to our little family next month. Now we did not expect the last little girl, and were astonished and some afraid when we first knew the one yet to come to us was on the way. We are very poor American people, and can't afford to bring up so many—unless unexpected luck should come to us, which is unlikely—even now, and certainly later when they get older and more expensive.

We might be able to do fairly well by the first two, but now we have too many for our means and income, and are fearful lest there might be others to follow, as time goes on, in spite of all we try to do. The fact is we don't know much of anything, about these things, either of us. We have received much advice from many sources, but it has not seemed to have availed us much.

Twenty-one

I am housekeeping, trying to send six children to school and have three little ones at home. At present am doing most of my work by keeping one of the children at a time out of school to help me. What I want you to do is to advise me what to do to prevent conception. If I don't use some sure preventive, there will be another baby next year. We now have more children than we can do justice by both mentally, financially and morally, and I cannot give my children the proper care, education and moral training they by right should have, and do my housekeeping too. We are really not financially able to hire my work done, though have tried, and failed so far, to get someone to help me. I have no chance to go to church or Sunday School, neither can I teach my children the Bible at home as I am always too busy.

Twenty-two

I was married when I was twenty to a man some few years my senior. I married greatly against my parents' and friends' wishes, since he was too poor, and, as father said, too shiftless to be a good husband and a good provider. The second accusation I yet deny, the first I can only admit, although I do not think that it is his fault so much as his hard luck. But a year after marriage I lost a child by miscarriage, a misfortune at the time but a blessing now. Since that time twins; two other girls and a boy have come to our home and with scarcely a year between them. Now I have five beautiful children and although I'll never give any of them up even though my better fixed relatives wish to adopt them, yet I do not want any more. Last winter we had scarcely enough to keep us living until spring, this year it is little better.

What would I do with more to feed and raise and finally to educate? I am determined to educate my children but I fear it will be altogether impossible if more children come. So if I wish to raise them right, to give them what other children have, and what they are by birth and abilities entitled to, I must not have more children.

Twenty-three

I am the mother of two sweet healthy boys, one fifteen months and the other three months. My health is fairly good but don't feel it would be if I should have to give birth to another baby very soon as I have all I can care for now, and our financial affairs are not so at present that another baby would be just the thing. We are both very fond of babies but don't feel it right to bring them into the world unless we can support them and give them advantages they should have. So I am writing to you to tell me of a certain and harmless preventive, as I thought all the time there was something of that kind. We have tried to obtain such information from doctors but they say there is no certain preventive. I don't believe I could commit abortion after having two sweet babies, so choose the preventive if I can obtain it as I value my husband's love very highly and I wish to do all I can to hold it.

Twenty-four

I am a farmer's wife and the mother of six fine bright children, if I do say it myself, the oldest twelve years and the youngest two months old. We are deeply in debt having bought a farm on contract last year. We just lost a valuable horse and with one thing and another are at our wit's end how to get along. Having passed all his exams, our oldest boy is attending high school, although he is so young. Now I do want to educate him and do my best for all the others. Another thing, too, I have had a bronchial cough from childhood and the doctor says am liable to have tuberculosis if I keep on having babies. So, if there is anything you can tell me or any way of my finding out means to keep from having more I beg you to tell me, as we need all our strength and money and more too, to care for those we have and I feel it would be unjust to them to have any more. If you can help me any I will be very, very grateful. I love my babies but it is because of that love I feel I haven't any right to have more. I thank you anyway for your true understanding of the problem of so many, many women.

Twenty-five

I am a mother of six children besides have lost three in ten years of married life. We care for children but find it impossible to care for them in any way as they should. They are good children and it seems a shame to have so many and not be able to feed and clothe them right. Our children have never been to a show of any kind or any pleasures such as all children love. Their father finds it impossible to get work in his business in the winter and if it were not for outside help I don't know what we would do. I am only 31 years old.

Twenty-six

We have two children (two and four years old). That isn't all of the family we want, because we love children and I think strong healthy parents should have four or five children, but I think they should be able to set the time for their births. Now if we could have four or five years yet without children we could get on our feet and probably finish our home (we have just two rooms built now).

Then if we had our home built we would be able to send our children through school. I want my children to have a college education. It is their right. Not only that but I think it is wrong to bring children into the world if one can't give them a good start in life. This is my story and I'll guarantee it is the story of a good many mothers in the United States, especially wives of working men. I wish that our laws would be changed so as to eliminate this worry for it is this worry that causes dissatisfaction and eventually divorce.

XVIII

Conclusion

We need prolong no further our explorations in this
Inferno of American motherhood. Nor need we emerge
from our pilgrimage with black despair in our hearts. For
close to us we now witness the rise in America of a new
generation of intelligent parents who are living intelligently planned lives. The voice of sorrow cries aloud for
deliverance; but it is the habit of happiness to protect
itself with a wall of silence. Therefore the public at large
hears little or nothing of those contented young families
which have been made possible by the voluntary control
of procreative faculties and the cultivation of the art of
parenthood.

These are the families of the future. They are fulfilling
their duty to our civilization; in their example lies all
the hope of our future. Refusing to submit to the closed
morality of the past, these parents no longer consider
themselves the playthings of fate.

Their children are brought into the world because they
are profoundly desired; because they can be born under
proper conditions, and reared in healthful surroundings;
because a sound mind and a sound body is assured to each
one of them; because each child, born of desire, is endowed
with a heritage of health and strength of spirit, fully

equipped to confront and surmount the obstacles with which every human being brought into this world must struggle. In brief, any intelligent observer whose eyes are trained to penetrate beneath the superficial and accidental aspects of American life to its most profound undercurrents, cannot ignore evidences of an awakened consciousness among young parents that each child must be assured the encouragement to express, "The spirit within which is the final endowment of every human being." The right to self-realization should be the birthright of every American child.

In the past we have had chaos, catastrophe, disaster, the invariable price paid for chance moments of happiness and bliss. The vicissitudes of the large family, the high infant mortality rate, the high maternal mortality rate, the appearance of the doctor for the annual accouchement, and the almost equally frequent appearance of the undertaker, were all considered "normal." This deplorable condition still persists in the unhappier strata of our society. Today we recognize that this type of procreation is no more "normal" than an epidemic of typhoid.

In this era of standardization, during which most lives are planned externally if not autonomously, it is inevitable that the whole problem of rearing children will become as ordered, as controlled, as planned, as any other phase of life. Just as our finest fruits and flowers have been developed by choice and selection from wild flowers and wild trees, and our finest breeds of livestock have been developed by conscious control, so is humanity learning that the old traditional folkways, based on trial and error, have been too expensively tragic to the race at large.

This burden has been borne to an overwhelming extent by the mothers' themselves. The reader who has attentively followed the records here presented must agree with this statement.

"Our purpose is to build in this nation a human society, not an economic system," that great statesman, Herbert Hoover, has recently pointed out to the citizens of this country. "We wish to increase the efficiency and productivity of our country, but its final purpose is happier homes. . . ." Now there can be no happy—not to mention happier—homes, in this or any other country without strong mothers. To go still further, we must recognize that the robust mother is in reality the happy wife, —happy in the security of her husband's love and the vital, life-giving bond which grows more abundant through mutual, bountiful expression—and such expression never curtailed nor rendered fragmentary and abnormal through a fear of unwilling pregnancy.

More planned lives and families we shall certainly see—indeed we may already see them if we are privileged—in our own day. But this plan must not be merely a standardized mechanical formula—the production of the regular number of children in the regulation number of years! No; variety we shall have, and vast differences. Some shall be childless, others with a comparatively large number of children.

Love will be the foundation of the plan—and happiness its end. Not the limited selfish happiness of "your" children or "my" children, but the great community of happiness in which all shall be able to develop into full realization all hidden potentialities, and the hard and fast differences between "yours" and "mine" shall be effaced in mutual aid and effort toward the common weal.

Toward the production of this state, no step is more immediately imperative than the emancipation of the women whose voices have been raised in these pages.

May this long and painful pilgrimage aid in the im-
· mediate abolition of enslaved motherhood.

Appendix

ANALYSIS OF LETTERS

THE following rough analysis of some five thousand letters, undertaken at the request of the author, is presented herewith as a summary of the general outstanding features typical of conditions and tendencies reported or suggested in the total of approximately 250,000 letters from mothers which I have received. No attempt has been made to reduce the evidence thus presented to statistical fact. But it is interesting to note that the fragmentary analysis of these mothers' letters agrees in general with the conclusions of more exhaustive and elaborate analyses of the birthrate and maternal conditions undertaken by biometricians and authorities in vital statistics.

Analysis of Typical Letters

BY MARY SUMNER BOYD

It has not been practicable to undertake a study of the whole body of about a quarter of a million mothers' letters, but a bundle of 7500 was chosen at random for rough analysis. Of these 2500 were read and rejected as giving too few facts. 5000 gave either many interesting facts or a full account of a few very important facts.

For these, classifications were made covering: (1) geographic distribution (2) economic status (3) mother's age (4) number of children (5) frequency of childbirth (6) family health (7) pathological conditions at pregnancy (8) miscarriages and stillbirths, parturition or after and a few psychological headings which would be difficult to reduce to figures.

Geographic Distribution

With the exception of a few from Canada and the West Indies the letters are from the United States. Every state is represented. The greatest numbers are from Pennsylvania, Illinois, New York and Texas. Ohio, Michigan, California, Indiana, West Virginia, Alabama, Missouri, Minnesota, Wisconsin, Kansas, Arkansas, Virginia, Nebraska, Iowa, Oklahoma, Kentucky, Tennessee, North Carolina, New Jersey and Massachusetts come next.

The various groups of states are each well represented and wherever there has been a special piece of local publicity the number is always large.

439

An article by Mrs. Sanger in Holland's Magazine of Texas, for example, puts that thinly populated state among the highest states on our list and has an effect on the adjoining states.

Though it is in many cases not possible to tell the nationality of the writers, in some it is. Among the correspondents are not only Americans from both North and South but Irish, Poles, Japanese, Germans, Scandinavians, German and Russian Jews, Italians, Canadians, both French and English, Spanish West Indians and representatives of the Slav countries of Europe settled in the United States.

Economic Status

Because the letters were not answers to definite questions it was necessary often to get certain facts by combinations of statements. Economic status of the family is an example of this. The combination used was the appearance of the letters, the father's occupation, his stated income and the mothers' or children's work for wages. Any or all of these were made the basis in averaging economic status and this average showed 80% of the writers to be very poor and only 2% prosperous. Often the poverty stricken appearance of the letter and a very generalized statement—such, for example, as "His wages keeps the six of us going very thinly" —had to be taken in lieu of concrete statements on wages or occupation.

The fathers' trades given are baker, printer, fisherman, butcher, railroad worker, foundryman, miner, bellboy, mill or factory worker, lumberjack, blacksmith, garageman, gardener, moulder, metal worker, soldier, weaver, waiter, and—most often of all—the general term laborer. Many fathers do odd jobs. There are a good number of World War veterans, many of them partly incapacitated, not all receiving a small government compensation.

APPENDIX

Slightly more independent in name, but in practice equally hard pushed by poverty are ministers in small communities, public school teachers, clerks, men who are trying to run small shops of their own, farmers, homesteaders and ranchers.

The following table gives rates of pay with the number of children in families receiving them. Some apply to many families:

$ 7.00 a week	....	8 children
10.00 " "	....	5 "
12.00 " "	....	3, 4, 5 and 6 children
12.50 " "	....	5 and 6 children
13.50 " "	....	4 children and pregnant
15.00 " "	....	3, 4 and 5 children
16.00 " "	....	6 children
17.50 " "	....	3 "
18.00 " "	....	3 "
19.50 to 25.00 (seasonal)	....	5 "
20.00 a week	....	4 and 5 children
21.00 " "	....	6 children and pregnant
22.00 " "	....	4 children
28.50 " "	....	3 "
35.00 " "	....	2 "

Many of the lower wages are given again and again. One of the most common is $15.00 a week.

Sometimes wages are given on a monthly or yearly basis:

5 children	......	$ 45.00 a month
3 and 4 children	..	50.00 " "
2 and 3 "	..	60.00 " "
3 children	......	75.00 " "
7 and 9 children	..	80.00 " "
4 children	......	90.00 " "
5 "	......	500.00 a year
3 "	......	1200.00 a year with house and garden

441

One-quarter of the women stressed the fact that they were wage earners, but references to incidental domestic industries, aside from the family care, raise this percentage to quite one third. The regular workers were seamstresses or dressmakers including piece workers at these trades, clerks, stenographers, teachers, factory workers, day's workers and laundresses. Incidental domestic industries were taking boarders, assistant in the husband's store or garage, raising chickens for market, milking and caring for barnyard stock, feeding, lodging and laundry work for farm laborers and themselves doing a laborer's work on the farm either all the year or as harvesters of crops such as berries, cotton, tomatoes etc. As extra labor for the wife—though not a source of income—may be named the care of the husband's or wife's "old people" or other relatives.

A few spoke of their children as working but the majority of the children were too young and the most striking references to child labor by the mothers were reminiscences of their own toil in childhood and fear that their children would have a like fate.

Age at Marriage and Motherhood

A thousand women gave their age at marriage. Eighty percent were married before they were 20, sixteen to nineteen being the commonest years, though one was married at 12 and others at 13, 14 and 15. A very much larger number of women gave their age at the time of writing the letter and this, taken in conjunction with either the number of children and their ages or the years married, worked out to show about the same proportion married before twenty.

One girl was a mother at 13, and others had children at 15 and 16. There were many mothers of seventeen and one of these had four children, another three pairs of twins.

APPENDIX

Size of Family

For 4,000 mothers who were *multiparæ* the average family was 5 children. In making this average 1,000 newly formed families with no or only one child were omitted. Of the 4,000 five hundred had borne 8 children or more. The largest family on record was 25; 19 and 17 were the next. The youngest mother of 8 children is 21; there are several in the later twenties with as many as this.

Frequency of Pregnancies

Sixteen hundred women gave definite statements as to the frequency of their pregnancies. Of these:

150 reported intervals of 2½ years or more
650 " " " 19 months to 29 months
800 " " " 18 " or less

Of this latter group 230 reported intervals of 10 or 11 months.

Family Health

Here again we have to rely in part on general statements, most of which speak of frail children or of undernourished or puny children. But in 100 letters definite illnesses or injuries are specified. These include cripples, children in need of operations (cause unspecified), children with rickets, TB, dropsy, heart trouble, blind, deaf, children with abscesses, convulsions (3 out of 6 in one family suffered in this way from some cause unknown), venereal diseases, kidney and stomach troubles, eczema, rupture, and a number said to be "very ill" or physically helpless.

Not so many letters tell of a sick husband but in some he is spoken of as frail or sickly; in others his sickness is named. Among the diseases are stomach trouble, gastric ulcers, cancer, piles, recovering from or needing an operation, accident or industrial disease (among these are mine accidents, lead poisoning and painter's colic), crippled from various other causes, inflammatory rheumatism, appendicitis, heart, kidney and liver trouble, rupture, asthma, blindness, spinal trouble, pneumonia, goitre, gallstones, venereal disease and the general head, "very ill and unable to work" at full or only part time.

A number of fathers were disabled in the World War. A few nervous invalids there were, many of them dating from the World War, shellshocked to the point of permanent or intermittent insanity.

Childbearing and Its Consequences

Eight hundred and fifty letters tell in detail of suffering in difficult pregnancy and parturition; and more than 150 make general references to difficult and injurious births. Many dread the complications of pregnancy more than those of birth. Diseases of pregnancy include: pernicious vomiting throughout the whole period, intolerable itching, St. Vitus's dance, epilepsy occurring only at that time, special liability to other diseases—such as "flu," the start of TB and goitre—asthma, heart, bladder and kidney trouble established for life, with uremic poisoning, occurring sometimes again and again. Other causes of suffering are weak, painful or paralyzed back, paralysis of other parts, piles, rupture, constipation, trouble with liver and stomach, varicose veins unhealed from a previous pregnancy, weakness to the point of helplessness, dizziness, numbness, deafness, blindness and insanity.

At childbirth or as a consequence of childbirth most of the diseases and injuries suffered in pregnancy and many besides are reported. Among these are infections, puerperal fever, lacerations, adherent placenta, *placenta prævia*, hemorrhages, abnormal presentations, fistula, prolapsed or retroverted uterus, blood poisoning, abnormal weakness of the muscles from exhaustion in labor, small or deformed pelvis demanding instrumental aid or Cæsarean operation, lameness as a result both of pregnancy and childbirth, milk leg and breast troubles.

These are emergencies which any woman may have to meet at birth. But 495 of the correspondents are invalids and as such approach childbirth with a special hazard of their own. Among the list of their diseases or injuries are goitre, increasing with each pregnancy, diabetes, stomach, liver, kidney or bladder trouble, gallstones, ovarian or uterine troubles, abdominal ptosis, heart disease, dropsy, pellagra, anemia, pneumonia, "flu," TB of lungs or bone, asthma, paralysis, rupture or piles, rheumatism, sciatica, a crippled condition due to accident or to spinal or hip disease, eczema, erysipelas, cancer, epilepsy and venereal disease.

Several women reported that they needed operations (unspecified). Only two of these sick mothers have less than two children and 50% of them have four or more. An interesting fact, noted but not classified in tabular form, was that a striking number of women described themselves as frail and gave their height as, in one case 4 feet 8 inches and, in a great many cases, 5 feet or 5 feet 1 or 2. Weights of 79 pounds, 80, 82, 85, 90, 95, 98, 102 105 and the like are common.

Miscarriages and Stillbirths

Three thousand and eighty women gave evidence on this point. In this group those who had two or three pregnancies had 3% of miscarriages or stillbirths. After three pregnancies the rates went up until at 9 it was 7%, at 10 or more almost 9%. Though relatively few told which of their conceptions failed to end in live births, these percentages may indicate that miscarriages are more frequent toward the end of a series of many births. Another possible indication is to be found in the following records given of loss by a group of twelve typical "breeders," as mothers of large families often call themselves:

Pregnancies	Living	Miscarriages	Fractional Loss
9	3	6	$\frac{2}{3}$
15	5	10	$\frac{2}{3}$
13	1	12	$\frac{12}{13}$
7	2	5	$\frac{5}{7}$
14	7	7	$\frac{1}{2}$
19	12	7	$\frac{7}{19}$
12	4	8	$\frac{2}{3}$
11	4	7	$\frac{7}{11}$
15	8	7	$\frac{7}{15}$
12	6	6	$\frac{1}{2}$
9	1	8	$\frac{8}{9}$
9	5	4	$\frac{4}{9}$

A glance at the Fractional Loss column shows that with one exception no mother had borne alive more than half the many children she conceived and most had lost far more than half.

It was not possible to obtain useful statistics on infant mortality. Though there were striking individual letters not a very large number of women reported on the fate of their children and few of those who did distinguished between infant and child deaths.

WOMEN AND HEALTH SERIES:
CULTURAL AND SOCIAL PERSPECTIVES
Rima D. Apple and Janet Golden, Editors

The series examines the social and cultural construction of health
practices and policies, focusing on women as subjects and objects
of medical theory, health services, and policy formulation.